EMPRESS
OF
BRITAIN

EMPRESS
OF
BRITAIN

CANADIAN PACIFIC'S GREATEST SHIP

Gordon Turner

Stoddart

A BOSTON MILLS PRESS BOOK

Canadian Cataloguing in Publication Data

Turner, Gordon, 1930-
  Empress of Britain

Includes bibliographical references.
ISBN 1-55046-052-8

1. Empress of Britain (Steamship).   2. Ocean
liners — Canada — History — 20th century.
I. Title.

VM383.E67T87 1992   387.2'432   C92-093919-8

Design by Gillian Stead and Mary Firth
Edited by Noel Hudson
Typography by Justified Type Inc., Guelph, Ontario
Printed in Canada by Friesen Printing

First published in 1992 by
Stoddart Publishing Co. Limited
34 Lesmill Road
Toronto, Canada
M3B 2T6

A BOSTON MILLS PRESS BOOK
The Boston Mills Press
132 Main St.
Erin, Ontario
N0B 1T0

The publisher gratefully acknowledges the support of The Canada Council,
Ontario Arts Council and Ontario Publishing Centre in the development
of writing and publishing in Canada.

In memory of Alan Howard, 1914-1986

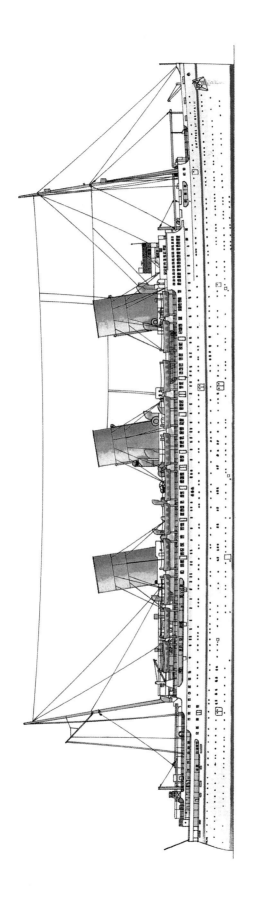
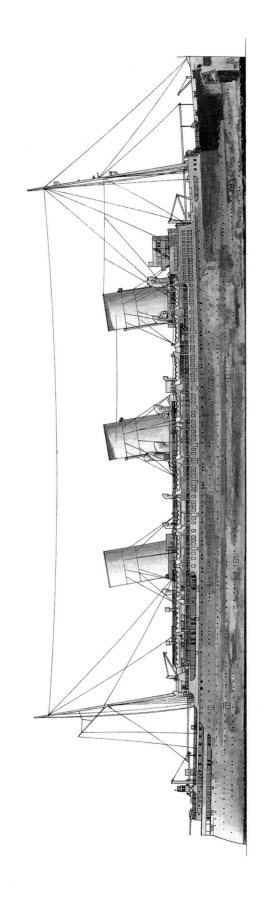

TABLE OF CONTENTS

Opposite: Profile drawings by Dietmar Borchert illustrate the Empress of Britain *in her attractive peacetime livery and in wartime grey paint, the latter, applied patchily and with streaks of rust showing, made the* Britain *less conspicuous but did not save her in the long run.* Dietmar Borchert

The Empress of Britain *lay serenely at Southampton in May 1931, awaiting passengers for her first Atlantic crossing.*
Author's Collection

INTRODUCTION

The *Empress of Britain* was no ordinary ship. In an era when some of the greatest passenger ships of all time took to the waters, she held her own with the best. Launched in 1930, her maiden voyage began a year later. After nine years of service, she was sunk on October 28, 1940. Then, curiously, the ship almost immediately disappeared from memory. In the years that followed, fewer stories were told about her and photographs were seldom seen.

To build the *Britain*, as the ship was sometimes called, Canadian Pacific approached John Brown & Co., Ltd., of Clydebank. In the 1920s this famous Scottish yard had built the passenger ships *Montcalm, Montclare, Duchess of Bedford, Duchess of Richmond* and *Duchess of York* for the company's North Atlantic service.

But the 42,348-ton *Empress of Britain* was different from these workaday ships. In size, speed and luxury, she surpassed by a wide margin any passenger ship previously seen in Canada. No other ship on the St. Lawrence, either in the Canadian Pacific fleet or among rival companies, even came close. She accommodated 465 First Class passengers, 260 Tourist Class, 470 Third Class and had a crew exceeding 700. The *Empress of Britain* was 760 feet 6 inches in overall length and 97 feet 6 inches in breadth.

Dimensions were not a matter of chance but of careful planning. Canadian Pacific knew that a ship of this great size could not run profitably between Canada and Europe year-round. From late spring to late fall she sailed from Southampton and Cherbourg to Québec, docked at Wolfe's Cove not far from the Citadel, then returned to Europe after a two-day stay at her Canadian terminal. In winter, when transatlantic traffic fell off considerably, she made four-month world cruises from New York. Cruise passengers, seeking warmer climates as well as broader cultural horizons, paid up to $12,850 each, although sometimes a minimum-price cabin could be obtained for less than $2,000 per person. The *Empress of Britain* was designed to pass through the Suez and Panama canals, which were on the most popular route for world cruises.

When cruising, the *Empress of Britain* was almost invariably the largest ship to call at the ports on her itinerary, thus inviting attention wherever she went. Her white hull, relieved by a band of royal blue, suggested an affinity for warm-weather ports, while her three immense buff funnels gave more than a hint of power. Many people were willing to apply the word "beautiful" to the ship, but a few resisted this description, perhaps because the funnels appeared to overwhelm the hull when viewed from some angles. It was certain beyond any doubt, however, that the Britain was imposing, dignified and majestic, and these were words that seemed particularly suitable for a ship that was, after all, an empress.

The *Empress of Britain* was planned when a spirit of optimism prevailed in Canada. Memories of the First World War were receding, and while prosperity was obviously not within the grasp of everyone, economic conditions were improving to such a degree that shipping companies felt justified in enlarging and modernizing their fleets. Cunard Line, the main competitor of Canadian Pacific, had placed six new ships on the St. Lawrence-Europe route in the early and mid 1920s. White Star Line and Donaldson Line had their following too. Canadian Pacific, as the country's foremost transportation company, wanted to remain in the lead. And why not? It offered what its competitors lacked: transatlantic, transcontinental and transpacific service. Passengers could travel between Europe and the Far East under the company's red-and-white checkered flag, with the rail link between Québec and Vancouver dividing the ocean journeys.

Edward W. Beatty, president of Canadian Pacific from 1918 to 1942, knew that simply building a ship was not enough to guarantee her success. It was essential to develop a loyal clientele and to appeal to potential passengers through shrewd and continuous advertising. The company's name was, of course, familiar to everyone in Canada but Mr. Beatty also wanted to reach travellers from the American Midwest who generally considered New York to be the only port of embarkation for Europe. The distance between Chicago and European ports was actually shorter by the St. Lawrence route and, moreover, the St. Lawrence River and Gulf were more sheltered than the North Atlantic. The thought of spending a day and a half in sight of land had a strong attraction for people who believed, no matter how wrongly, that a North Atlantic crossing was inseparable from a bout of seasickness. The slogan "39 Percent Less Ocean" was coined to allay the fears of the timid.

The *Empress of Britain* entered service in May 1931 and alternated between seasons of North Atlantic voyages and annual world cruises until the Second World War broke out. It was her misfortune to sail at a time when the Depression had reduced passenger lists considerably, an economic disadvantage she shared with all transatlantic ships of the period. On most crossings she was less than half full, and there were sailings when the passenger total dropped below 200. Her globe-circling cruises managed to attract an average of about 400 passengers, but occasionally the threat of war reduced this number.

The outbreak of the Second World War saw the ship filled beyond her stated capacity when she reached Québec on September 8, 1939. A few months later she was requisitioned as a troopship. Following two crossings from Halifax to Scotland, she sailed from England to the Middle East, then to Australia and New Zealand. After returning to Britain she again set out for the Middle East, carrying a large contingent of soldiers. She was due to return to Britain once more, but her final voyage was never completed. On October 26, 1940, she was bombed off the coast of Ireland and, while being towed to port, was sunk two days later by a German submarine.

Ten years after her launching, the *Empress of Britain* lay at the bottom of the Atlantic. She had the unenviable distinction of being the largest passenger ship sunk on the high seas during the war. Had she survived, her life would likely have been more than twice as long. In those ten years she had carried a king and a queen, prime ministers and governors general, industrial tycoons and wealthy widows, stars of stage and screen, and writers and artists, to say nothing of thousands of passengers of less exalted station. This book tells her story; it shows in word and picture the kind of ship she was and recalls the voyages she made in her brief yet remarkable life.

Several places mentioned in the book have changed their names since the 1930s. In Québec, maps show Father Point as Pointe-au-Père, Murray Bay as La Malbaie, and Crane Island as Ile-aux-Grues. Elsewhere in the world, Palestine is Israel, Abyssinia is Ethiopia, and Ceylon is Sri Lanka. Straits Settlements is part of Malaya, Siam has become Thailand, and Cambodia is Kampuchea. Batavia, on the island of Java, is Djakarta. Among the Chinese cities, Peking (also called Peiping) is Beijing, Chinwangtao is Qinhuangdao, and Canton is Guangzhou. In Brazil, Bahia is now known as Salvador. A few other places have altered the spelling of their names in minor ways.

The *Empress of Britain* accepted both Canadian and British currency. For most of the 1930s, one pound sterling (£1) was worth about five dollars; one dollar was equal to approximately four shillings.

Most of the nautical terms in the book are self-explanatory. A few that are not are included in the Glossary.

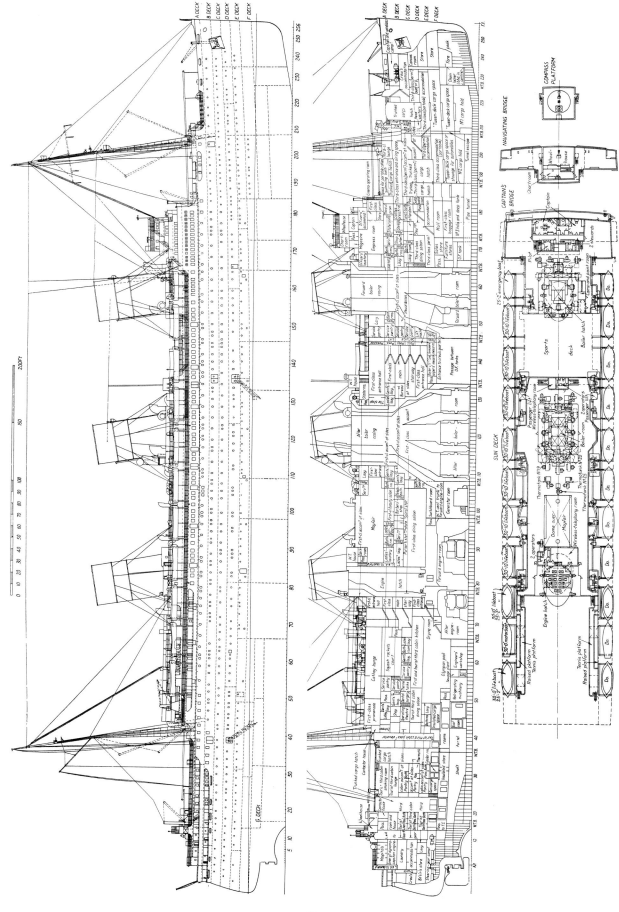

Outboard and inboard elevations and deck plans of the Empress of Britain *show the complexity of her layout.* Marine Publications International Ltd. *(see next pages)*

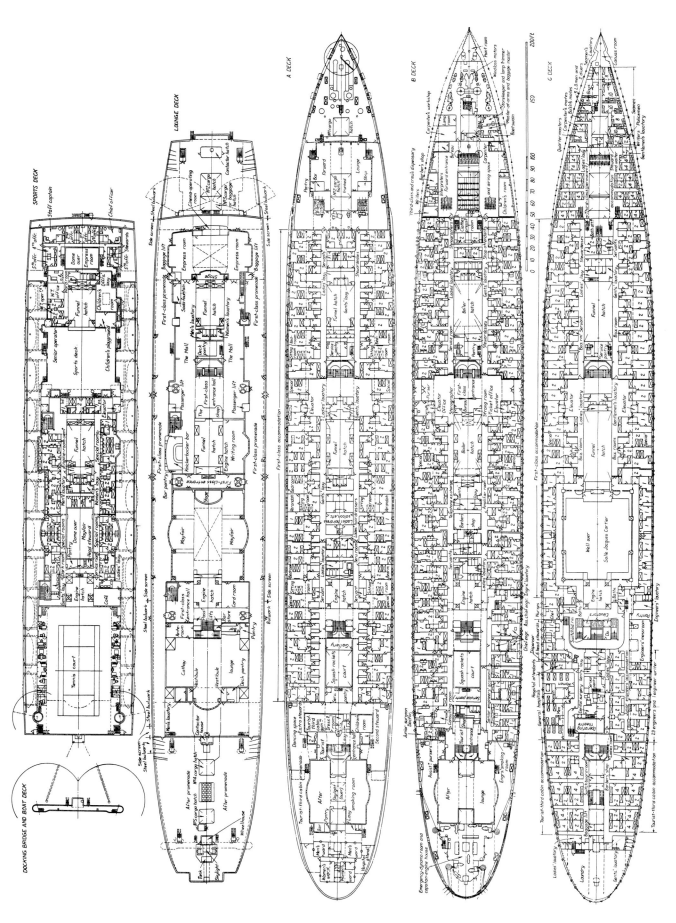

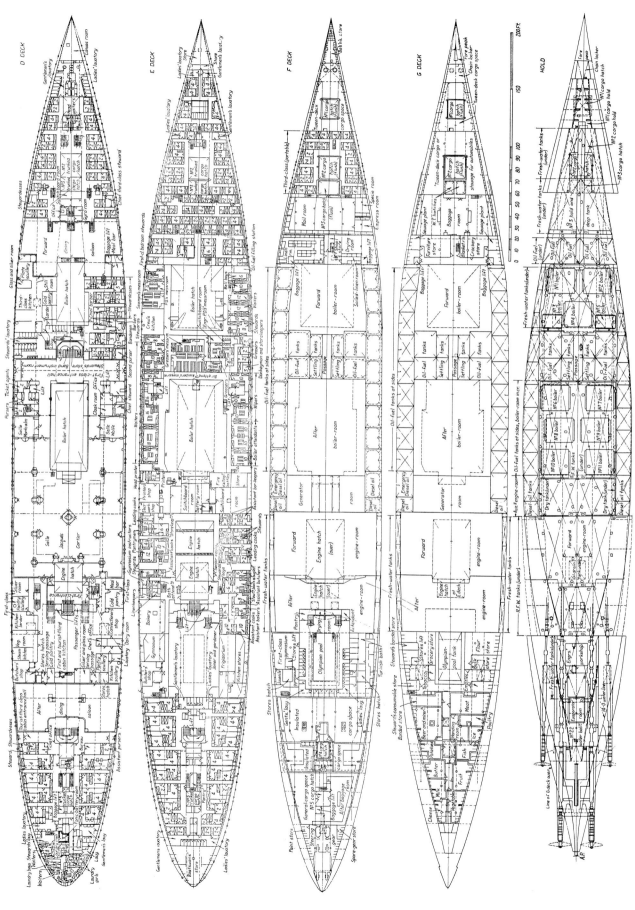

— 13 —

At the launching on June 11, 1930, the greased ways eased the Britain's *passage from land to water while the drag chains attached to the hull restricted her movements in the confining waters of the River Clyde.*
Jay Bascom Collection

CHAPTER 1

THE SHIP TAKES SHAPE

On November 28, 1928, with grey skies threatening to break into rain at any moment, a small group of workmen laid some flat steel plates in a straight line on heavy wooden blocks in the shipbuilding yard of John Brown & Co., Ltd., at Clydebank, a few miles downriver from Glasgow. There was no ceremony to denote the occasion. It was simply part of a day's work, but it was also the start of a job that would occupy the yard and its workers for the next two and a half years. The plates marked the beginning of the keel of the *Empress of Britain*, Canadian Pacific's greatest ship.

John Brown's yard was no newcomer to the construction of notable passenger ships. Among its earlier successes were the *Lusitania* and *Aquitania* of Cunard Line. It had the facilities and expertise to build the *Empress of Britain*, the largest ship ordered in Britain since end of the First World War.

Workmen had prepared a building berth, spanned by large cranes, for Hull No. 730, as the 760-foot-long ship was known to Brown's. Construction was planned in the minutest detail. The laying of the first keel plate was only the beginning of a long and intricate process. Detailed drawings were now translated into girders, beams and plates.

The keel formed the backbone of the ship. It was then time to complete the skeleton and add the skin. Mindful of the *Titanic* disaster, which had happened less than 20 years before, and with the knowledge that the *Empress of Britain* would sometimes sail through ice-infested waters off the coast of Newfoundland, Canadian Pacific ordered the ship's outer steel plating to be of double thickness at the stem and for 150 feet back at either side up to the waterline level. The ship also received a double bottom, consisting of two metal skins with 4 to 5 feet between them. This space, divided into 44 main compartments, would be used to carry oil, fresh water and ballast water.

The decks, ten in all, and the main bulkheads, or watertight internal walls, were fitted into position. All 26 doors that were later placed in these bulkheads could be closed from the bridge simultaneously in an emergency. The hull continued to grow, and when finished it contained over 19,000 tons of steel. Iron moulders, riveters, rivet heaters, fitters and other skilled and semi-skilled workers toiled steadily for a year and a half until the launching date.

While the hull was under construction, the yard placed orders for the multitudinous pieces of equipment to be manufactured elsewhere. Delivery dates were assigned to ensure that items arrived at the yard at suitable times. The accounting department kept careful records of expenditures. The contract required Canadian Pacific to pay for the ship in six instalments, the first when the keel was laid and the last when she was handed over to her owner. When the figures were finally added up, the ship cost £2,130,723 (about $10,653,000), leaving Brown's a slim profit of £63,485 (about $317,000).

The manufacture of equipment might have followed routine procedures, but delivery to the shipyard sometimes presented problems. The rudder, weighing 67 tons, was too large to be taken by rail to Clydebank from the factory in Darlington, in the north of England, so a 14-wheel truck, 58 feet in length, was used. Although the police provided an escort, the truck still needed seven days to make the 200-mile journey to Clydebank along the roads of England and southern Scotland.

Four-bladed manganese-bronze propellers for the *Britain* took more than three months to make. The two larger inboard ones, which could rotate at 150 revolutions per minute, weighed over 25 tons each and had a diameter of 19 feet 3 inches. The two outboard ones, capable of reaching 200

The spectacle frames for the inboard propeller shafts were clearly visible in the stern framework on May 31, 1929.
Glasgow University Archives/
Scottish Record Office

Most of the ship's stern had been plated in by January 8, 1930, but a number of portholes had not yet been cut out.
Glasgow University Archives/
Scottish Record Office

On December 7, 1928, nine days after work began on the Empress of Britain, *construction of the keel was well advanced.* Glasgow University Archives / Scottish Record Office

revolutions per minute, weighed more than 17 tons each and were 14 feet in diameter. When installed, the propellers were balanced so sensitively that they could be turned by the pressure of one finger. A complete extra set, to be carried aboard the ship, was made in case of emergency.

June 11, 1930, the *Empress of Britain*'s launching date, arrived with construction already well advanced. The delivery date, a year away, could be maintained. Some internal fittings and woodwork that would otherwise have been installed after the launching were now inside the ship.

The launching received more publicity than any in Britain since the *Aquitania* 17 years before. In addition to newspaper and magazine reporters and photographers, a radio team from the British Broadcasting Corporation arrived at Clydebank. The proceedings were broadcast to a large audience in Britain and relayed throughout the world. At least 16 stations in Canada and more than 60 in the United States carried an account of the events, as did stations in Australia, South Africa and Mexico.

Ships were usually launched by women, but the Prince of Wales, later to become King Edward VIII, consented to perform the ceremony. He held the title of Master of the Merchant Navy; hence his selection as sponsor could not be criticized. It was, in fact, a coup for Canadian Pacific to obtain the Prince's services at a time when his popularity with the public was running high and demands on his time were numerous. France, Italy, Germany and Britain were all in the course of planning, building, or had just completed, large, fast and prestigious ships for the North Atlantic run, and Canadian Pacific was keenly aware of the favourable publicity that attended a royal launching.

Preparations had started well in advance of the actual date. The Clyde had been dredged where the *Britain* would enter the river; the ship's hull had been painted and the wooden launching cradles

The Empress of Britain *rose dramatically above the shipyard buildings of Clydebank, dwarfing the men on the roadway below.*
Glasgow University Archives/ Scottish Record Office

Rows of shipyard cranes stood on guard as the warmly dressed crowd watched the ship enter the water.
Jay Bascom Collection

Shortly before the Empress of Britain *was launched, Canadian Pacific's* Empress of Japan *was towed down the River Clyde to undergo trials prior to entering transpacific service.* Jay Bascom Collection

greased. Massive chains had been attached to the ship's sides to arrest her progress if she should overrun the estimated distance and become stuck in the mud on the opposite bank.

A crowd greater than 20,000 gathered to view the launching. The platform where the official party stood was packed, but spectators could easily identify one figure in the front row, the slightly built Prince of Wales, wearing a light topcoat and bowler hat. Beside him stood E.W. Beatty, chairman and president of Canadian Pacific, in a three-piece suit, and Lord Aberconway, the distinguished-looking 80-year-old chairman of John Brown's, dressed, like the Prince, in a topcoat and bowler.

The ceremony was delayed for a few minutes, but eventually the "all clear" signal appeared on the indicator at the front of the platform. The Prince proclaimed the traditional words, "I name this ship *Empress of Britain*, and may success attend her and all those who sail in her." He then cut the red, white and blue ribbon which held a bottle of Canadian wine. The bottle swung against the side of the great liner and shattered on impact. The Prince now pulled the automatic lever which set the release gear in operation. To the resounding cheers of the crowd, the ship, whose launching weight was 21,000 tons, began to move slowly, stern first, down the slipway, picking up momentum with each passing second as she left the land and entered her natural element. In that highly critical period, brief though it was, the hull was subjected to stresses and strains that far exceeded anything the ship would likely experience in her lifetime.

As the cheers faded, tugs took the ship in tow, then nudged her into the yard's fitting-out basin, where she would spend the next ten months. The assembled dignitaries had since descended from the platform to a luncheon where Lord Aberconway, the Prince and E.W. Beatty delivered speeches and proposed toasts, their words frequently interrupted by bursts of applause. It was a memorable day.

On December 19, 1930, the ship appeared outwardly to be nearing completion, although the lifeboats had not yet arrived from their manufacturer. Glasgow University Archives/Scottish Record Office

CHAPTER 2

THE LAST WORD IN SHIPBUILDING

Plans for the *Empress of Britain* were in the hands of several naval architects, all experienced men with high reputations. Hugh R. Macdonald of Canadian Pacific applied his specialized knowledge of the company's requirements in passenger accommodation. He worked alongside Charles S. Douglas, who had advised Canadian Pacific on the construction of ten earlier ships, and J.M. McNeill of John Brown's. Mr. Macdonald and his staff prepared plans for such diverse areas as bars, kitchens, hospital, storerooms, offices and shops, while Mr. Douglas attended to the ship's speed, stability and strength.

John Johnson, Chief Superintendent Engineer of Canadian Pacific, was responsible for the *Britain*'s propelling machinery and auxiliary machinery. His instructions were clear: make the new ship operate as economically as possible and make her easy to manoeuvre in crowded waterways. From an imaginative yet disciplined mind came his invention, the Johnson boiler, which put into practice his theories on the use of high-pressure steam. When the *Britain* entered service, this boiler generated twice as much steam as the standard type, with no less efficiency. The ship had eight conventional Yarrow boilers as well as one Johnson boiler and, in addition, two smaller auxiliaries, all burning oil. Steam produced in the boilers supplied four sets of single-reduction geared turbines which drove four propellers. These turbines generated 62,500 shaft horsepower, giving the ship a service speed of 24 knots.

Three enormous 68-foot-tall funnels were partly assembled on land and lifted aboard by crane in sections. If laid on their sides, three railway sleeping cars or two double-deck buses could have run abreast through any one of them. While the first two served conventionally as uptakes for fumes, the third formed part of the ventilation system and also contained the *Britain*'s 21-tube radio broadcasting equipment. Of equal importance, the third funnel gave a sense of balance to the ship's profile.

The hollow steel foremast rose 213 feet 9 inches above the waterline. Enclosed lookout platforms, or crow's-nests, were located at 80 feet and 130 feet above deck level. The lower platform was reached by a ladder inside the mast, but to arrive at the upper one, a sailor had to climb an external ladder for the last 50 feet. The lower crow's-nest contained a telephone, giving the lookout direct contact with the bridge. As an additional safety feature, it also had a battery-operated indicator with a transmitter in the crow's-nest and a receiver on the bridge. If the lookout wanted to warn the officer on duty on the bridge of anything at sea needing more careful scrutiny, he turned the indicator in that particular direction, then pressed a buzzer to get the navigating officer's attention.

No fewer than 407 electric motors supplied power for ventilation, kitchens, refrigerators, elevators, steering gear, boat-hoisting apparatus, and for various machines on deck and in the engine rooms, boiler rooms and workshops. Cooking equipment was entirely electric. The main kitchen on D Deck ran the width of the ship, with much of the space at the sides occupied by storage rooms and sculleries. Insulated and refrigerated storerooms were capacious enough to hold provisions for a four-month cruise. The refrigerators had 13 compartments to maintain proper temperatures for

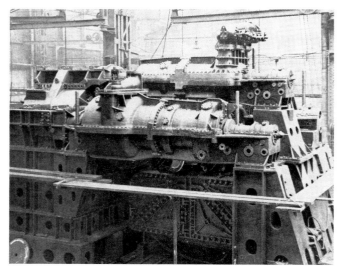

The inboard turbines, gear case and condenser stood in the workshop, awaiting installation in the Empress of Britain.
Author's Collection

One of the Yarrow high-pressure boilers waited beside the fitting-out basin before being lifted aboard.
Author's Collection

The Johnson boiler, weighing 166 tons, had a combustion space almost completely filled with water tubes.
Author's Collection

A dockside crane swung the top section of the middle funnel into position on October 31, 1930.
Glasgow University Archives / Scottish Record Office

The First and Tourist Class kitchen was installed after consultation with marine caterers, kitchen engineers, dining saloon and kitchen staff and even some gourmets. Glasgow University Archives/Scottish Record Office

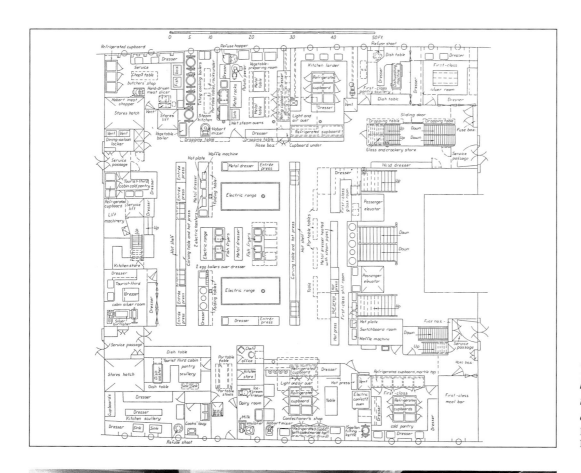

The layout of the kitchen was planned to make the best use of a limited space.
Marine Publications International Ltd.

The wheelhouse looked rather untidy and the wheels were tied down while construction continued elsewhere in the ship.
Glasgow University Archives/Scottish Record Office

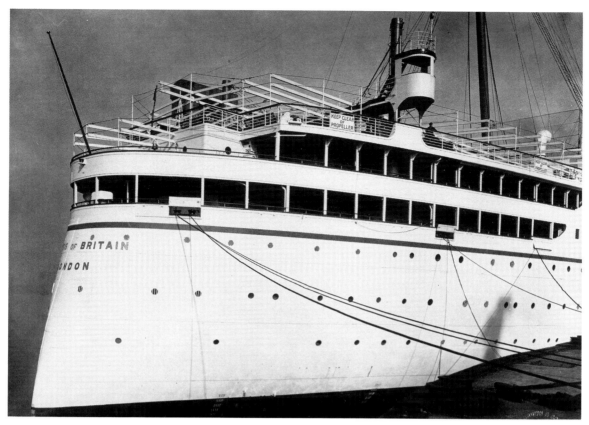

The Empress of Britain*'s cruiser stern was less elegant than the counter sterns that were popular only a few years earlier.* Glasgow University Archives/Scottish Record Office

each kind of food. Actual working space in the kitchen, dominated by two large electric ranges, was only about 50 feet long and 50 feet wide.

The *Britain* was designed to carry mail and a small amount of general cargo, so derricks of various lifting capabilities were ordered. Twenty-six handsome teak lifeboats with canvas covers were manufactured in Glasgow, not far from the shipyard. In addition, there were 22 rafts, each certified to accommodate 22 people. Other safety apparatus included fire extinguishers, hoses, axes, smoke detectors and alarm signals, as well as 1,951 life jackets.

From Waygood-Otis came 12 elevators of the latest design. Five served passengers and were capable of travelling 200 feet per minute. Lengths of chain, wire, rope and four large anchors reached the yard. The anchors required windlasses and capstans, and the electric motors to drive them. Navigation instruments, built to the highest specifications, arrived at Clydebank by rail and road. Magnetic compasses, a gyro compass, an echo-sounding machine and direction-finding apparatus were purchased, delivered and installed. Carefully packed ship-to-shore telephone equipment came in sturdy boxes. The first of its kind to be placed in the cabins of a transatlantic ship, it allowed passengers in the most expensive accommodation to make and receive calls in the privacy of their own quarters.

The fitting-out list seemed almost endless: turbo-driven and diesel-driven generators, batteries, 320 miles of electric cables, chronometers and clocks, gauges, fans, pumps, pipes, valves, filters, glass, burglar alarms, vacuum cleaners, motion-picture projectors, washing and drying machines for the laundry, a printing press. Installing everything was a complex process, but the shipyard was confident it could be achieved before the date of the maiden voyage, tentatively scheduled for June 1931. One aspect of fitting-out that extended well beyond the requirements of most passenger ships was the First Class public rooms and cabins, where high luxury was the keynote.

The dome of the Mayfair Lounge was of amber glass panels, each with a stylized golden sun in the centre. The carpet, woven in Persia, was of a 16th century Polish design. Jay Bascom Collection

CHAPTER 3

EVERY INCH AN EMPRESS

Canadian Pacific knew that the ship's accommodation, both public rooms and cabins, had to be planned and executed with exceptional care, particularly in First Class. On a five-day Atlantic crossing a passenger might tolerate minor inconveniences, but on a four-month cruise a petty annoyance could take on the proportions of a major catastrophe. Passengers willing to spend thousands of dollars to circle the globe had to be convinced that life aboard the *Empress of Britain* represented the highest standards in luxury, comfort, taste and service. The company had several years' experience running world cruises and realized that space was a leading criterion in passengers' demands. The new ship was indeed roomy. First Class passengers had more space per person in the *Britain* than in any ship afloat. How best, then, to use it?

To decorate and furnish the public rooms, £250,000 (about $1,250,000) was allocated. Design of the passenger space would ordinarily have fallen to P.A. Staynes and A.H. Jones, the owner's decorative architects, but the *Empress of Britain* was not an ordinary ship. Canadian Pacific commissioned five of England's best-known artists, assigning particular rooms to each of them. The artists had a fairly free hand, one of the few instructions being to combine simplicity with dignity in their work. Mr. Staynes and Mr. Jones would co-ordinate the artists' work by designing the entrance foyer, stairways and corridors to establish a sense of unity when passengers moved from one room to the next. They were also responsible for the Writing Room, Card Room and Olympian Pool, as well as the deluxe and special suites.

The principal First Class public rooms were located on the Lounge Deck. They were, in the words of Canadian Pacific, "suited to different purposes or moods, all of them rich in quiet luxury." Luxury was certainly present, but the décor, although outstanding in its workmanship, did not place the ship in the absolute forefront of the most recent trends in design. A handful of designers elsewhere had made tentative overtures towards eliminating the floating Grand Hotel concept in passenger ships, making the public rooms less ornate and more functional. North German Lloyd, for example, had put the *Bremen* on the North Atlantic route in 1929, a ship whose interiors were decorated along what traditionalists considered quite severe lines, perhaps in retrospect too austere for the complete comfort of some passengers. The *Empress of Britain*, by comparison, was fairly conservative in most of her public rooms but did make certain concessions to the latest in contemporary style. Canadian Pacific knew its passengers. On a four-month world cruise they were people with time and money to spend. The majority were over 50 years old, and the ship's decorative work had to appeal to their long-formed tastes.

At the forward end of the Lounge Deck was the Empress Room, about 70 feet wide and 40 feet long. One of England's leading painters, Sir John Lavery, perhaps known best for his portraits, was engaged to decorate the room. The colours he chose were coral pink, blue and silver, in a pattern described by one critic as rhythmical yet restrained. In the centre of the ceiling was a large blue dome bespangled with planets and constellations. The room was to serve also as a ballroom and had a parquet floor of Austrian oak laid in squares. Tall mirrors arranged along one wall reflected the highly polished wood. On stage stood a beige Steinway grand piano. Silver light standards, topped with clusters of pink ostrich plumes, cast a soft

The Empress Room was noted for its versatility. Sometimes a ballroom, and periodically a lecture room, it also served as a cinema. Jay Bascom Collection

The starboard Mall, looking forward to the Empress Room, exemplified the spaciousness of First Class in the Empress of Britain. CP Rail Corporate Archives

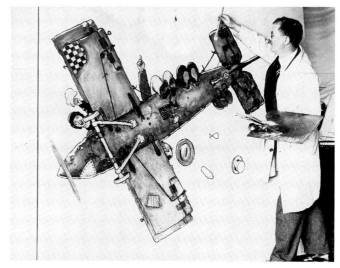

The Knickerbocker Bar was small in size but became big in popularity. Author's Collection

W. Heath Robinson applies the finishing touches to a ceiling panel of the Knickerbocker Bar. According to the artist, this panel illustrated exhilaration and uplift. Author's Collection

The entrance to the Empress Room, seen from the Mall. The plants at each side of the door were cared for by the ship's gardener. Author's Collection

glow over the room. A small projection booth was installed so that passengers could enjoy the latest talkies.

Leading aft from the Empress Room were two corridors known as the Mall. Not quite rooms in their own right, yet more than passageways, the two arms met in a foyer which formed the main entrance to the rooms of the Lounge Deck. Settees, easy chairs and writing tables were placed throughout the Mall. Crystal pendants set in recessed panels in the ceiling illuminated its limed oak walls. In the foyer was a shop, in reality a counter with display cases, stocked to provide the necessities and luxuries that passengers wanted at sea. Illuminated glass turrets on either side of the counter offered a touch of Art Deco amid the ship's often traditional furnishings. Opposite the shop, at the head of the main stairway, a large mural by Maurice Greiffenhagen depicted the arrival of Samuel de Champlain and his young wife, Hélène Boullé, at Québec in 1610.

Between the main entrance hall and the Mayfair Lounge were the Knickerbocker Bar on the port side and the Writing Room to starboard. The Writing Room included the Library, and to suggest the coziness of a book-lined room in an English country home, a stone fireplace was installed, but the warm glow came from an electric fire, not from coal or wood.

The Knickerbocker Bar, sometimes called the American Bar, owed its distinctiveness to its decorator, W. Heath Robinson. The inventive cartoonist's whimsically comic drawings were familiar to millions of newspaper and magazine readers. He went to work in his London studio, painting his designs on large sycamore panels, which he then dispatched to Clydebank. Mr. Robinson spent three or four days in the shipyard, putting the finishing touches on his work and supervising the installation of the panels. They illustrated the history of the cocktail with a series of remarkably ingenious gadgets, starting with a bent-over cherry tree branch held in position by a crooked stick in the hands of a stout, mustachioed gentleman. Attached to the stick were a string, net and pair of scissors, rigged up so that a tug on the string manipulated the scissors into cutting the stem of a cherry, which then dropped into the net. At the end of the frieze the artist had painted a complicated arrangement of pulleys, gears, levers, bathtub, pipes, pumps and tank, all patched up and tied together with string, which tested the cocktail by letting it drip into the gaping mouth of a volunteer

Thoroughly Spanish in its treatment, the card room gave little evidence of being part of a ship. The ceiling louvres and the rod anchoring the centre table to the floor were clues that the room was indeed on board a ship. Author's Collection

A preliminary sketch for the Cathay Lounge depicted the Chinese theme, but by the time the room was completed a number of details had been altered. Author's Collection

lying on a couch and attended by two physicians, one with a stethoscope against the man's chest, the other checking his pulse.

The largest public room was the Mayfair Lounge. This 83-by 70-foot lounge, with no pillars in its central area, gave Sir Charles Allom a large, well-proportioned space in which to exercise his talents. He selected the Renaissance style, with rich walnut panelling embellished with silver. Sofas and chairs of subdued colours, along with card tables, coffee tables and writing tables were arranged around the lounge. A superb tapestry showing the hunting prowess of Emperor Maximilian I hung as a backdrop for the stage. Above the centre of the room, the ceiling consisted of an arched dome of amber glass. In the surrounding frieze, Sir Charles had included snowshoes, canoe paddles and maple leaves, an acknowledgement of the *Empress of Britain*'s Canadian ownership.

Between the Mayfair and Cathay lounges stood the Card Room, Spanish in motif, with arches, red leather, wrought iron, and black and gold tiles. Six walnut card tables were covered in red baize, a fabric that also decorated the face of the clock.

The Cathay Lounge was, in fact, the Smoking Room. In earlier ships the Smoking Room was generally labelled as such and was an exclusively male preserve, but times were changing and so were social mores. If not exactly encouraged to use the room, women were at least tolerated. An artist's rendering made in 1930 showed men as its sole inhabitants, but even on the maiden voyage women began to use the room. Nevertheless, when the ship was built, there was a lavatory for men in the Cathay Lounge but none for women.

Edmund Dulac was commissioned to decorate the Cathay Lounge. He was best known as a book illustrator, but occasionally designed his own furniture. A Chinese fretwork theme pervaded the room. Decoration and furnishing attempted to blend the exotic with the functional. Walls were panelled in grey ash, while the ceiling was of pale gold leaf. A four-sided clock, rather institutional in appearance, hung from the centre of the ceiling. Four columns, faced with black glass and banded with silver were connected at the top by an ornamental fretwork canopy. The lacquered vermilion-and-ebony furniture repeated the canopy's angular designs. Tall red Chinese vases stood on each side of a green-and-gold glass fireplace. The floor was of Macassar ebony and oak with an inlaid pattern. The effect was quite overwhelming at first glance, although the room did exhibit a sense of symmetry.

The other large First Class room was the Dining Saloon on D Deck, about 20 feet above the waterline. To reach it from the Lounge Deck, a passenger either took an elevator or descended four decks via the main staircase. Known as the Salle Jacques Cartier, it accommodated 452 diners, 416 in the main room and 18 in each of two smaller private rooms, Salle Wolfe and Salle Montcalm. Its decorator was Frank Brangwyn, an eminent British painter then at the height of his fame.

The Salle Jacques Cartier, 120 feet long and running the full width of the ship, was advertised as the largest room afloat without supporting pillars. It rose two decks high at the centre, thereby relieving the low ceiling height of 10 feet elsewhere in the room. The port and starboard sides of the central well had murals displaying incidents in the life of Jacques Cartier, the French explorer of the St. Lawrence River. Walls were of light oak, while the ceiling consisted of panels divided by solid-looking oak beams.

A rubber-based composition with the trade name Rublino covered the floor. It was made to a pattern devised by Mr. Brangwyn, an unusual commission for a respected member of the Royal Academy. More typical of his work were several murals illustrating human figures, flowers and fruit, all colourful in appearance and bold in style. In the middle of the room stood a tall buffet on an octagonal oak base, with three tiers of gold mirrors, brilliantly lit at the apex. The artist also designed the light oak armchairs, upholstered in moquette, and tables which accommodated from two to seven diners.

Sports facilities lessened whatever burden of guilt accompanied overindulgence in the dining saloon or bars. Walking, the simplest of exercises, could be done on the Lounge Deck, four circuits of the promenade equalling one mile. The 40- by 20-foot Olympian Pool on F Deck was one of the largest installed in any ship. At one end a large sea turtle, carved in Portland stone and inlaid

Frank Brangwyn designed the Salle Jacques Cartier, perhaps the most contemporary of the ship's public rooms. The letters C.P. were worked into the lighting fixtures near the ceiling. Jay Bascom Collection

A placid terrazzo-glass turtle spouted an endless stream of sea water into the Olympian Pool. The changing cubicles epitomized the fine woodwork that could be found throughout the ship. CP Rail Corporate Archives

The Olympian Pool was large, symmetrical and inviting. Changing cubicles lined each side, while four individual shower rooms stood at one end. The fluted columns were embedded with turquoise mosaics. Jay Bascom Collection

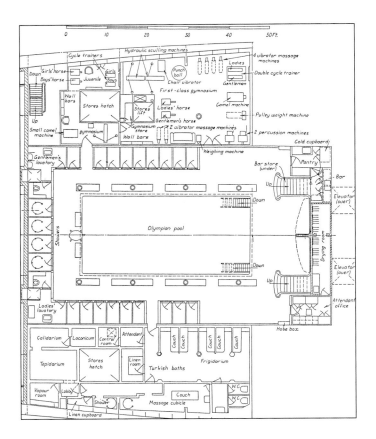

F Deck towards the stern was the location of the Olympian Pool, the gymnasium and the Turkish baths.
Marine Publications International Ltd.

The First Class gymnasium offered a diversity of equipment to any passenger needing a workout.
CP Rail Corporate Archives

The First Class Children's Room possessed all the latest toys. Behind the curtain was a recess with four cots.
Glasgow University Archives/Scottish Record Office

The barbershop on B Deck had the most modern equipment available in 1931.
CP Rail Corporate Archives

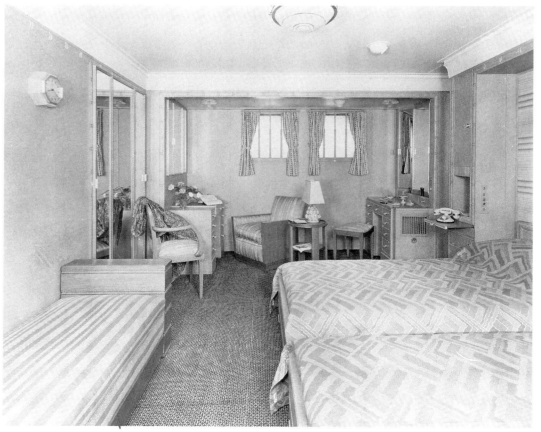

Cabin 345 on C Deck was designated as a special stateroom, which meant that it ranked higher than a regular First Class cabin but lower than a suite.
Author's Collection

with blue mosaic, spouted a continuous stream of sea water into the pool. Turkish baths with a massage table stood to the starboard side of the pool and a well-equipped gymnasium occupied the port side. The gym possessed 2 horse-riding machines, 1 camel-riding machine, 1 double-cycle racing machine, 6 belt vibrators, 1 chair vibrator, 2 hydraulic rowing machines, a punch ball, skipping ropes, 16 pairs of Indian clubs, 16 pairs of dumbbells, 6 medicine balls of various weights, 3 sections of wall bars and, perhaps most essential of all, a weighing machine. Adjacent was a children's gym, similarly furnished but with the apparatus built on a smaller scale.

Above the Lounge Deck was the Sports Deck, 455 feet long, whose main attraction, just aft of the third funnel, was one of the first full-size tennis courts on any ship. Galleries for spectators lined the sides of the court and a small cafe stood at the forward end. The Sports Arena, between the first and second funnels, was the location for shuffleboard, deck tennis, quoits and bullboard. On A and B decks, immediately beneath the Cathay Lounge, was a championship-size indoor squash court, complete with a spectators' balcony. The hardwood walls were lined with fibre sheets and pads to reduce noise.

On the starboard side of the Sports Deck was the Children's Room, decorated by Heath Robinson. The artist had let his imagination run free in the Knickerbocker Bar, but here he kept to traditional themes. Bo Peep, Mother Hubbard, Little Boy Blue and other nursery rhyme characters looked down serenely from the walls. The furniture was child-sized and there were toys for youngsters of all ages.

First Class cabins, situated on the Sports Deck and on A, B and C decks, surpassed in luxury anything previously found on the St. Lawrence route. Canadian Pacific decreed that the words "cabins" and "staterooms" were not appropriate and that "apartments" should be used. Passengers, however, ignored the edict and continued to speak of cabins. Many were more than 25 feet long, although often narrow and L-shaped rather than rectangular. All were outside cabins; that is, with portholes and a view of the sea. Most were furnished to accommodate two passengers, but there were also 69 single-bed cabins. About three-quarters of the cabins had en-suite bathrooms, the majority with tubs and the rest with showers.

The most sumptuous cabins graced A Deck, the location of the six suites. Each of the two deluxe suites consisted of an entrance vestibule, sitting room, double bedroom, bathroom with separate toilet, sun verandah and box room. Smaller suites had less floor space and no sun verandahs. All First Class cabins had beds six and a half feet long rather than bunks, with the beds placed lengthwise in relation to the ship's hull, instead of crosswise. This, it was claimed, made for greater passenger comfort in heavy seas. Larger cabins each had a triple-mirrored dressing table with stool, fitted wardrobe, sofa, armchair, bedside tables and lamps, and a full-length wall mirror. Heat rose from radiators and cool air flowed from an adjustable ball-louvre system of ventilation. Carpets, bedspreads, and upholstered chairs and sofas all had one attribute in common: the fabric for each item seemed to have been chosen without regard for the overall appearance of the cabin. Circular, angular, linear and floral patterns competed and often clashed within a limited space.

Beams, girders and pipes in First Class cabins were all hidden from view, a feature that did not exist in every Atlantic liner. Craftsmen had used an astonishing variety of woods to finish the walls; not only the common walnut, ash, sycamore, mahogany, birch, oak and maple, but also the more exotic black bean, paroba, satinwood, pearwood, sapele, zebrano, angelim, Macassar ebony, locust and avodire.

Twelve rooms scattered throughout First Class did not conform to the degree of grandeur elsewhere. Small in size and plainly furnished, these were servants' quarters, available to passengers who felt it essential to take along a maid or valet when they travelled.

Whether making a North Atlantic crossing or taking a lengthy cruise, First Class passengers would have been hard put to find a ship that excelled or even matched the luxury of the *Empress of Britain*.

The sitting room of a deluxe suite represented a style of comfort familiar to wealthy passengers. The sideboard to the left of the electric fireplace had a hinged door which concealed a hot plate. CP Rail Corporate Archives

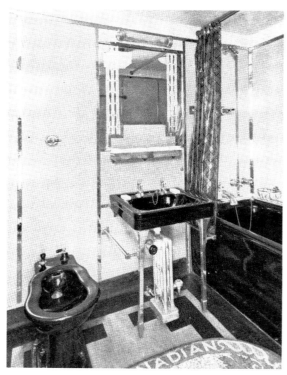

Black was a colour seldom found in ships during the 1930s, but the bathroom fixtures of one suite used it extensively. Author's Collection

A sitting room could be converted easily to a dining room when the occupants decided to eat in their own quarters. CP Rail Corporate Archives

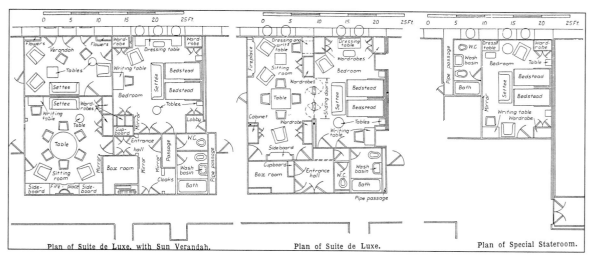

Layout plans of the most expensive accommodation disclose that space was used generously in the Empress of Britain, *compared with other ships.* Marine Publications International Ltd.

The Tourist Class Dining Saloon lacked the grandeur of the Salle Jacques Cartier but was nevertheless a satisfying room. The chains that fastened the chairs to the small holes in the floor had not yet been installed.
Glasgow University Archives/Scottish Record Office

CHAPTER 4

DESIGNED IN DETAIL

Most skilled artisans at the fitting-out basin worked in First Class, but Brown's assigned some to Tourist and Third. The noted artists who had designed the First Class rooms took no part in the planning of these classes; this was was left to P.A. Staynes and A.H. Jones. Tourist Class—whose official but seldom-used name was Tourist Third Cabin Class—was located towards the stern. The lavish expenditure that characterized First Class showed more restraint here.

The Smoking Room on A Deck was panelled in limed oak and furnished with tapestry-covered easy chairs and settees. Its marble fireplace helped perpetuate the illusion that the passenger was in a substantial middle-class home or a good country hotel rather than on the high seas. On the opposite side of the entrance hall were a gymnasium and a children's room, both generously supplied.

Directly below stood the Lounge, identical in size to the Smoking Room, a room of solid comfort with deep, inviting walnut easy chairs and settees upholstered in green and orange moquette. It had a marble mantelpiece with an etched mirror, grand piano and a few card tables. At the back of the lounge, a portable Roman Catholic altar was stored behind a screen.

The Dining Saloon seated 164 people at tables for two, four and six. It did not boast a special name, as did its grander First Class counterpart, the Salle Jacques Cartier, but the two restaurants shared the same kitchen. The First Class menu, however, showed a greater choice of dishes.

Cabins, many accommodating four people, were comfortably furnished with bunk-style beds, mirrored wardrobes, chests of drawers, and armchairs. Veneered plywood, mainly oak and beech, covered the walls. Some larger cabins had two washbasins, but there were no private bathrooms for the 260 Tourist Class passengers; they shared 20 baths, 32 toilets and 5 bidets.

Smaller cabins measured about 10 feet by 10 feet, bigger ones 16 by 10. Compared with the same class in other North Atlantic ships, these were fairly large dimensions. Canadian Pacific believed that on world cruises, when class barriers were literally taken down, and the *Britain* operated as a one-class ship, roominess became an important factor in selling these cabins to less wealthy passengers. Upper berths were then removed to make the cabins look larger.

Like the public rooms and cabins, open deck space was located near the stern. The passengers had 16,000 square feet for strolling and for deck games, mostly on the Lounge Deck. The ship's propellers throbbed more noticeably in Tourist Class, but passengers were spared the pitching motion that sometimes characterized Third Class accommodation.

Not that there was anything wrong with Third Class cabins, but their position well forward on C, D, E and F decks made them uncomfortable when the ship began to rise and fall in rough seas. Regardless of this tendency, Third Class cabins on C and D decks were still considered good enough to be sold for world cruises. All had upper and lower berths, were a uniform 6 feet 5 inches wide, and varied in length from 6 feet 6 inches to 13 feet 2 inches. Walls were faced with painted plywood, but furniture was of polished hardwood. A strip of blue carpeting ran down the centre of each floor.

Every cabin had hot and cold running water but, as in Tourist Class, there were no private bathrooms. Only 5 baths and 28 toilets served 470 Third Class passengers. Beams and rivets of the ship's sides and deckheads, or ceilings, were clearly visible in the cabins. If bookings ran high,

The Smoking Room in Tourist Class, subdued and conservative, contrasted noticeably with the flamboyance of the Cathay Lounge, its First Class counterpart. Author's Collection

The marble fireplace of the Tourist Class Smoking Room had a grate with a "Magicoal" electric fire. Author's Collection

A Tourist Class cabin on C Deck gave its occupants some privacy at night with individual curtains for each bunk. CP Rail Corporate Archives

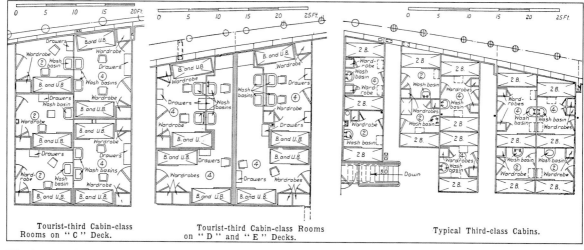

Tourist-third Cabin-class Rooms on "C" Deck.

Tourist-third Cabin-class Rooms on "D" and "E" Decks.

Typical Third-class Cabins.

The layout of Tourist Class and Third Class cabins showed that space was a prime consideration in establishing the difference between classes. The sloping lines of the hull indicate that the accommodation is close to the extremities of the ship, near the stern in Tourist, near the bow in Third. Marine Publications International Ltd.

Children who used the Third Class sycamore-panelled playroom had a good assortment of toys to choose from.
CP Rail Corporate Archives

11 portable cabins far forward on E Deck and 21 on F Deck, occupying space that could be converted to hold cargo, were pressed into service.

Passengers had deck space forward on the open end of the Lounge Deck and a more sheltered area below on A Deck. A small lounge on A Deck seated about 80 people at a pinch. At one side of the entrance stood a bar and at the other a shop. Third Class shared a dispensary with the crew but had its own barbershop. The Children's Room, dominated by a large black rocking horse, had an annex with five cots. The well-lit Dining Saloon on D Deck, with mahogany walls and a frieze of sycamore, seated 234 at oak tables, mostly for six or eight people.

More than 700 officers and crew had to be accommodated in the ship, and they were generally housed wherever space could be found in the extremities or depths of the hull. Officers fared better than ordinary crewmen. The Captain's quarters, consisting of a bedroom, sitting room, bathroom and box room, were on the Sports Deck, directly below the navigating bridge. The Chief Engineer had a suite of rooms aft on B Deck, with his senior staff in nearby cabins.

Most officers either had cabins to themselves or shared with another officer, but the vast majority of the rank-and-file crew had no privacy at all. The carpenter and bosun were among the few who had their own cabins, and a small number of the more senior crewmen were accommodated in cabins for two, but far more common were the "glory holes" on E Deck. Furnished with two-tier metal bunks, they housed 6, 8, 10, 12 or even 18 men. These crowded quarters, spartan in appearance, had very limited living and sleeping space and few storage facilities, but they were at least equal to the crew accommodation on other Atlantic liners, or possibly a little better. Officers had 19 baths and 20 toilets but the rest of the crew, more than 600 strong, had just 7 baths, 7 showers, 9 urinals and 32 toilets.

A Third Class cabin was small, functional and basic. CP Rail Corporate Archives

The slope of the ship's side indicated that the Third Class barbershop was far forward in the hull. Glasgow University Archives / Scottish Record Office

Planned for comfort, the Third Class Lounge could accommodate only a fraction of the Third Class passenger complement. Author's Collection

The Dining Saloon for Third Class passengers looked somewhat utilitarian, although the table decorations softened the effect.
Author's Collection

The staff captain, next in rank to the ship's master among the deck officers, had a large cabin that was a combined office, sitting room and bedroom. The curtain at the left could be drawn to conceal the sleeping area.
Glasgow University Archives / Scottish Record Office

On the control platform of the forward engine room, everything was in readiness for the speed trials. CP Rail Corporate Archives

CHAPTER 5

TESTS AND TRIALS

Late in March 1931 the fitting out of the *Empress of Britain* was nearly complete and the work of the shipyard almost finished, but a series of rigorous trials had to take place before the ship could be handed over to Canadian Pacific.

On Sunday, April 5, 1931, four tugs took up position alongside the *Britain* and waited for the incoming tide. At 12:15 p.m. the blast of their whistles indicated that they were ready to tow the ship to the Tail of the Bank, a deep-water area where the river met the Firth of Clyde. The *Britain*'s farewell to Clydebank resembled a victorious parade rather than a simple towing job. The crowd, estimated at several hundred thousand, lined both banks of the River Clyde for the entire 16 miles to observe the ship's departure. Elders of one church persuaded the minister to revise the time of the service so that the congregation could see the *Britain* as she passed. A railway company, sensing good business, advertised three special trains from Glasgow to Langbank, a good vantage point, but demand for tickets was so great that ultimately it ran 12 trains. By bus, train, streetcar, automobile, motorcycle, bicycle and on foot, people of all ages arrived, intent on witnessing one of Clydeside's greatest ships leave her birthplace, never to return, they thought, after her trials were completed.

For the tugs to tow the *Britain* from the fitting-out basin to a mid-channel position in the river took a mere 15 minutes. During the early stages only a few inches of water lay between the liner's keel and the river bed, but in minutes the margin grew to 4 or 5 feet. The tugs gradually increased their speed to eight knots, and in less than two and a half hours the procession reached the Tail of the Bank, where the tugs released her. In addition to the large number of crew members aboard, there were representatives of John Brown's yard and Canadian Pacific, all ready to measure, monitor and evaluate the ship's performance.

Captain R.G. Latta, who had been appointed the *Empress of Britain*'s master four months earlier, was on the bridge, accompanied by two Clyde pilots. "Jock" Latta began his seagoing career as an apprentice in the sailing ship *Ardencraig*. In 1904 he joined Canadian Pacific with the rank of Fourth Officer. He served in several of the company's ships before being appointed Chief Officer of the *Montezuma* in 1910. Seven years later he became master of the *Monmouth*, and in 1923 took command of the first *Empress of Britain*, a ship which changed her name to *Montroyal* in 1924 and went to the breaker's yard in 1930. He had commanded ten Canadian Pacific ships in all before taking up his newest appointment. A quiet, decisive man, respected by his crews and popular with his passengers, Captain Latta's experience and personality made him an excellent choice as master of the new ship.

H.G. Donald, the *Britain*'s Chief Engineer, stood on the control platform of the forward engine room, sometimes leaving his post to inspect the equipment he was gradually getting to know. Mr. Donald, John Johnson and the shipyard representatives had to nurse the machinery through the trial stages and make the necessary adjustments until its performance met or surpassed the established standards.

Initial trials began on April 6 to test the anchors and steering gear, then the ship proceeded to the Gladstone Graving Dock at Liverpool, where she had her hull cleaned and painted. Sea trials started several days later, when the *Britain* returned to Scotland. Reporters gathered at Skelmorlie

The Salle Jacques Cartier accommodated 416 diners at one sitting. The room was 19 feet high in the central area.
Jay Bascom Collection

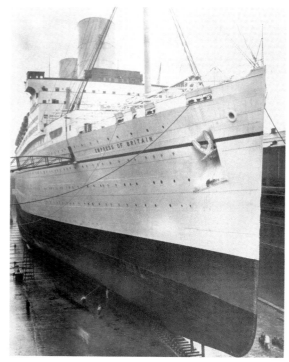 

Before the speed trials were held the Empress of Britain *entered the dry dock at Liverpool to have her hull inspected, cleaned and painted.*
CP Rail Corporate Archives

The size of the rudder and propellers became apparent when the Britain *was in dry dock.*
CP Rail Corporate Archives

on the Firth of Clyde, stopwatches in hand, ready to calculate the ship's speed between the two points known as the measured mile. To their dismay, the *Britain* carried out her speed trials off the less-populated coast of the island of Arran, also in the Firth of Clyde but about 15 miles from Skelmorlie, leading some writers to conclude that the trials were held in secret to conceal possibly disappointing results.

The ship had avoided the traditional measured mile because her speed and size would have started a wash powerful enough to capsize small boats and perhaps erode the shoreline. In the more open waters off Arran, she spent two days undergoing exhaustive tests. With all four propellers in use, her speed averaged 25.271 knots over the mile. The next day, using the inner propellers only, she averaged 22.595 knots. Since these figures were each attained in a rough sea with a strong breeze, both builder and owner expressed satisfaction with the results.

The trials continued. A 12-hour test to measure fuel consumption determined conclusively that the ship was economical beyond expectations. In seven days, the *Empress of Britain* covered 1,700 miles, meeting every demand made of her in open and narrow waters, sailing both day and night in favourable and adverse weather. Canadian Pacific believed that it had a winner on its hands, and the company waited with quiet confidence to see if the travelling public shared its opinion.

The Empress of Britain *shared the harbour at Southampton with an array of smaller ships as the start of the maiden voyage drew near.* Author's Collection

CHAPTER 6

THE MAIDEN VOYAGE

Preparations began on both sides of the Atlantic well in advance of the *Empress of Britain*'s maiden voyage from Southampton and Cherbourg to Québec and back. The ship was registered in London and received the official number 162582. Her radio call sign was GVCN and her international signal letters GMBJ. Insurance amounting to $10 million was placed with under-writers to cover her first year of service. The Montréal and London offices of Canadian Pacific reported a steady stream of bookings for the *Britain*'s first North Atlantic season, particularly in First and Tourist classes.

In and around Québec, one of North America's oldest ports, construction work accelerated to meet a new deadline. The ship's initial arrival date had been advanced from late June to June 1. Along the shore of the St. Lawrence River the Québec Harbour Commission had built Wolfe's Cove Terminal, 4,300 feet long with water 40 feet deep at low tide, to accommodate the *Britain* and any other large ships that might follow her. A rail link from the terminal to the main line was necessary, so Canadian Pacific bored a tunnel more than a mile long through solid rock, completing it and laying the rails only a few days before the *Britain*'s first appearance at Québec.

Meanwhile, at Southampton, 60 miles southwest of London, work continued apace for the maiden voyage. A week before the ship was due to leave, special trains brought guests to an inaugural luncheon aboard ship. Sir George McLaren Brown, the company's general manager in Europe, urged them to remember that the distance between Southampton and Québec was shorter than the distance between Southampton and New York, and that nearly 1,000 miles of the *Britain's* voyage would be made in sheltered waters. He emphasized that the speed of the *Empress of Britain* on the St. Lawrence route and the *Empress of Japan* on the Pacific, linked by the company's cross-Canada rail service, brought the Orient nearer to Europe than ever.

The idea of the ship drawing the British Empire closer together was taken up on the editorial page of the May 27 issue of the *Daily Express*, one of Britain's mass-circulation newspapers, whose owner was Canadian-born Lord Beaverbrook:

> An event of Imperial moment takes place today. The *Empress of Britain* sails on her maiden voyage from Southampton to Canada. The same vision and faith that flung the railways across Canada from ocean to ocean in superb confidence that settlers and trade would follow have inspired this magnificent vessel. The skill and experience of British shipwrights have built her.
>
> The finest ship on all the seas, she is also a vibrant proof of what Canada and Britain working together can achieve... New York made more accessible from England via Canada than by direct route; the St. Lawrence transformed into one of the greatest of trans-Atlantic and Imperial thoroughfares, such are but a few of the possibilities assured by this commanding stroke of commercial genius.
>
> But above all as she feels her way down the Solent the *Empress of Britain* will stand out as a pledge to the British and Canadian peoples that their destiny is one, their interests indissoluble, their co-operation is invincible.

The Britain, *with
steam up, dressed
overall and her
paintwork at its
immaculate best,
waited for the first
passengers to arrive.*
Author's Collection

*Captain R.G. Latta,
master of the* Empress
of Britain, *E.W. Beatty,
and Captain J. Gillies,
general manager of
Canadian Pacific
Steamships, stopped
briefly for the camera
before the ship left
Southampton.*
Author's Collection

The *Empress of Britain*, with fuel, stores and her predominantly British crew aboard, beckoned her first passengers. The Prince of Wales decided the night before that he would like to see the ship leave on her maiden voyage. His visit was to be a surprise, with only a few people notified of his intentions, but somehow a rumour of his impending arrival circulated through the waiting dockside crowd.

Shortly before the Prince was due, a chauffeur-driven limousine made its solitary way along the dock. To the consternation of the assembled dignitaries, it was not the Prince of Wales who emerged, but four crew members who had been imbibing in a local bar and who were now quite tipsy. They were quickly hustled out of sight and soon afterwards a second limousine arrived, this one carrying the Prince. E.W. Beatty met him at the foot of the gangway and escorted him on a rapid half-hour tour of the ship. The Prince expressed his regrets at not being able to accompany Captain Latta on the maiden voyage. His inspection caused a short delay in the ship's departure, but finally, at 1:12 p.m. on Wednesday, May 27, 1931, the *Empress of Britain* left Southampton. Her only stop was at Cherbourg, 89 miles to the south. She reached the French port at 5:51 p.m., took on more passengers, and sailed at 8:27. The crossing had now begun in earnest.

Because the maiden voyage sailing date had been altered at short notice, only about one-third of the cabins were filled, with 201 passengers in First Class, 86 in Tourist and 63 in Third. Douglas Fairbanks and his Toronto-born wife, Mary Pickford, then among Hollywood's brightest luminaries, had booked at the last moment. Their presence lent a touch of glamour to a passenger list that, at least in First Class, reflected the worlds of business, politics and the press. Mr. Beatty, accompanied by a valet, was making the trip along with a number of friends. Viscount Rothermere, proprietor of the *Daily Mail* of London, was on board and dutifully sent dispatches about the *Britain*, which his newspaper published. "I have no hesitation in describing her as the finest vessel ever launched," His Lordship wrote the second day out. He also mentioned that vibration, a frequent problem on fast new ships, was limited to a faint tremor when he placed his hand on the deck. He was perhaps premature in his judgement. Vibration was noticeable in the shallow waters of the St. Lawrence, although never more than a minor nuisance.

Three Canadian reporters experienced the first crossing: Thomas T. Champion of Canadian Press, C.H. Peters of the Montréal *Gazette* and C.H.J. Snider, news editor of the Toronto *Evening Telegram*. Their daily reports heightened the sense of anticipation felt by many people throughout Canada who had followed the ship's progress in their newspapers since the day she was ordered. To Mr. Snider, the ship embodied "a bold Canadian bid for a topmost seat in the sun of shipping supremacy."

Captain Latta met the journalists on the third day. "I am more than satisfied with the ship's performance during this, her maiden trip," he told them. "Taking into account the weather conditions, in fact, my expectations have been surpassed. Her speed is being entirely maintained and is even increasing, and I was never better pleased with a ship." The weather he spoke of had ranged from overcast to misty to clear with moderate breezes and a slight to moderate sea.

The *Empress of Britain* continued to make excellent time across the Atlantic, but Captain Latta had no intention of asking Chief Engineer Donald to extend the ship to full speed on her first crossing. In four days in unrestricted waters the ship's daily run was 588, 584, 592 and 590 miles. It was obvious to all on board that a record passage was imminent, barring delays caused by fog.

As the ship neared Newfoundland, crew members prepared to haul up over 600 pounds of airmail letters from one of the holds. Mail bags had been put aboard at Southampton, and the Post Office hoped to have them in Montréal four days after they left England. Arrangements to execute the plan were nothing if not thorough. The Canadian Coast Guard ship *Aranmore* stood by at Sydney, Nova Scotia, ready to put to sea at short notice. Two Stearman planes of Canadian Airways had touched down at Sydney after a flight from Montréal. If the *Britain* reached Cabot Strait late Saturday night or early Sunday morning, the *Aranmore* would meet her, receive the mail bags and dash back to Sydney, where they would be transferred to the waiting planes. But it was not to be. The *Britain* arrived later than expected at Cabot Strait, causing the plans to be cancelled, and the four-day mail service between England and Canada was out of the question, at least for the time being.

The shop on the Lounge Deck seemed to have an unusually large number of necklaces for sale. The illuminated glass turrets drew the passengers' attention to the shop's location. Author's Collection

The best-known passengers on the first crossing were Douglas Fairbanks and his wife, Mary Pickford. At left, Mrs. Dorothy Walker Buhler of Toronto; at right, Eric Brown of Ottawa. Author's Collection

The First Class main entrance hall was a convenient location for passengers to gather before going down to dinner four decks below. Author's Collection

The letters were eventually taken ashore when the pilot boat met the *Empress of Britain* at Father Point, near Rimouski, on the St. Lawrence River. Meanwhile, the planes had flown from Sydney to Rimouski. In order to salvage what he could from the situation, Captain Arthur Ingram loaded 280 pounds of mail into his Stearman, took off from the tiny airport and flew out over the St. Lawrence, circled the *Britain* at deck level, then sped on his way to the St. Hubert airport near Montréal, where he landed at 3:10 p.m. on June 1. He handed over the mail to a Post Office official 5 days, 7 hours, 58 minutes after it had left England. The other pilot, Bernard Martin, reached St. Hubert with 327 pounds of mail 20 minutes later. He, too, flew around the *Britain*, but used the opportunity to photograph the ship.

While the *Britain* sailed through the Gulf of St. Lawrence, the newsmen gathered in the walnut-panelled sitting room of E.W. Beatty's deluxe suite to question the president of Canadian Pacific. Mr. Snider inquired, "What would be the price of accommodation like this suite we are in on a world cruise?"

"I shudder to say it," said Mr. Beatty, "but I think it is $20,000." That was the price for two occupants, but he added that it included tours at every port the ship visited. Moving from financial to technical matters, he told the newspapermen that fuel consumption made the difference in operating a steamship and that John Johnson's boiler design would lead to impressive savings. "The *Empress of Britain*," he continued, "with one and a half times the tonnage of the *Empress of Japan*, has actually a lower fuel consumption, and the *Empress of Japan* broke all previous records." The interview ended when Mr. Beatty received a telephone call from Ottawa, more than 600 miles away. The Governor General, the Earl of Bessborough, was welcoming the ship to Canadian waters.

A popular meeting place for men travelling in First Class was the Knickerbocker Bar. Here, between drinks, they dusted off the hoary old jokes that had made the rounds of large North Atlantic passenger ships for years and trotted them out once more. "This ship is so big that I had to ask a steward to direct me to the ocean," was one. "An elevator will take me up to the Lounge Deck, but then I need a taxi to get around it," was another.

A broadcast from the *Britain* was scheduled for Monday afternoon between four and five. A few days earlier, when the ship was about 500 miles out in the Atlantic, a trial broadcast had reached England with such clarity that the organizers were confident of equal success when she neared Québec. Thirty-seven radio stations in Canada and 15 in the United States were linked up to carry Monday's program. The orchestra played selections by Schubert, Massenet and Jerome Kern. Mr. Beatty and Viscount Rothermere spoke glowingly of the ship, as did Miss Pickford, who said, "As a Canadian, I am proud of the *Empress of Britain*. She is the last word in luxury and comfort." Her husband praised the ship in a somewhat circuitous manner, stating that the trip was too short because of the many attractions she offered and that these same attractions robbed one of the sense of being at sea. The program ended with the orchestra playing "O Canada."

In the narrower reaches of the St. Lawrence it was compulsory to carry a pilot, and the one who came aboard at Father Point was 79-year-old Captain J.E. Bernier, well known for his Arctic voyages earlier in the century. The *Britain*'s draft, 32 feet, was the deepest of any ship to use the St. Lawrence, but Captain Bernier knew the channels intimately and the ship did not even stir the mud as she made her way up the river.

As the *Empress of Britain* neared Québec, there was a crowd estimated at more than 100,000 waiting to see her arrival. C.H.J. Snider, hoping to write a story that was different from the other reporters', searched for a position that would give him an unusual perspective to observe the docking of the ship. He found one in the *Britain*'s foremast. Mr. Snider climbed up the ladder inside the mast until he emerged, 112 rungs later, at the lower crow's-nest. Looking down, he saw two white tugs come alongside, ready to push the ship against the dock.

Captain Latta was not to be hurried. Using a searchlight to counter the setting sun, he picked out a bollard over which he meant to place his first mooring line. Slowly and with deliberate care, he brought his ship to a position almost parallel with the dock and about 50 yards offshore. Because

The Knickerbocker Bar was a favourite rendezvous for men. An unusual clock was incorporated in the circular panel above the cash register. Author's Collection

it was too far for a sailor to throw a rope ashore, the first tug took the *Britain*'s thick mooring line, secured a lighter rope known as a heaving line to it, and moved towards the dock. When she reached it, a crewman tossed the heaving line, weighted at one end, upwards to a dockworker, who immediately grabbed it. Several dockworkers hauled it ashore and placed the loop of the attached mooring line around a bollard. The second tug carried out the same operation. The ship's capstans wound in the lines, and shortly before 10 p.m. on Monday, June 1, the *Empress of Britain* completed her first Atlantic crossing. Mr. Snider now descended from the foremast and began writing his article.

The crowd waiting at Wolfe's Cove was not limited to spectators who simply wanted to see the great new white ship. It also included many movie fans who hoped to catch a glimpse of their idols, Douglas Fairbanks and Mary Pickford. The police cordon barely managed to keep them behind the barriers, while newspaper reporters and radio announcers eased their way through and hurried aboard. A woman journalist, claiming to be a fortune-teller, quickly won Miss Pickford's confidence, and by adroitly phrasing her questions soon had the details she wanted for an exclusive story. Reporters employing more conventional means to reach the actress and her husband had to wait.

After concluding their interviews, they sought out Canadian Pacific's president. One reporter found him coming up a stairway and asked him about the ship's speed. "The boat was clamped down all the way, so far as speed was concerned," he said. Nevertheless, it was the fastest crossing on record between Europe and Québec. According to C.H. Peters of the Montréal *Gazette*, the actual time from Southampton to Québec was 5 days, 13 hours, 25 minutes.

The ship had taken the Cape Race route, around the southern shore of Newfoundland. When the seasonal danger of icebergs had passed, the *Britain* would take the shorter Belle Isle route, sailing through the strait between Labrador and Newfoundland. With an optimism that belied his habitual caution, Mr. Beatty claimed, "We'll make passage from Cherbourg to Québec in four and a half days."

For the next three days, the *Empress of Britain* lay at Wolfe's Cove while thousands of visitors came aboard to inspect the wonder ship. The Imperial Order of Daughters of the Empire organized public tours and sold 15,000 tickets at 25 cents each, raising $3,750 for charities. After the last of Tuesday's visitors had left, final touches were put in place for a gala banquet that evening. Among those at the head table in the Salle Jacques Cartier were E.W. Beatty, of course; the Earl of Bessborough; R.B. Bennett, Prime Minister; Sir Robert Borden, former Prime Minister; the Lieutenant-Governors of Québec, New Brunswick and Prince Edward Island; L-A. Taschereau, Premier of Québec; and Captain Latta. The dining room was filled to capacity, with leaders in business, politics and society at every table. Tuesday, June 2, marked an evening of triumph for Canadian Pacific, its newest ship and its president, who, in the course of his remarks, announced that Captain Latta was now appointed Commodore of the Canadian Pacific fleet, the first person to hold this rank in company history.

More than 500 ticket agents and reporters from Canada and the United States arrived at Québec in four special trains early on Wednesday, June 3. They enjoyed breakfast aboard the *Britain*, toured the ship, then assembled in the Salle Jacques Cartier for lunch. William Baird, the company's steamship passenger traffic manager, reminded his guests that a delegation of agents had visited John Brown's yard two years earlier and had made a number of suggestions about the ship's layout and facilities, some of which had been incorporated in the *Britain*. He emphasized that Canadian Pacific offered the shortest and most attractive route to Europe, with excellent rail connections at both ends of the sea journey. He spoke also of the ship's speed. "The land-to-land crossing was made in three days, six hours and twenty-five minutes," he said, referring to the time taken between Bishop Rock in the Scilly Isles off the westernmost tip of England and Cape Race. A good salesman, Mr. Baird delivered a speech that fell on receptive ears, but agents knew it would be difficult to sell tickets as long as the Depression dragged on.

Reporters touring the *Britain* at Québec wrote flattering accounts for newspapers in Canada and the United States. Some were balanced and thoughtful, while others dealt only with trivial

A group of passengers waited expectantly as Douglas Fairbanks posed for the photographer before diving into the Olympian Pool.
Author's Collection

Le Caviar Frais de Sterlet
La Tortue Claire en Tasse
Les Paupiettes de Sole Nantua
Les Médaillons de Boeuf aux Champignons Frais
Les Petits Pois Nouveaux au Beurre
Les Pommes Fondantes
Les Asperges Vertes Sauce Velour
La Coupe Glacée Empress
Les Friandises
Dessert
Demi-Tasse

S.S. Empress of Britain
Quebec June the second
nineteen hundred and thirty-one

Unlike the wide selection of dishes available on a First Class crossing, the dinner menu for the notables of government and business, held aboard the Empress of Britain *on June 2, 1931, offered no choice at all.*
Jay Bascom Collection

CANADIAN PACIFIC STEAMSHIPS, LTD

———◆———

EMPRESS OF BRITAIN

Length 760½ feet.   Beam 97¾ feet.   Net. Tonnage 22,545½   Gross. Tonnage 42,348½

ABSTRACT LOG

SOUTHAMPTON TO QUEBEC VIA CHERBOURG.

SAILED MAY 27, 1931   VOYAGE No. 1

DATE	LATITUDE	LONGITUDE	DIST.	BARO.	Temp'ature Sea	Temp'ature Air	WEATHER REMARKS
May 27	Departure	Southampton		29.86	53	61	Left Southampton 1.12 p.m. ; Arrived Cherbourg 5.51 p.m.
		Cherbourg	89				Left Cherbourg 8.27 p.m. ; N.E.xE.4 ; overcast and clear
„ 28	50.15 N	10.36 W	352	29.50	56	65	S.S.W. 4 ; 5.23 a.m. Bishop Rock ; misty weather to clear
„ 29	50.48 N	26.00 W	588	29.83	56	57	S'ly/N.N.W. 4.7 ; slight to moderate sea ; fine and clear
„ 30	49.19 N	40.58 W	584	29.35	59	55	S'ly to E'ly 4 ; overcast with rain ; slight sea
„ 31	46.30 N	54.54 W	592	29.95	45	51	N.W'ly 4 ; Cape Race 8.48 a.m. ; overcast, fine, clear, slight sea
June 1	To Father	Point	590	29.76	47	49	Var. 3 ; overcast, clear, misty showers
		To Quebec	158				Arrived Father Point 11.35 a.m. ; Left Father Point 12.04 p.m.
							Total distance Southampton to Quebec 2,953 miles.

Beaufort Scale :—   0 Calm   1 Light Airs   2 Light Breeze   3 Gentle Breeze   4 Mod. Breeze   5 Fresh Breeze   6 Strong Breeze
7 Mod. Gale   8 Fresh Gale   9 Strong Gale   10 Whole Gale   11 Storm   12 Hurricane.

Before disembarking, the passengers received a printed abstract of the ship's log, setting out details of the first Atlantic crossing. Author's Collection

matters but all emphasized the size, luxury and speed of the ship. The Montréal *Gazette* gave its readers a list of superlatives, the first of which was unwittingly calculated to irk the proud Scottish residents of Clydebank, where the ship had been built. The unnamed reporter, weak in his knowledge of geography, said that she was the largest built in England since the war. In a more informed vein, he added that the *Empress of Britain* was one of the fastest ships in the world, had a laundry capable of washing 10,000 articles a day, and had 4,500 light bulbs in the Salle Jacques Cartier.

Public inspection of the *Britain* concluded on Thursday, June 4. Earlier that day some of the best swimmers, tennis players and squash players in the province of Québec sampled the sports facilities and pronounced them superior in every way. That evening, a dinner, dance and cabaret were held on board, again under the auspices of the I.O.D.E. The $4 admission included a chartered bus service between Place d'Armes, in the centre of the city, and the ship.

Now it was time to get ready for the ship's return to Southampton on the second leg of the maiden voyage. She left Québec on Saturday, June 6, at 4:30 in the afternoon with 533 passengers, 238 of them in First Class. The crowds watching her leave equalled those that had seen her arrive earlier in the week. Sightseers stood expectantly on the Plains of Abraham and the slopes of Battlefield Park. Spectators packed the streets of the Lower Town. Departure from Wolfe's Cove was uneventful, but when the ship was about 12 miles downstream, low water in a stretch of the river known as the Traverse forced her to anchor for two and a half hours and wait for high tide.

No further setbacks occurred until the *Britain* was only a few miles from Southampton, when heavy fog compelled her again to drop an anchor. When raising it after the fog lifted, the pin of a shackle holding the lengths of chain snapped and the ship resumed her passage, leaving the anchor and 60 fathoms of chain on the seabed. The *Empress of Britain*'s time from Father Point, where the St. Lawrence pilot left, to Southampton by way of Cherbourg was 5 days, 6 hours, 3 minutes—another record.

The calm waters of the St. Lawrence River were ruffled by the Empress of Britain *off Crane Island in bright sunshine on June 1, 1931.* Jay Bascom Collection

Decoration of the Cathay Lounge was a radical departure from the traditional smoking-room style of Atlantic passenger ships. Below the clock is a sculpture nicknamed ''Neptune's Tooth'' by E.W. Beatty. Author's Collection

Bellboys were usually between 14 and 16 years old, small of stature and quick of mind. Their chocolate-brown uniform with gold trim and white gloves had to be spotlessly clean at all times. Author's Collection

CHAPTER 7

THE WORLD'S WONDER SHIP

Following the maiden voyage, the *Empress of Britain* embarked on a series of 16 Atlantic crossings. Her passenger lists remained well below capacity, a problem that continued to challenge Canadian Pacific throughout the decade of the ship's existence. Nevertheless, she showed an operating profit of $396,158 for her first season. Whether the ship ran profitably or not was of little concern to most passengers. To them, the opportunity to travel aboard a luxury liner meant a five-day break from the routines that determined their lives ashore, and they strove to enjoy it.

Newspapers, which had reported every particular of the maiden voyage, now relegated the *Empress of Britain* to the inside pages, but magazines began publishing stories about the wonder ship of the St. Lawrence. Most articles dwelt at length on First Class, with a final paragraph or two describing Tourist and Third, but some also mentioned other features. In *MacLean's Magazine* of August 1, 1931, Leslie Roberts wrote:

> In the argot of the day, she has everything—speed, size, stability, but, above all, luxury to the *n*th degree... Nothing that makes for luxury has been forgotten; nothing that makes for comfort has been overlooked.
>
> Forty-five engineers divide the watch duties. Their engine rooms are the abiding places of innumerable dials and indicators, each finely tuned to speak in terms of minute accuracy to those who understand the intricate language of machines, boilers and pressures. No longer is "the chief" the dour, hard-bitten gentleman who stalks among his boilers wearing a chunk of oily waste in his grimy hand as badge of his trade. The new ship's engineer, à la *Britain*, is a well-groomed technical executive, driving his ship through the seas from a business man's desk, in constant consultation with these dials and indicators whose name is legion on this gigantic liner.
>
> Safety devices abound. New type gravity davits enable her crew to lower boats to the water, far below, in greater security from crash than ever before in the history of the sea. Motor-propelled lifeboats and regulation ship's boats in far greater number than the required government complement swing out from her sides. Gyro-compasses and every imaginable gadget devised by the brain of the nautical scientist provide new aids to safety in navigation at sea or inshore.

Before the ship left Southampton on June 17, a reporter asked Captain Latta about the chances of the *Britain* setting a new record. His laconic reply was, "Wait and see." Although he kept his intentions to himself, he was hoping to take the Belle Isle route and cut about five hours from the first westbound crossing, but his knowledge of fog, which often hung for days off the coast of Newfoundland, prevented any rash prediction. Passengers were confident, however, and had their optimism rewarded when the time from Cherbourg to Father Point was announced as 4 days, 12 hours, 33 minutes. Captain Latta had taken the Belle Isle route, as he had privately expected.

On the basis that this was a faster Atlantic crossing than the record-breaking time of the North German Lloyd ship *Europa*, some journalists declared that the *Empress of Britain* now held the

One of the ship's youngest passengers lay contentedly in a baby carriage as the nursemaid in a properly starched uniform studied her charge.
Author's Collection

The camber, or slight upward curve, of the deck is clearly visible on the promenade at the front of the enclosed section of the Lounge Deck.
CP Rail Corporate Archives

CANADIAN PACIFIC STEAMSHIPS, LTD

◆

EMPRESS OF BRITAIN

Length 760½ feet.   Beam 97¾ feet.   Net. Tonnage 22,545½   Gross. Tonnage 42,348½

ABSTRACT LOG

SOUTHAMPTON TO QUEBEC VIA CHERBOURG.

SAILED JULY 8, 1931.   VOYAGE No. 3 WEST

DATE	LATITUDE	LONGITUDE	DIST.	BARO.	Temp'ature Sea	Air	WEATHER REMARKS
July 8	Departure	Southampton Cherbourg	83	29.85	61	52	Left Southampton 1.30 p.m. ; W.S.W. 5 ; fine and clear. Arrived Cherbourg 4.20 p.m. G.M.T. ; Left Cherbourg 6.29 p.m.
,, 9	51.23 N	12.05 W	423	29.73	61	60	2 20 a.m. Passed Bishop Rock Light ; E.N.E. 3 ; fine and clear ; slight sea.
,, 10	53.26 N	28.28 W	612	29.89	60	60	N'ly 3 ; fine and clear ; slight sea.
,, 11	53.10 N	45.20 W	605	30.10	56	52	S.S.W. 3 ; fine and clear ; slight sea.
,, 12	52.01 N	53.32 W	306	29.82	58	48	W.S.W. 3 ; Dense fog ; slight sea.
,, 13	51.24 N	56.49 W	130	29.63	59	54	S.W. 3 ; Dense fog ; slight sea ; 3 a.m. (approximately) Belle Isle abeam.
,, 14	To Father To	Point Quebec	505 158	29.65	58	53	S.W'ly 3 ; Arrived Father Point 8.49 a.m. ; Left 9.14 a.m. Approximate arrival Quebec 6 p.m. Total distance Southampton to Quebec 2,822 miles.

Beaufort Scale :— 0 Calm 1 Light Airs 2 Light Breeze 3 Gentle Breeze 4 Mod. Breeze 5 Fresh Breeze 6 Strong Breeze
7 Mod. Gale 8 Fresh Gale 9 Strong Gale 10 Whole Gale 11 Storm 12 Hurricane.

The log abstract gave the departure time, but because it was issued to passengers before the ship docked, the arrival time was approximate. Author's Collection

Blue Riband of the Atlantic, the mythical award for the fastest crossing. The *Britain* undeniably took 4 hours, 33 minutes less between Cherbourg and Father Point than the *Europa* did from Cherbourg to the Ambrose Channel light vessel near New York, but the *Britain* had a shorter route and the *Europa* was a faster ship. The award was still rightfully the *Europa*'s, because only New York was recognized as the North American terminal for Blue Riband claims.

The *Empress of Britain* arrived at Wolfe's Cove on June 22, 4 days, 22 hours, 59 minutes after leaving Cherbourg, again a record. When questioned by newsmen, Captain Latta, always economical with words, simply stated, "There is no need for me to say anything; the *Empress* has said it for herself."

About mid-August, Canadian Pacific announced a reduction in First Class fares, ranging from nearly six percent to ten percent, for the rest of the season. The minimum one-way fare dropped from $265 to $250. Upholding shipboard custom, the fare did not include the use of a deck chair. To reserve one, a passenger had to pay $1.50 for the chair, $1.50 for a cushion and $1.50 for a steamer rug. Most of the heavy, polished hardwood chairs were placed on the Lounge Deck, whose promenade was largely glass enclosed as a protection against the frequent damp, raw winds and cold weather of the North Atlantic. In mid-morning, bouillon was served to the well-wrapped passenger. No extra charge was made for the hot drink.

Speed records continued to fall. When the *Britain* reached Québec on August 31, newspapers announced her time from Cherbourg to Father Point as 4 days, 9 hours, 23 minutes. Not every crossing set a record, however, and sometimes the *Britain* had to contend with unco-operative weather. This was brought forcibly home late in August when gales in the English Channel whipped up immense seas which obliterated the Cherbourg breakwater. Not wanting to risk his ship, Captain Latta cruised up and down for several hours before deciding to cancel the call at the French port and proceed directly to Southampton. The 133 disappointed passengers who had packed their bags

**Empress Hotel
Victoria, B.C.**

MENU

Grape Fruit   Apples

Baked Apples, Hot or Cold

Compote of Prunes, Apricots, Plums

Oatmeal Porridge   Milk Toast   Wheatena

Post Toasties   Grape Nuts   Krumbled Bran

Corn Flakes   Pep   Bran Flakes

Findon Haddock in Milk   Fish Kedgery

Eggs : Boiled, Fried, Turned or Poached

Omelettes : Plain, or Grand Mere

Canadian Breakfast Bacon   Beef Ham

Minced Beef with Walnuts

Dorset Sausage

COLD :

York Ham   Leicester Brawn

White and Graham Rolls   Plain or Buttered Toast

Brown, Pulled or Raisin Bread   Bath Buns

Griddle Cakes

Preserves

Tea   Coffee   Cocoa

Breakfast   **Tourist Third Cabin**

Empress of Britain   Sunday, August Thirtieth, 1931

Canadian Pacific

*The Tourist Class breakfast menu is illustrated with a drawing of the Empress Hotel in Victoria.
With railways, steamships and hotels under one management, Canadian Pacific advertised itself
as "The World's Greatest Travel System."* Author's Collection

But the cruise had a few serious aspects as well. The ship's library held an extensive supply of books about lands along the route, and the principal lecturer, Martin DeMuth, was a fountain of information in the talks he gave before the *Britain*'s arrival at each port. Whether it was history, economics, climate or shopping, he usually had a ready answer to every question. In addition, the cruise staff issued memograms, complete with maps and illustrations drawn by Mr. DeMuth, describing places of interest in the ports of call.

A newspaper, *Empress of Britain World Cruise News,* appeared daily during lunch when the ship was at sea. Small though it was, consisting of a double sheet 10 inches by 6 inches, it had an experienced reporter as editor, J. Fergus Grant of the Montréal *Gazette.* While shipboard events were always found in its columns, most space was allotted to world news, which arrived by radio. Grim statistics of unemployment, the Japanese occupation of Manchuria, and exchange rates for the dollar and pound contrasted with details of the ship's daily mileage, reminders to advance the clocks one hour at midnight and notices for the concert in the Mayfair Lounge.

After a record-breaking time of 5 days, 9 hours, 55 minutes from Port Tewfik, the *Britain* arrived at Bombay on Thursday, January 7. The ship sat too deep in the water for her to tie up at a dock, so she anchored in the harbour and passengers went ashore by tender. Reporters and spectators milled around the tourists as they disembarked at Ballard Pier. They focused their attention on one in particular, Barbara Hutton, heiress to the $50-million Woolworth fortune, who was travelling with her mother. A recent debutante, she made news wherever she went, and India was no exception. Four trains were waiting to take the passengers on tours of India. Their sleeping cars were of the non-corridor type and each two-person compartment was equipped with a small shower. A manservant was assigned to every two compartments. These arrangements delighted Miss Bridie, but Barbara Hutton and her mother travelled in much greater luxury, with a saloon car attached to the train for their exclusive use.

Following a week of extensive sightseeing, passengers returned to Bombay with trinkets and souvenirs of their visit to India. Silk scarves, embroidered shawls, brass trays and little ivory elephants proved to be the most popular items.

The *Empress of Britain* was not air-conditioned, and while fans and ventilators were useful, the heat was oppressive at times, particularly in port. Chefs now prepared iced soup, iced coffee and a variety of cold dishes. Passengers frequently ate lunch on the open decks, but most avoided the sun except for short periods. One regular foursome of bridge players always remained indoors, however, oblivious to everything except their cards.

Passengers fell into a routine while the *Britain* was at sea. Some had breakfast in their cabins, while others ate in the dining saloon. One, in an idle moment, counted 115 items on the breakfast menu. Although the Salle Jacques Cartier could hold all passengers at once, there were two sittings for lunch, at 12:30 and 1:30, and two for dinner, at 6:15 and 7:30. Smoking was permitted in the dining saloon only on the second sitting at lunch and dinner and was forbidden at breakfast. Each evening one of the orchestras, consisting of two violins, a cello and a piano, entertained diners.

After breakfast, some passengers took a daily swim in the Olympian Pool or in the smaller temporary outdoor pool forward on the Lounge Deck. Others played squash or tennis. For the less vigorous, a deck steward provided equipment for shuffleboard, bullboard and deck quoits. At 11 in the morning, waiters came round with ice cream or bouillon, according to the weather.

Following lunch, people chatted with friends, read, wrote letters, played cards or strolled around the Lounge Deck until tea was served at four. After dinner, an evening program entertained or enlightened passengers. Mr. DeMuth delivered his well-researched lectures. The projectionist screened Hollywood and British films in the Empress Room. The ship's classical orchestra, led by violinist Stuart Jones, gave concerts. Fred English not only played double bass but also sang in a fine baritone voice. Some evenings fancy dress balls were held, and often there were private cocktail parties. Attendance as a guest at a private party implied, at least in the minds of some passengers, the obligation to act as host at a later date. The bars continued to do good business

A popular trip was the excursion to the Pyramids of Egypt. On the Britain's *first world cruise, someone took a snapshot of the tents in which a group of passengers spent the night.*
Author's Collection

The open-air swimming pool was a temporary structure erected on the forward section of the Lounge Deck each year after the world cruise began.
Author's Collection

Cabin 7 on the Sports Deck was located directly above the Knickerbocker Bar. Here, as elsewhere in the ship, the grain of the wood was strongly evident.
CP Rail Corporate Archives

with duty-free prices. Planned entertainment usually ended at 10:45 each night, leaving time for a late swim before passengers retired to their cabins.

As the *Britain* sailed south from Bombay to Ceylon, Miss Bridie brought her diary up to date. On January 17 she wrote:

> Day after day of perfect sunshine and cloudless blue skies. Not a sign of rain or even greyness. Very hot but never uncomfortable as there is a soft breeze, and there is a fan and three ventilators in my stateroom. To-day has been another absolute foretaste of Heaven. This morning I spent half an hour in the gym, then had a swim before church, and after lunch I wore my blue figured muslin, and sat in my lounge chair on deck for two to three hours reading peacefully. It was unutterably perfect. I shall always be tremendously glad that I came. During all the years I have waited and worked towards it, I never thought it would be so much better worthwhile than I anticipated.
>
> I am feeling splendidly well and strong, in fact just my own energetic self again. Every day I swim and tramp, cycle and row (in gym), play tennis, and in intervals make friends. Of all the delights of the trip, I enjoy the days at sea best of all. Surely I have more salt water than blood in my veins. I could go to the topmost deck and shout aloud with exultation.

The traditional ceremony of crossing the line was planned for the day when the ship reached the equator. Entering into the spirit of the occasion, Captain Latta announced that he had received a telegram from Father Neptune asking, "Are you applying for safe conduct through our equatorial domains?" He had replied, "Yes, please, passenger list 379 souls, crew of 649." But the good-natured revelry that would have accompanied crossing the line had to be postponed. A heavy swell of the Indian Ocean, together with stifling heat, caused the event to be rescheduled to a week later, when King Neptune, looking uncommonly like the ship's Chief Officer, held court with his ducking chair displayed prominently beside the outdoor pool. Volunteer victims, forewarned about the nature of the festivities, sensibly wore swimsuits under their already limited clothing as they sat in the chair, waiting to be lathered with soap and shaved with a 6-foot wooden razor before being tipped backward into the pool.

Stops at Padang, Batavia, Singapore and Bangkok came and went. When the *Britain* reached Manila, thousands of spectators lined up to see her arrival. The shore excursion at the capital of the Philippines departed from the familiar kind of sightseeing tour by including a visit to the Bilibid Prison with its 3,000 inmates. The prison workshop did a brisk business in the sale of canework and inlaid boxes, and while passengers shopped, the prison band entertained them with a selection of military airs. Female prisoners, confined to their own section of the jail, scrambled to the bars of their cells to stare at the tourists when they left.

As the ship was steaming towards Hong Kong, rumours spread that the visit to Shanghai would be omitted because of the fighting that was raging around the city. These stories were temporarily put aside when the *Britain* entered Hong Kong harbour and dropped her two bow anchors. Dozens of sampans immediately surrounded the ship, children holding up nets to catch coins the passengers threw down.

The stay in Hong Kong was extended from four to five days because the call at Shanghai was indeed cancelled. Passengers explored the British colony and ventured inland as far as Canton. The Peak in Hong Kong, its commanding view one of the main objectives of the sightseers, was unfortunately shrouded in mist when one group reached the summit, so everyone descended and went on a shopping expedition. Though most passengers were wealthy, they were not averse to bargain hunting. Marion Bridie, not one of the more prosperous, had an eye for thrift and a taste for luxury. She bought some embroidered-silk nightdresses for seven shillings and sixpence each (about $2) and a three-piece set in fine silk for £1 (about $5). "Oh," she wrote, "but those silky

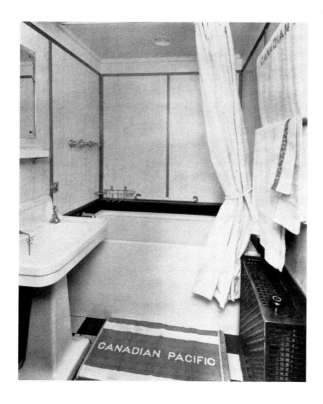

After a day of sightseeing in the Orient, a long soak in a bathtub sounded inviting, but not every tub in the ship was full length.
CP Rail Corporate Archives

garments are luscious." Other passengers came aboard laden with jade, ivory, kimonos, silk shawls and dresses. Some even carried canaries in little wooden cages.

The *Empress of Britain* attracted considerable attention from the residents of Hong Kong. Passengers were permitted to bring friends aboard for a tour of the ship and a meal; during the stay waiters served 800 additional meals. Other intending visitors, though, had to apply for a pass before they were allowed on board.

Miss Bridie, who had spent two days living ashore with the granddaughter of the half-brother of her grandmother's cousin, returned on Monday morning and found a place on the Sun Deck to take a prolonged look at Hong Kong as the ship sailed. Unwittingly, she had neglected the ninth point on the printed sheet "Ten Important Points" which had been placed in every cabin on the first day of the cruise. It read: "Passengers are respectfully requested to advise their room stewards of their re-embarkation on the ship preparatory to its sailing." A muttered "Thank goodness" from her distraught cabin steward, who spotted his errant passenger after a hurried search of the ship, reminded Miss Bridie of her thoughtlessness.

Cabin stewards' duties kept them steadily occupied from the time they delivered breakfast or gave wake-up calls until they turned down the bed covers at night. Most First Class cabins had en-suite bathrooms, usually with access from the vestibule off the ship's corridor as well as from the bedroom. This arrangement allowed the steward to enter the bathroom and fill the bath without disturbing occupants of the cabin. The task completed, a knock on the inside door and "Your bath is ready, ma'am" informed the passenger that the tub was filled to the required depth and heated to the requested temperature. It was the kind of service that First Class passengers expected and that Canadian Pacific ensured they received.

The *Britain* avoided Shanghai and sailed north to Chinwangtao, a port about 150 miles from Peking. Mr. DeMuth gave an engrossing lecture on Peking but the ship's arrival in Chinwangtao was, in a literal sense, chilling. The 90 degrees Fahrenheit in Manila had given way nine days later to 23 degrees in the northern Chinese port. Ice floes, several inches thick, dotted the harbour.

Wool and fur coats that passengers had placed in storage more than two months earlier now became essential. The statement in the brochure advising members of the cruise that "winter has departed from China by the time the cruise ship arrives" was forgotten, however, as travellers stepped ashore for the train journey to Peking and a five-day stay in the bustling city.

To Miss Bridie, Peking was old and cold, dirty and dusty, but it was also thrilling and fascinating. She and her fellow passengers travelled throughout the city in rickshaws, visiting the Imperial Palace, the Summer and Winter Palaces and the Marble Barge. They spent one evening at a Chinese theatre, but the members of the audience, who were gossiping, buying and selling food, eating, and wiping their faces with damp hot towels during the performance, held their interest far more than the play itself. No visit to Peking was complete without a trip to the Great Wall, and the tourists, abandoning fashion for warmth, donned fur-lined coats, caps, gaiters and galoshes as they trooped aboard a special train for the short journey north on a bitterly cold day. Before leaving Peking, some cruise members attended an informal talk by American writer Pearl Buck, whose novel *The Good Earth* had recently been published to critical and popular acclaim.

The train that took everyone back to Chinwangtao was guarded by a small group of soldiers. As well as passengers, the train contained their abundant purchases of furs, jade, antiques, silk, satins, linens and embroidered work to the value of $50,000. Before boarding the *Britain*, passengers had to pay the Chinese government seven and a half percent duty and ten percent Flood Relief Tax on nearly everything.

At 8 p.m. on February 23, the ship departed, pushing her way through crackling ice floes in the harbour. She now had an 800-mile journey to Beppu, a small Japanese town at the entrance to the Inland Sea. Cold though the weather remained, passengers forgot about it on seeing row after row of tiny children welcome them with songs and flags. When they came ashore, visitors went by automobile to the town's auditorium, where the mayor, speaking through an interpreter, greeted them effusively. Dancing and music delayed the sightseeing tour but failed to diminish the passengers' enjoyment of their visit to this small holiday resort.

The ship remained in Japanese waters for nine days, calling at Kobe and Yokohama. Kobe was a disappointment, but the *Britain*'s visit there was principally to allow sightseers to visit the nearby historic cities of Kyoto and Nara. While the ship made her way to Yokohama, the guides who had shepherded passengers around Kyoto and Nara travelled to the port by train and for the second time in a few days welcomed the visitors as they stepped ashore. Tokyo was only a short distance away and the passengers spent the next four days touring the Japanese capital.

Yokohama to Honolulu, a distance of nearly 3,400 miles, was the longest unbroken run of the cruise. Outdoors, a new series of sports competitions began. Indoors, one more bridge tournament started. Miss Bridie entered a spelling bee and won second prize, a memorandum book. Another fancy-dress evening was held, and considering the purchases the women had made in India, China and Japan, it presented no difficulties in creating original costumes.

A deck officer conducted tours of the bridge. He reassured Miss Bridie about the watertight compartments into which the ship was divided and the smoke detection devices that allowed fires to be located quickly. She was surprised to hear that the water in the Olympian Pool weighed 300 tons and that the ship used 300 tons of water a day, but that the total passengers, complete with their baggage, weighed less than 300 tons.

The *Britain*'s ship-to-shore telephone became highly popular with passengers. While on the Indian Ocean, Fergus Grant had a 20-minute conversation with a representative of the Canadian Marconi Company at Yamachiche, Québec, 7,000 miles away. Some weeks later, he phoned a telephone company official in the Philippines. Newspapers in Manila reported the story, which led to a flood of calls from the city to the ship. Midway between Japan and Honolulu, American passengers began to phone friends in Hawaii, ostensibly to let them know the ship's arrival time but mostly to impress them with the fact that the call came from a ship in mid-ocean. Subsequent news stories in the Honolulu press created an added interest to an already well-advertised ship.

Saturday, February 27, 1932

YESTERDAY we were at beautiful Beppu, quaint hot spring city on the Island of Kyushu, where the Japanese gave us a most friendly welcome. The charm of Beppu's scenery was augmented by the gracious hospitality of her people.

NOW by daylight the *EMPRESS OF BRITAIN* is wending her way through the Inland Sea between the Islands of Hondo and Shikoku. The day is ideally clear. We are truly fortunate in seeing this wondrous miniature Mediterranean under such excellent weather conditions.

The panorama is ever-changing...snow-capped mountains in the background, hundreds of intimate islands, decorated with picturesque villages...... Toy-like sail boats glide by us in the sparkling water of emerald, turquoise, jade..... mirrored paintings of fairyland.

We arrive in Kobe this afternoon. Kyoto and Nara, Japan's former capitals, will be visited on included excursions by special trains from Kobe.

On Wednesday, March 2nd, we shall proceed to Yokohama.

If Mr. DeMuth's memogram for February 27 were typical, there was practically no need for a passenger to keep a diary of the cruise. Les Carson

Marion Bridie continued to write, or, as she put it, "peg away at," her diary each evening between 7:15 and 9 o'clock. Canadian Pacific had surely no better advocate than this middle-aged Scottish lady. The day the ship crossed the International Date Line, thus giving passengers and crew March 11 twice over, she wrote:

There have been many halcyon days but this has been the best of all... After three good sets of tennis the Olympian Pool (well named) was simply intoxicating, and then a little friendly converse sauntering around among the many with whom I have found mutual interests... The soft winds and the gentle motion of the ship lulled one into

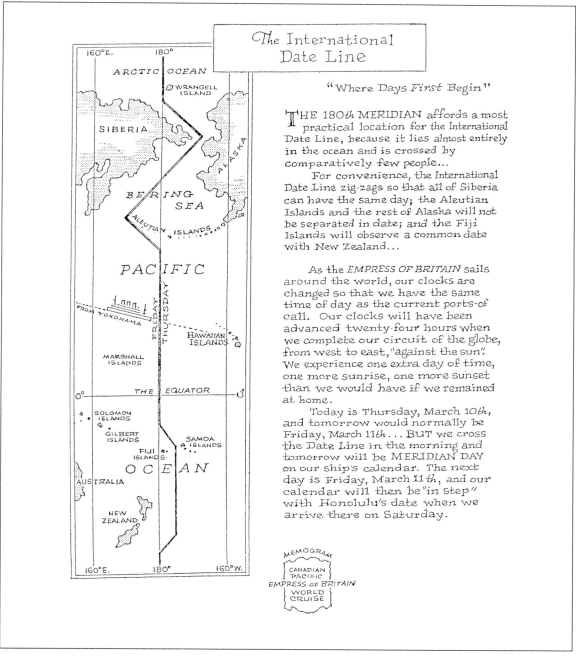

The International Date Line

"Where Days First Begin"

THE 180th MERIDIAN affords a most practical location for the International Date Line, because it lies almost entirely in the ocean and is crossed by comparatively few people...

For convenience, the International Date Line zig-zags so that all of Siberia can have the same day; the Aleutian Islands and the rest of Alaska will not be separated in date; and the Fiji Islands will observe a common date with New Zealand...

As the EMPRESS OF BRITAIN sails around the world, our clocks are changed so that we have the same time of day as the current ports-of call. Our clocks will have been advanced twenty-four hours when we complete our circuit of the globe, from west to east, "against the sun". We experience one extra day of time, one more sunrise, one more sunset than we would have if we remained at home.

Today is Thursday, March 10th, and tomorrow would normally be Friday, March 11th... BUT we cross the Date Line in the morning and tomorrow will be MERIDIAN DAY on our ship's calendar. The next day is Friday, March 11th, and our calendar will then be "in step" with Honolulu's date when we arrive there on Saturday.

MEMOGRAM
CANADIAN PACIFIC
EMPRESS of BRITAIN
WORLD CRUISE

The International Date Line gave passengers a new topic of conversation and the memogram tried to explain it in simple terms. Les Carson

day dreams. A school of dolphins lolloped past, not another being in sight and hardly a sound. Soft, baby clouds made fleeting shadows on the ocean. I was almost driven to wonder whether Heaven could offer more.

Honolulu gave a traditional Hawaiian welcome on March 12, with young ladies draping leis around the visitors' necks as they stepped ashore after seven days at sea. Friendly though the welcome was, many passengers were more concerned about receiving mail that the ship's agent brought aboard. After two days in Honolulu and one in Hilo, the *Britain* left Hawaii for San Francisco.

The Empress of Britain*'s visit to San Pedro, the port for Los Angeles, attracted large crowds who were eager to see the biggest ship to call at a Californian port.* Author's Collection

The cruise staff distributed an analysis of passengers by sex and age, and to no one's surprise, women outnumbered men by two to one. The average passenger was 49 years, 7 months; the oldest, a man of 84; and the youngest, a child of four.

Shortly before the ship reached San Francisco, Marion Bridie sat one evening in the dining room, where she ate alone by preference, and asked Heald, her waiter, for a dinner of radishes, bread and cheese. He remonstrated as far as his position allowed but finally complied with her wishes. Moderation at the table was difficult to practise when the menus were so inviting:

BREAKFAST

FRUIT
Water melon, papayas, mangoes; sliced fresh Hawaiian pineapple, oranges, apples, grapefruit; iced orange juice, grapefruit juice; compote of prunes, peaches, pears, figs, apricots, pineapple, baked apples (hot or cold); iced sauerkraut; clam juice, tomato juice.

SOUP
French onion soup, clam broth.

CEREALS
Oatmeal porridge; Wheatena; boiled rice, milk toast; Grape Nuts, Puffed Rice, Puffed Wheat, Post Toasties, Shredded Wheat, Force, Bran Flakes, Pep, Corn Flakes, Rice Krispies.

FISH
Broiled kippered herring, fried flounder, fish cakes, anchovy sauce.

EGGS
Boiled, fried, turned, poached, scrambled (en cocotte), shirred (country style).

OMELETTES
Nature, au cibolette, Parmesan, louvournaise, bonne femme, sweet.

READY DISHES
Creamed minced chicken on toast, Salisbury steak with smothered onions.

GRILL TO ORDER
Premium, Wiltshire and Ayrshire bacon; beef, ham; calves' liver meunière, Cumberland ham, sheep's kidneys on toast, Deerfoot and Palethorpe sausages; French lamb chop; breakfast steak.

POTATOES
Baked jacket, mashed, lyonnaise.

COLD MEATS
York ham, sliced turkey, galantine of capon, spiced beef, Melton Mowbray pie.

BREADS AND PASTRIES
Graham, white, whole wheat, cottage, French, raisin, Energen; Vienna rolls; plain, buttered, French, cinnamon, Hovis and Melba toast; corn muffins, Scotch baps, croissants, brioche, bran muffins, yeast tablets; lemon scones, toasted Sally Lunns, streusel kuchen; griddle, buckwheat and wholemeal cakes; waffles, Demerara sugar; banana waffles.

PRESERVES
Honey (clear or cloudy), honey in comb, coconut honey, various jams and jellies.

COFFEE
French, American, Sanka, Kellogg's Kaffee Hag, instant, Postum.

TEA
Orange pekoe, Ceylon, China, green, Tilleul, mint.

Cocoa, chocolate, Ovaltine, Horlick's malted milk, iced tea, iced coffee, iced chocolate.

The *Empress of Britain* arrived at San Francisco on Sunday, March 20, the largest ship to sail through the Golden Gate. Tugboats brought her into a recently dredged dock and gently pushed the ship against Pier 32. Mayor Angelo Rossi came down to welcome the *Britain*, and for the next two days thousands of San Franciscans visited the Embarcadero to see the ship for themselves. At night, she could be identified from several miles away when her searchlights focused on the three towering buff funnels.

Los Angeles did not match San Francisco's popularity with the passengers, but the ship's late-evening departure displayed the extravagance of a Hollywood premiere when searchlights of 20 naval vessels swept the skies then bathed the *Britain*'s hull with light, while a fireboat shot great streams of water into the air. A six-day passage took the ship to the Panama Canal, where, unlike the Suez Canal, passengers remained aboard for the transit. The *Britain* was the biggest vessel to traverse the Panama Canal, and was therefore assessed the highest fee, $18,941.25, a sum reached by multiplying the ship's net tonnage (15,153 according to the United States rules of measurement which prevailed in the Canal Zone) by $1.25.

Representatives of the canal administration came aboard at Balboa to hand out descriptive folders and give commentaries during the eight-hour trip through the 18-year-old canal. The 40-mile journey began at six in the morning, with many passengers who had placed early wake-up calls already on deck. Five small but powerful electric locomotives positioned on tracks at each side of the two 110-foot-wide Miraflores Locks at the Pacific end assisted the *Britain*, the forward locomotives pulling and the others holding the ship steady while she went through the locks. After the ship left the next lock, the Pedro Miguel, Miss Bridie found the canal voyage to be an exhilarating experience, her enjoyment marred only by the guides' incessant chatter on the loudspeakers, giving information that was self-evident and repeating what was already printed in the folders. Near the Caribbean end of the canal, the ship dropped through three more locks, then spent a few hours at the nearby city of Cristobal before leaving for Havana.

At the Cuban capital, a number of passengers who resided in the southern United States left and about 150 people came on board for the 1,200-mile trip to New York. During the circling of the globe, passengers had come and gone at various ports. Most of those who had embarked at New York and Monte Carlo some months earlier took the entire cruise, but Canadian Pacific knew there was profit to be made by accepting people who wanted to take only one particular segment.

On Friday, April 10, a cold, grey morning, the big white ship reached New York. Warmly wrapped passengers stepped ashore to be welcomed in many cases by friends and families who had seen them off four months previously. After 128 days, the *Empress of Britain*'s first world cruise was over, a huge success in the eyes of her passengers. E.W. Beatty, as president of Canadian Pacific, said he was satisfied with the financial return, and the shore staff had already planned most of the details of the next world cruise.

The ship now crossed the Atlantic, carrying the hundred European passengers who had made the complete circuit of the globe, along with about 350 on a routine crossing from New York to Cherbourg and Southampton. For Marion Bridie, after the heady experience of a four-month cruise to fascinating lands, the Atlantic crossing was something of an anticlimax. The *Britain* reached Southampton about four in the afternoon of April 15. Passengers saw their baggage taken ashore then waited impatiently for the formalities to be completed before they set foot again in England.

Miss Bridie, meticulous as ever, had made lists by category of everything she had bought, with each article's purchase price in local currency and in sterling. Consequently, she went through customs inspection in less than ten minutes then boarded the special train for London. Recollections of the memorable cruise and the sense of anticipation at coming home competed in her mind and neither won.

The *Empress of Britain* would now spend a month in Southampton, undergoing minor renovations for her season on the North Atlantic. Her crew dispersed to their homes for several weeks before rejoining the ship for the May 21 departure for Québec.

And Marion Bridie found a few moments to complete the diary she had kept so assiduously for four months:

> My *Empress*, oh, my *Empress*, how I love you. On your long, lonely voyages my thoughts will be with you. On sunny mornings and on grey stormy days you will know that in spirit I am tramping up and down your decks... But nothing can ever really be grey again for the backward memories will remain forever like a golden crimson sunset.

The walnut-panelled Library had the latest works of fiction and non-fiction as well as a selection of classics and reference books. Author's Collection

CHAPTER 9

THE SECOND
ATLANTIC SEASON

Publicity surrounding the *Empress of Britain*'s first season on the North Atlantic tapered off in 1932, but the ship continued to make news. Before sailing from Southampton on May 21, she spent some days in dry dock having the outer propellers restored to allow her to maintain her exacting timetable during the 20 scheduled crossings.

In First Class, minimum one-way fare fell to $200. By contrast, fares for the *Empress of Australia*, an older and smaller ship on the same route, began at $148. The lowest-priced Tourist Class ticket from Québec to Southampton for the *Empress of Britain* cost $103; oddly enough, it was $111 for the slightly shorter journey to Cherbourg. Third Class passengers paid $71.50 for an eastbound crossing to Southampton, but a westbound sailing cost $1 more. The success of the ship-to-shore telephone service during the world cruise brought a reduction to $3 a minute for calls to most of eastern Canada and the northeast United States when the Britain was within 500 miles of the North American coastline.

Only 313 passengers made the first trip from Southampton and Cherbourg to Québec. Procedures at Cherbourg followed a set pattern. The *Britain* anchored instead of tying up at a dock, then a tender ferried passengers, baggage and any mail bags out to the ship. The call seldom took more than two and a half hours.

Because of the *Britain*'s speed, postal authorities on both sides of the Atlantic used her frequently as a mail ship. They resumed the previous year's experiments, involving the use of aircraft when the ship arrived in Canadian waters. Extensive planning went into the scheduling and costs were high, but the Canadian Post Office persisted in its efforts to establish a four-day mail service between London and Montréal.

On June 24, the *Britain* sailed from Southampton with letters mailed that morning in the English capital. Four days later, in the Strait of Belle Isle, 14 mail bags were transferred to a Royal Canadian Navy minesweeper, which in short order handed them over to a waiting seaplane in Bradore Bay. After a flight to Havre St. Pierre, the mail was put aboard a second seaplane, which intended to touch down at Rimouski. The pilot, realizing that the St. Lawrence waters were too rough, flew his plane inland to Lac Laguille. There the bags were quickly thrown into a car which took them to Rimouski, where a land-based aircraft was warming up. The sacks were promptly loaded, and the plane set off for the St. Hubert airport, arriving at 3:45 in the afternoon. Montréal mail was removed and taken away for sorting and delivery, leaving another plane to fly the remaining bags to Ottawa. It arrived at 4:45 on June 28, and thus the four-day mail service between the capital cities was established. Whether it was worth continuing, in view of the expense and logistical difficulties, was another matter.

Attention of a less welcome kind came to the ship on her fourth westbound crossing in 1932. Government delegations from Britain, South Africa, India, Northern Ireland and Southern Rhodesia were on board, and therefore the passenger list contained more than its usual share of notables. Delegates were to attend the Imperial Conference in Ottawa, the British group led by Stanley Baldwin,

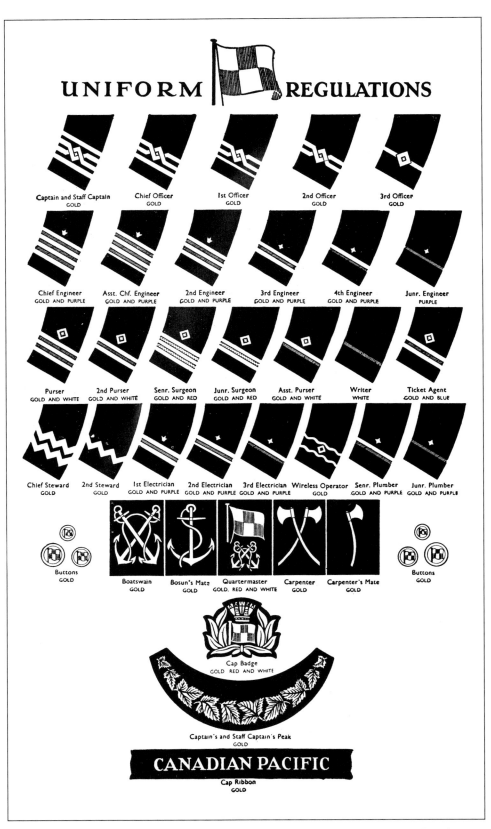

The passenger list usually included a page depicting sleeve insignia for easy identification of officers and crew. Author's Collection

The Empress of Britain's *arrival at Wolfe's Cove, Québec, meant regular employment for local tugs. The propeller of the* Busy Bee *churned the water in the foreground.*
CP Rail Corporate Archives

There was little damage to either ship when the Empress of Britain *and the 4,000-ton* Briarwood *collided near the mouth of the Saguenay River on July 18, 1932.*
Steamship Historical Society Collection, University of Baltimore Library

formerly Prime Minister and now Lord President of the Council. One reporter left a list of questions for Mr. Baldwin to answer as the ship approached Québec. While most of his comments were platitudes ("A delightful passage" and "We are deeply grateful to Canadian Pacific and Captain Latta for the comfort in which we have spent the last few days"), he knew the advantages the *Britain* offered in combining business with pleasure. "We have done much useful work on board," he said, a reference to the meetings the delegates had held in the ship.

Afternoon tea was a daily ritual. It was served in the lounges as well as on deck. CP Rail Corporate Archives

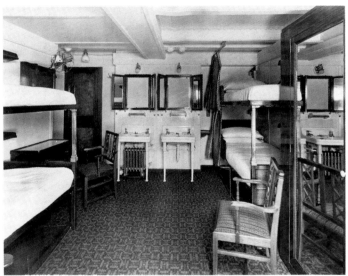

Cabin 520 in Tourist Class was located on the starboard side of E Deck, less than 100 feet from the stern. The door at left connected with Cabin 524.
Glasgow University Archives/ Scottish Record Office

MENU

Grape Fruit Grenadine

Petite Marmite Henri IV

Poussins en Cocotte Beurre Noisette
Petits pois   Haricots verts
Cœur de Laitue

Asperges, Deux Sauces

Soufflé Grand Succès
Friandises

Mr. G. W. Essery

Mrs. Essery

Miss Amy Essery

Miss Doris Essery

Miss Margaret Essery

Empress of Britain   Friday, June 17th, 1932.

The Essery family had a private dinner one day after the Empress of Britain *left Québec on June 16, 1932.*
Author's Collection

What he did not mention was the fire that broke out in the *Empress of Britain* on July 17 during a concert that evening in the Empress Room, over which Mr. Baldwin presided, a job normally given to a well-known passenger with some ability to speak in public. The ship's concert, a custom observed on almost every crossing, gave passengers an opportunity to display whatever vocal, instrumental or comedic skills they possessed—or thought they did. Just before this particular program ended, someone saw smoke curling near the stage. Mr. Baldwin spotted it too and announced at once, "That ends the concert." The passengers filed out of the crowded lounge without signs of fear or panic. Stewards and a watchman put the fire out with a water hose and a chemical extinguisher. An investigation showed that it was caused by a fused electric wire in the switchboard.

The fire, although minor, was not the only problem the *Britain* faced during this crossing. Icebergs, then heavy fog, had delayed her. Finally the fog lifted, but it returned as the ship sailed up the St. Lawrence River. Off the mouth of the Saguenay, when many of the passengers were eating breakfast, the *Empress of Britain* and a 4,013-ton cargo ship, the *Briarwood*, collided. The ships avoided a head-on collision but nevertheless struck each other a glancing blow, the *Briarwood* receiving the worse of the encounter. When it became clear that neither ship was in any danger, the *Britain* carried on towards Wolfe's Cove, while the outbound *Briarwood* returned to Québec for inspection. Although the cargo ship had a large dent in her starboard bow and had lost part of an anchor, she was soon able to resume her passage to England. The *Britain* also had a dented starboard bow, but was not in any danger. A Marine Department representative said that because damage was slight, an inquiry was unlikely.

It had been an eventful crossing for crew and passengers, but reporters at Québec were more interested in getting the delegates' opinions about the forthcoming Ottawa Conference for their newspapers' front pages than in listening to comments about icebergs, fog, fire and collision. Stories about the passage itself were buried in the centre pages.

Most voyages passed without incident, which was precisely what Canadian Pacific wanted. If the ship's name were to be in the news, it should be in a favourable context. One such occasion arose when Melville Caverhill, a 22-year-old would-be author, won a round-trip ticket from Southampton to Québec for a magazine essay. He indulged his passion for tennis on the Sports Deck, notwithstanding a tendency to serve double faults frequently. A condition of the prize was that on his return he had to write a second essay. He had no misgivings about doing so, and the fact that 14 editors and all his relatives had advised him against a career in journalism did little to temper his enthusiasm. Canadian Pacific received a good measure of attention from his efforts, although, like most publicity, it was difficult to assess its effectiveness in terms of tickets sold.

As the 1932 season on the North Atlantic drew to a close in October, statisticians calculated the *Britain*'s best times for the year. When she took the pilot aboard at Cherbourg on June 21, her time from Father Point, 158 miles downriver from Québec, was 4 days, 7 hours, 58 minutes, beating her previous record by 1 hour, 22 minutes. Captain Latta noted that this was 9 hours, 8 minutes less than the best passage between the Ambrose Light, about 22 miles from New York, and Cherbourg. Her best westward time, from the Cherbourg breakwater to Father Point, also in June, was 4 days, 8 hours, 27 minutes.

Despite the newness of the *Britain* and the high reputation she had gained, only 11,294 passengers sailed in her in 1932, 3,235 in First Class, 3,542 in Tourist and 4,517 in Third.

Planning for the second world cruise was now virtually complete, and the *Empress of Britain* left Southampton on November 23 for New York, with her outer propellers again removed. The passenger list was headed by Noel Coward, travelling to New York to direct one of his plays. Among the lesser known was Lt. Col. Georges Vanier, Secretary to Canada's High Commissioner in London, who 27 years later became Governor General. The 276 passengers disembarked and three days later the second world cruise began.

The Empress of Britain *made her solitary way through the Panama Canal one week before the world cruise ended.*
Steamship Historical Society Collection, University of Baltimore Library

CHAPTER 10

THE PLAYWRIGHT PASSENGER

If the ship herself was the star of the first world cruise, a passenger was the star of the second. George Bernard Shaw, 76 years old, made headlines wherever the *Empress of Britain* sailed. The Irish playwright, accompanied by his wife, did not embark until Monte Carlo; therefore, when the ship left New York, reporters wrote extensively about the *Britain* and said little about the ticket holders.

Despite the best efforts of Canadian Pacific, fewer than 190 American and Canadian passengers booked for the complete globe-circling journey. About 100 others were headed for the Mediterranean and India, including Cornelius Vanderbilt Jr., who had surprised his wealthy and famous family by becoming a journalist, then later establishing newspapers in California. He intended to leave the ship at Athens and travel through Europe, interviewing the 15 most important political leaders in the major European countries if, as the *New York Times* somewhat unkindly remarked, "he can decide by that time who they are."

With Captain Latta on the bridge, assisted by a pilot for the trip down the Hudson River, the *Empress of Britain* sailed at noon on December 3, 1932. As she backed away from the pier, a red Bellanca plane of Aerial Explorations circled the ship and a photographer began taking shots of her. Aerial coverage of a ship's departure was not uncommon, but on this occasion the pilot did not return immediately to the airport. Instead, he followed the ship while the photographer removed the film from his camera and placed it in a bag with long streamers attached. When the *Britain* neared Staten Island, the plane flew in low and, in the brief moment it was over the tennis court, dropped the bag onto the deck. One of the ship's photographers retrieved it, hurried down to his darkroom, then quickly developed the film and made several hundred prints. He distributed them at once to passengers, who now owned pictures of the departure before the ship's pilot had even left the *Britain*.

The itinerary of the second cruise was almost identical to the first. Funchal, Gibraltar and Algiers were the *Britain*'s first three ports. The European contingent, 60 strong and mostly British, came aboard at Monte Carlo and the ship set course for Naples, Athens and Haifa. Most passengers disembarked at Haifa for their Christmas visit to the Holy Land and missed the Empire-wide December 25 radio program, culminating with King George V's speech, in which five minutes were allocated to a broadcast from the *Empress of Britain*. George Bernard Shaw and his wife were among the few remaining aboard until she reached Port Said.

With most passengers ashore, Shaw now had time to get on with his writing, which was one of his reasons for taking the cruise, but he also took regular brisk walks around the deck and a daily swim in the pool. Bar stewards, always alert to the opportunity to make a little extra money, devised a plan to enrich themselves from Shaw's presence, but without cost to the playwright. He had stated firmly that he would not give one single autograph during the cruise. In the *Britain*'s bars, passengers were not allowed to pay for their drinks with cash; instead, they signed a card and settled their accounts periodically. The stewards proposed to supply Shaw with the drinks he

On the tennis court, one of the Empress of Britain*'s most popular amenities on cruises and Atlantic crossings, it was not necessary to wear whites. The door at the far side of the court was the entrance to a small cafe.*
Author's Collection

The Empress of Britain *drew a large number of spectators when she made one of her annual southbound transits of the Suez Canal.*
Reginald V. Badcock

ordered and retain the signed cards, with the intention of paying for the drinks themselves and selling the cards later for their autograph value. Their scheme collapsed when they discovered that the playwright was a teetotaller. He was also a vegetarian, and when other passengers sat down to their New Year's dinner of roast turkey, Chef Michel Kern prepared a meal of cream of barley soup, gnocchis aux tomates, broccoli aux beurre, almond souffle and Postum for Shaw.

While passengers were away for a week in Palestine and Egypt, finishing touches were added to the open-air swimming pool at the forward end of the Lounge Deck. The canvas-lined pool, 32 feet long, 18 feet wide, and 7 feet 9 inches deep, was ingeniously built into the Number 2 and Number 3 hatchways, or openings, that led to the cargo holds. Waiters served lunch on the open deck on hot days, making it possible for passengers to spend the entire day outdoors, dressed in swimwear or sports attire, without having to face the inconvenience of putting on indoor clothing and descending to the Salle Jacques Cartier for lunch.

On January 7, 1933, the *Britain* arrived at Bombay and remained at anchor for eight days. Passengers went ashore and split up into several groups, which travelled by special trains to tour Delhi, the Taj Mahal, Benares, Darjeeling, Calcutta and Madras, visitors to the last two cities planning to rejoin the ship when she reached Colombo. Shaw and his wife, however, remained in Bombay. The newsworthiness of the ship's best-known passenger did not subside at any time during the cruise and he attracted reporters and photographers at every port. Passengers tried not to intrude on Shaw when he was writing. To give him the privacy he desired, at least once a steward placed the writer's deck chair on the docking bridge, a seldom used but rather exposed structure near the ship's stern. He did most of his writing, though, in the seclusion of his cabin and at a sheltered corner of the Lounge Deck promenade.

The adage that a cruise ship was the ideal setting for romance was confirmed when the *Britain* arrived at Colombo. Two American passengers became engaged when the ship was travelling through the Red Sea, and the marriage ceremony took place in the Empress Room with the registrar of Colombo officiating. Although made at the last minute, the arrangements were carried out with considerable style. The ship's orchestra supplied the music, and a sailor striking four bells in the forenoon watch served unknowingly as the carillonneur. Captain Latta, his Staff Captain and the Chief Officer were among the guests.

Local reporters, prompted by the wedding, inquired about other shipboard romances. Cornelius Vanderbilt Jr. was still aboard. He had not disembarked at Athens and gone off to interview Europe's leading politicians. Rumours swept through the ship that he had become engaged to Adonnell Massie, a beautiful 19-year-old platinum blonde booked for the complete cruise, but he refused to confirm the stories. He simply stated that he was so impressed with the cruise that he had decided to remain aboard. Mr. Vanderbilt, separated from his second wife, eventually remarried, but Miss Massie did not become his bride.

Rituals of crossing the line were observed off the coast of Sumatra when the ship reached the equator. One difference from the previous year was that the crew member portraying King Neptune had been made up carefully as a recognizable caricature of Shaw. The dramatist kept his camera in action throughout the performance.

For the crew, a world cruise was less strenuous than a North Atlantic crossing. One junior engineering officer had originally been assigned an inner cabin located above the kitchen. It became uncomfortably warm in the tropics, and with fewer engineers on board because of the closing of the after engine room, he was given a vacant outer cabin. It had not only a porthole, but also a wind chute, a type of metal scoop attached to the open porthole to catch any breeze when the ship was moving and draw air into the cabin. One disadvantage of the chute was that it tended to collect anything that passengers on the upper decks discarded overboard.

After calling at Singapore, Bangkok and Manila, the *Empress of Britain* sailed to Hong Kong, arriving on February 11 at seven in the morning. Reporters flocked on board to interview Shaw and found him in an affable mood as he aired his opinions on the League of Nations, Communism,

The docking bridge, near the stern, was where the officer in charge aft stood when the ship was entering or leaving port. Communication with the navigation bridge was by a telegraph located in the cab which extended beyond the ship's side.
CP Rail Corporate Archives

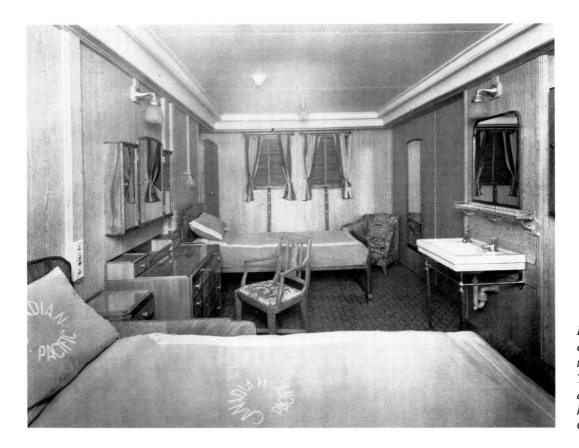

Bed coverings were clearly labelled with the company's name. The chest of drawers and night stand both had glass tops.
CP Rail Corporate Archives

tensions between China and Japan, the Great Wall of China, and the state of literature. He hoped that the war in the north would not prevent him from visiting Peking. "All wars stop for the *Empress of Britain*," he added.

In spite of Shaw's claim, it was still doubtful whether the ship could land her passengers at Chinwangtao, where they would board trains for Peking. A radio message finally came, informing Captain Latta that passengers could travel in safety although Japanese forces had recently waged an offensive against the Chinese within five miles of the port. When they did leave the ship, the first question most of the tourists asked was, "Where's the war?" The war zone had, in fact, moved 200 miles to the northeast, and the sightseers visited Peking and the Great Wall without incident. Following her previous year's itinerary, the *Britain* reached Japan, visiting Beppu, Kobe and Yokohama. Hawaii was next, then San Francisco.

The ship's arrival at San Francisco was marred by the loss of her starboard anchor when too much strain was put on the cable, but the tug *Sea King* recovered it the next day. In her early years, the *Britain* had a greater propensity than most ships to lose an anchor. The chain holding the anchor was in 15-fathom lengths connected with heavy U-shaped metal shackles which had a removable bar across the upper part. This bar tended to break, but the problem was solved when a patent shackle, consisting of two D-shaped halves joined in the centre along the straight edge, replaced the older type.

No one knew if George Bernard Shaw would actually go ashore when the *Britain* reached San Francisco. At the Hawaiian port of Hilo the playwright sprained a leg when he attempted to dodge a ponderous group of hula dancers. In addition to his disability, he discovered that he lacked a United States visa. The State Department in Washington, urged on by the influential publisher William Randolph Hearst, saved the day by cabling permission for Shaw to land at San Francisco and rejoin the *Britain* at Los Angeles. It was not easy for the playwright to avoid the press in California, but his difficulties increased two weeks later when the ship reached Cuba. Some enterprising New York reporters and newsreel cameramen came aboard at Havana and spent the next three days trying to interview and photograph him before the ship docked at New York on May 11. There Captain Latta ordered the ship's master-at-arms to guard the door of Shaw's cabin. Reporters departed without their interviews but shortly before sailing time on May 12 they returned and the playwright resigned himself to their barrage of questions.

Most passengers ended their cruise at New York, although the European group stayed on until the *Britain* reached Cherbourg and Southampton. George Bernard Shaw and his wife disembarked at the English port and returned to the comparative solitude of their own home. He had kept to his resolve to write during the cruise, and left the ship with the manuscript for *A Village Wooing* and a draft of *On the Rocks* in his luggage.

The *Empress of Britain* had steamed only 9 miles fewer than the year before. She had consumed far less oil, however, an average of 179 tons a day for the ship's propulsion compared with 210 tons on the preceding cruise. In transatlantic service she used 356 tons per day. Furthermore, almost nothing had been spent on engine room maintenance. The *Britain* now entered dry dock for the installation of her outer propellers and routine upkeep. Two weeks after the cruise ended, she was ready for another six months on the North Atlantic.

Crowds at Southampton watching the Empress of Britain *leave included relatives of the crew as well as families and friends of the passengers.* Associated British Ports Collection/Southampton City Museums

CHAPTER 11

THE FIVE-DAY FLYER

The *Empress of Britain* left Southampton at 12:30 p.m., May 3, 1933, crossed the English Channel to Cherbourg, then set course for Québec with only 345 passengers. Effects of the Depression were now all too obvious. The *Britain* made 26 Atlantic crossings in 1933, six more than the year before, but Canadian Pacific had laid up several of its ships, knowing that there were simply not enough people to fill the cabins. It did not have the market to itself. The Cunard Line ships *Alaunia*, *Antonia*, *Ascania*, *Aurania* and *Ausonia*, Donaldson Line's *Athenia* and *Letitia*, and White Star's *Calgaric* and *Laurentic* all advertised sailings from the St. Lawrence to a variety of ports in Britain and continental Europe, although they too suffered from a lack of passengers.

Québec, the *Britain*'s Canadian terminal, was, then as now, a largely French-speaking city. The ship carried a number of bilingual crew members. Waiters and cabin stewards who spoke French wore red collars instead of blue and white respectively on their jackets; stewardesses had red turn-backs on their caps, while stenographers had red shoulder tabs on their dresses. Passenger lists, distributed early in the crossing, contained not only the names of everyone in the ship but several pages of information on passports, meal times, safekeeping of valuables, cheques ("Passengers are respectfully advised that the Purser has no authority to accept private cheques in payment of accounts, or for exchange"), lifeboat drill and other matters of concern to the traveller trying to adapt to a new environment for five days. Sometimes these pages were printed in English and French; at other times the information in French was restricted to one or two pages or omitted entirely.

The great majority of passengers spoke English, but in 1933 there were at least two groups whose mother tongue was French. On July 1, more than 50 French-speaking people left Québec for Cherbourg in the *Britain* on a seven-week tour of Europe organized by the newspaper *L'Evénement*. Two months later, the ship took a hundred modern-day pilgrims to Cherbourg on the first leg of a Holy Year visit to Rome and Palestine. On their return, the ship's concert took place on the last night at sea, October 25. The chairman was not one of the several Roman Catholic priests aboard but Rev. L.M. Watts, a young Anglican clergyman from Perdue, Saskatchewan. Unfortunately he had no knowledge of French and his attempts to pronounce the names of some of the singers and their selections had the audience tittering. Regardless, everyone contributed generously to the collection for seamen's charities taken up during the intermission.

The July 1 sailing from Québec, which took the Belle Isle route, included three other organized groups: Boy Scouts, nurses and the Canadian Authors' Association. The writers had just ended a convention at the Chateau Frontenac in Québec and 70 of them were leaving for an extensive tour of Europe. Two of the country's most prominent authors, Dr. C.W. Gordon, better known as Ralph Connor, and Charles G.D. Roberts, were among the passengers, both in Tourist Class.

Perhaps the best-known person to cross the Atlantic in the *Empress of Britain* in 1933 was Prime Minister R.B. Bennett, who was returning to Canada from the World Economic Conference in London. He was one of 253 in First Class when the ship left Southampton on August 26. Fast though the *Britain* was, she was not speedy enough for Mr. Bennett. He had a speaking engagement in Montréal and wielded his authority by summoning the Coast Guard ship *Druid* to take him ashore

The commanding view at Québec revealed that the St. Lawrence was a busy river. Canada Steamship Lines' 1,982-ton cargo ship Edmonton *lay at the dock in the foreground.*
CP Rail Corporate Archives

at Murray Bay. The *Britain* had to make an unscheduled stop in the St. Lawrence at 5:30 a.m. on September 1 to disembark the Prime Minister, who travelled by automobile from Murray Bay to Québec, then by train to Montréal, arriving in time to address his audience.

The Prime Minister's return to Canada made the front pages, and because he had sailed to England in the *Duchess of Bedford* and come back in the *Empress of Britain*, Canadian Pacific gained welcome newspaper coverage. There were times, however, when secrecy was considered essential. Earlier in the season, the *Britain* had carried a cargo of $3 million in gold. About 6 a.m. on May 11 two trains pulled into Wolfe's Cove, Canadian Pacific's carrying $2 million, Canadian National's $1 million. Railway police, armed with machine guns, rifles and revolvers, accompanied the trains from Ottawa and stood guard while the gold bars were taken aboard and locked in the specie room on F Deck. The transfer concluded without incident and the gold reached the Bank of England in London five days later.

The *Empress of Britain* continued to make fast crossings. Ships of Cunard, White Star and Donaldson Lines could not equal her speed, or even come close. Of the other Canadian Pacific ships, the *Empress of Australia*, launched 20 years earlier but not completed until after the end of the First World War, managed only 16 1/2 knots and needed seven days between Québec and Southampton. The *Duchesses of Atholl, Bedford, Richmond* and *York* each had a service speed of 18 knots and a maximum of 19. Their eastbound sailings began at Montréal and they took eight days to arrive at Liverpool, with prior calls at Glasgow and Belfast.

To illustrate the *Britain*'s speed, Stanley Pearch, the Purser, told a story to reporters travelling from Québec to Father Point. The *Duchess of Richmond* had sailed from Montréal the previous day and a passenger had inadvertently left a suit behind. It was sent on to Québec and put aboard the *Britain*. "That lady should be pleasantly surprised when she reaches London next Friday," said Mr. Pearch, "for the suit will be waiting at her hotel a day before she arrives."

In the eyes of the ship four members of L'Evénement*'s group posed for the camera: Aileen Bettesworth (top), Louise Monette (left), Robert Kirouac and Yvette Bettesworth (seated).* Mrs. Aileen Grassby

Chief Engineer H.G. Donald knew how to make the ship's engines perform at maximum efficiency. Record times, however, were not planned in advance, according to a Canadian Pacific spokesman: "If the *Empress of Britain* makes a new record we are always glad, but it is not the company's policy deliberately to aim at spectacular passages." On this topic, Captain Latta was non-committal. "If the *Empress of Britain* has favourable weather conditions, she makes fast passages, sometimes records," was all he would say.

To emphasize the reliability of the ship's engines, George Stephen, traffic vice-president of Canadian Pacific, spoke to the press on August 20: "Starting with the commencement of this round trip from Southampton last Saturday, the *Empress of Britain* for the next twelve weeks will be engaged in what is to all intents and purposes a continuous voyage of 40,320 miles. In the ninety-four days from last Saturday to November 14 she will start Atlantic crossings from one side or the other every Saturday and a total of eighty days will be spent actually under way."

This service, he pointed out, not only involved fine navigation on the part of Captain Latta and his officers but called for exact co-ordination between ship and shore staffs so that the liner would be prepared for each crossing between her Thursday arrival and her Saturday departure. "The steaming upon which she is now engaged," he added, "will be a demonstration of the economical value of her machinery in a highly competitive machine age."

It was all a noticeable contrast to events a century before when the tiny Québec-built wooden paddle steamer *Royal William* left Pictou, Nova Scotia, on August 18, 1833, for Gravesend, England, where she arrived on September 12 with seven passengers, thus becoming the first steamship to cross the Atlantic from Canada to Britain. To commemorate the centenary, a special dinner was held aboard the *Empress of Britain* on August 16.

Towards the end of the season, the passenger count dwindled, sometimes falling below 300. Lacking distinguished names to interview when the ship docked, reporters had to search for trivial

Third Class passengers gathered on the forward section of the Lounge Deck when the Empress of Britain *was on the St. Lawrence.*
CP Rail Corporate Archives

The Sun Deck, aptly named when this photograph was taken, was for the exclusive use of First Class passengers.
CP Rail Corporate Archives

ENTERTAINMENT - Held in the THIRD CLASS

EMPRESS OF BRITAIN

On Wednesday October 25, 1933, at 8.30 p.m.

Chairman : Rev. L. M. WATTS

Aged widows.
Orphans.
Lifeboat Institutions

Overture	"Selected"	
	EMPRESS OF BRITAIN ORCHESTRA	

Song   "Selected"
Mr. D. WILSON

Violin Solo   "Czardas"   Monti
FREDERICK PEARSON

Song   "Votre Sourire"
Miss M. A. LeBUEF

Comedian   "Parson of Puddle"
Mr. M. J. N. STURT

Song   "Silver Hair and Heart of Gold"
Mr. L. METCALFE

CHAIRMAN'S REMARKS

Community Singing whilst the Collection is being taken
in aid of Seamen's Charities of Canada and England

Song   "I Hear You Calling Me"
Mr. R. WILLIS

Songs at the Piano
Mr. J. ENGLAND

Song   "Selected"
Mrs. BEGIN

Song   "Selected"
Mr. P. COUPER

Humourous Selections
Mr. G. PEARCE

At the Piano : Mr. J. England

"GOD SAVE THE KING"

Rev. L.M. Watts, chairman of the Third Class concert, wrote down the names of the charities that would be supported by the collection. Rev. L.M. Watts

news to fill their columns. One such item appeared following the *Britain*'s arrival at Québec on October 26. When the ship was about 750 miles out of Southampton, two exhausted crows alighted on the deck. They took up residence on, appropriately enough, the crow's-nest, remaining aloft during the crossing except for short flights down to the bridge to peck at scraps of raw meat. They flew off when the ship reached the Strait of Belle Isle and land came into sight.

The *Empress of Britain* arrived at Southampton on November 14, closing her third Atlantic season. She had spent 135 days, 18 hours at sea, and 59 days, 16 hours in port. In steaming 73,327 nautical miles she had consumed 46,643 tons of oil, 1,405 tons of diesel fuel and 46,795 tons of fresh water. Passenger numbers had risen only fractionally from the previous year, 11,451 compared with 11,294, in spite of six additional crossings. The *Britain*'s speed made her popular with the Post Offices of Canada and Britain; in 1933 she took 59,955 bags of mail. Her cargo capacity was never fully utilized, and she carried only 3,192 tons, in addition to 78 uncrated automobiles.

Passage times, good in 1932, were even better in 1933:

Cherbourg to Father Point (Cape Race route): 4 days, 21 hours, 5 minutes.
Father Point to Cherbourg (Belle Isle route): 4 days, 7 hours, 32 minutes.
Bishop Rock to Cape Race: 3 days, 6 hours, 4 minutes.
Bishop Rock to Belle Isle: 3 days, 2 hours, 40 minutes.
Belle Isle to Bishop Rock: 3 days, 1 hour, 34 minutes.
Québec to Father Point: 6 hours, 30 minutes.

A formal atmosphere prevailed when the Empress Room served as a ballroom. The blue dome showed the stars as they were on June 11, 1930, the day the ship was launched. Author's Collection

MENU

Hors d'œuvres

Cream Portugaise

Boiled Cod, Lobster Sauce

Beef Olives, Mashed Swedes

Roast Lamb, Mint Sauce
Peas
Boiled and Chateau Potatoes

Salad

Ginger Pudding
Ice Cream

Dessert   Coffee

Red Wine may be obtained at 30 cents per bottle.

Dinner   **Third Class**

Empress of Britain   Monday, May 8, 1933

The Third Class menu offered a limited choice of good, plain, unsophisticated food. Len Childs

The Chief Steward's department carefully added up the quantities of food the passengers and crew ate:

Flour	97,750 lb.	Poultry and game	47,500 lb.
Cereals	30,400 lb.	Codfish	8,740 lb.
Sugar	36,000 lb.	Haddock	8,255 lb.
Groceries	26,800 lb.	Salmon	5,600 lb.
Potatoes	61,575 lb.	Other fish	35,050 lb.
Tomatoes and turnips	21,125 lb.	Eggs	179,150
Cabbage and		Milk powder	13,860 lb.
beans	32,630 lb.	Butter and margarine	34,150 lb.
Other vegetables	82,410 lb.	Cheese	5,240 lb.
Beef	78,150 lb.	Coffee	6,555 lb.
Veal	6,105 lb.	Tea	3,760 lb.
Mutton	22,290 lb.	Jam	8,590 lb.
Lamb	14,275 lb.	Apples	497 cases
Bacon	20,975 lb.	Oranges	439 cases
Pork	11,150 lb.	Other fruit	493 cases

Captain Latta said in an interview after the *Empress of Britain* docked at Southampton on November 14: "As far as weather conditions have been concerned, the season this year has been exceptional. It is seldom that such little delay has been experienced on the North Atlantic and Canadian routes. The absence of fog, or the successful manner in which we have dodged it, has enabled us to pass Bishop Rock with such regularity that the inhabitants of that part of the land are said to be timing their clocks by our passing."

He was exaggerating about the clocks, of course, but it was true that his ship had kept highly consistent time throughout the season. Now he returned to his home in Cheshire, where he spent the next few weeks gardening before taking the *Britain* to New York for a short cruise to the West Indies, to be followed by another world cruise.

The Tennis Court Cafe, a popular room when the Britain *was on a cruise, had hand-painted Japanese wall coverings and light-green wicker furniture.* Jay Bascom Collection

CHAPTER 12

AROUND THE WORLD IN 130 DAYS

The first two world cruises had departed early in December, but Canadian Pacific now believed that passengers would sooner spend the holiday season at home than in Palestine and Egypt. They would still be able to see Bethlehem and to visit the Pyramids, only in late January instead of late December. Some people, however, looked forward to a short sea break at Christmas. Not wanting the ship to lie idle during the holidays, Canadian Pacific scheduled an 11-day cruise from New York to the West Indies to meet the demand.

The *Empress of Britain* arrived at New York on December 21 with 319 passengers and 6,000 bags of mail, leaving late the next day for Kingston, Port-au-Prince and Nassau with a large number of American and Canadian vacationers. Apart from calls at Havana during world cruises, this was the *Britain*'s first visit to the Caribbean; interest in the ship ran high, as it had in every other place she visited.

Nearly 300 people embarked at New York on January 4, 1934, commencing at 9 o'clock. It was a hectic three hours with taxis coming and going, cabin trunks, suitcases and hat boxes carried aboard, trucks delivering bunches of flowers and baskets of fruit, hundreds of relatives and friends touring the ship before the final goodbyes, newsreel cameras rolling, last-minute supplies arriving and guests departing, but promptly at midday the gangway was lifted and the third world cruise began. More than 70 Canadian passengers were aboard, half of them booked for the complete cruise.

Once more, Edward Henderson was Cruise Director. Speaking to a reporter, he offered clothing tips for men contemplating buying a ticket for the next cruise: "Our man passenger must remember to bring a number of cool garments for tropical wear. Soon after leaving New York, the ship enters the Gulf Stream and heavy clothing is discarded. Gibraltar, Algiers, Monte Carlo and the Holy Land call for light wool or flannel suits... A sun helmet should certainly be included. India's warmth requires tropical clothing but those making the across-India journey need an overcoat."

More than 70 of the 130 days were to be spent at sea and entertainment had to be planned. Martin DeMuth, reappointed lecturer and artist, brought aboard a collection of lantern slides to supplement his talks on each of the 30 ports. Mrs. Lucy Kerr of Banff, Alberta, Directress of Entertainment, organized costume balls, cabarets, vaudeville shows, bridge competitions and gala dinners. Stuart Jones and his orchestra were engaged again. To care for passengers' and crew's health, two medical doctors and a dentist were appointed. Dr. Roy McDougall of Ottawa had an unexpected assignment while the *Britain* cruised between Monte Carlo and Naples, when he made and fitted a set of upper and lower dentures for a patient and thereafter claimed to be the first dentist to accomplish this task on the high seas.

Fares for the cruise began at $2,100 per person with shore excursions and at $1,600 without. Only four cabins were available at the minimum rate, numbers 654, 655, 656 and 657, all on D Deck and fewer than 100 feet from the ship's stem. In summer, these cabins formed part of Third Class, but on cruises all passengers were considered First Class; occupants of cheaper cabins had a free run of the ship and were entitled to the same level of service as passengers in the best suites.

Cabin 147 was the bedroom of a deluxe suite. For British passengers boarding at Monte Carlo, the suite was priced at 4,464 guineas (about $23,435) for two people on the 1934 world cruise. CP Rail Corporate Archives

For 915 guineas (about $4,815) per person, two people could share Cabin 340 on C Deck from Monte Carlo to Southampton for 124 days. CP Rail Corporate Archives

A few days in Egypt inspired many costumes for the masquerade ball in the Mayfair Lounge. Some may have been bought ashore, but it was also possible to rent costumes from the ship's shop. Author's Collection

Canadian Pacific's advertising told prospective travellers what to expect:

> Then there's the food. If you're a bit of a bon vivant, the *Empress of Britain* food is famous. If you don't want a regular meal, you can have a little special steak or chop grilled for you. If you like to make your own French dressing as a rite, at table, you can. If you like to entertain, there are plenty of private rooms. Private bridge-teas, dinners, or small dances. . .the *Empress of Britain* knows how to handle them all with style.

The typical passenger was financially secure, retired or both. Although the ship had a skilled medical staff and never spent more than seven consecutive days without visiting a port, the prospect of death among the elderly had to be considered. Deep down in the ship, far from the view of cruise members, six lead caskets were stored, exclusively for deceased passengers. If, however, a crewman died at sea, his body was placed in a canvas sack weighted down with heavy iron bars which, after an early morning burial service, was slid over the ship's side into the sea. A superstition among the crew was that a death was imminent if a shark followed the ship. A sailor spotted one shortly after the *Britain* left Los Angeles on the 1934 cruise and soon afterwards a crewman died.

On world cruises, crew always outnumbered passengers, as they did on most Atlantic crossings. There was a surplus of sailors in the early 1930s and many could not find a seagoing job. One who did was Fred Sammé, who joined the *Empress of Britain* as an Able-Bodied Seaman in 1932 and remained with her for four years. Initially he signed on for £9 a month (about $45), but as the Depression continued, his pay was cut to £8 (about $40). He collected overtime when he worked beyond ten hours a day. On Sundays, only essential routines were carried out unless an emergency arose. For waiters, stewards and engine-room crew, Sundays at sea were, of course, simply regular working days.

Mr. Sammé and seven other sailors shared a cabin, about 18 feet by 12 feet, located not far above the ship's waterline. Sometimes, when the sea became rough, the occupants were too slow in closing the porthole and got drenched. Bunks in the cabin had spring mattresses at a time when straw-stuffed ones were the seaman's usual lot. Food was above average. If three meals a day were not enough, a hungry sailor could drop into the mess and fix himself a snack of bread and cheese.

The arrival of the Britain at a port was a financial bonanza for store owners, tour operators and restaurateurs. Alan Maurice Irwin, a reporter on the 1934 cruise, saw this for himself when the ship reached Funchal, the first stop after leaving New York:

> Poverty-stricken, happy, but clean, the native Madeirans think Santa Claus is still alive every time a cruise liner comes in. Most people on holidays tip pretty well and here, even when the giver feels a litle ashamed that he is only handing over a quarter to the two men who pulled or checked his *carrinho do monte* down the four-thousand-foot cobble-stone slide, what usually seems like a minimum tip is apt to be a full day's pay. What makes it all the better for them is the fact that they have been paid and tipped by the cruise company as well.

The *carrinho do monte*, a popular tourist attraction in Funchal, was a two-seat wicker sled with greased runners which made a 20-minute descent of the steep streets of the city. Two husky young men controlled each sled with ropes attached to the front of the runners.

On the previous cruise, some passengers had flown from Batavia to Bali, and they spoke so glowingly about the island that Canadian Pacific included it in the 1934 timetable. Organizational problems had to be solved, though, before the visit took place to "this Eden of the East Indies," as one writer described it. Bali lacked enough automobiles to take everyone on sightseeing trips at once so half the passengers landed at Boeleleng on the northern side of the island, from which they travelled by car to Padang Bay on the eastern side. While this was happening, the ship proceeded

Able Seaman Fred Sammé enjoyed a moment off duty while a friend took his photograph.
Fred Sammé

The ship's photographers, with cameras ready, always accompanied the passengers on shore excursions. At the pagoda in Bangkok, all five tourists had pith helmets, then considered an essential item of dress in tropical lands.
Les Carson

The Farewell Dinner for May 20, 1934, was actually the second of its kind. The first had been held a week earlier, before the American and Canadian passengers disembarked at New York.
Jay Bascom Collection

Diner au Revoir

on board the

Empress of Britain

Sunday, May Twentieth

Nineteen hundred thirty-four

Eleventh Round the World Cruise

MENU

Prawn Cocktail   Florida Cocktail
Smoked Salmon   Bayonne Ham
Canapés Moscovite
Iced Celery   Olives   Salted Almonds

Clear Ox Tail au Sherry
Cream à la Reine Margot

Fillet of Sole Meunière, Clara Ward
Poached Salmon, Sauce Mousseuse

Lamb Cutlets, Oyster Plant, Parisienne Potatoes
Breast of Chicken à la Stanley   Tournedos Judith

Punch Romaine

Sirloin of Beef à l'Anglaise
Roast Turkey, Cranberry Sauce

Runner Beans   Asparagus Hollandaise
Vegetable Marrow, Sauce Crème
Potatoes : Persillées,   Sablées,   Château

Salads : Lettuce and Tomato, Rachel, Escarole
Avocado Pear

Pudding Soufflé aux Amandes
Gateaux St. Honore   Bombe glace Orientale
Petits Fours

Fruits de Saison

Dessert   Coffee

to Padang Bay. Here the remaining travellers took local tours for the rest of the day. The overland group arrived late in the afternoon and everyone was aboard in time for dinner. Passengers exchanged itineraries the next morning and the *Britain* returned to Boeleleng to pick up the second day's overland party.

The *Empress of Britain* could not dock at either Boeleleng or Padang Bay, and with no suitable local tenders, passengers went ashore in the ship's motor lifeboats, each commanded by a junior engineering officer. The lifeboats lacked awnings to protect people from the blistering sun, however, so the red leather seat cushions were kept reversed until the minute passengers stepped aboard.

The *Britain* arrived at Hong Kong on March 17 for a four-day stay and was immediately surrounded by a fleet of sampans. Local boatmen, trying to make a living in precarious times, held out bamboo poles with nets on the end beneath the ship's garbage chutes. They carefully sifted through the refuse, searching for anything that could be salvaged and reused. This experience was new for most passengers but a familiar sight to sailors accustomed to Far Eastern waters. Calls at Shanghai and Chinwangtao occurred without the menace of war that had clouded earlier visits. It was cherry blossom time when the Britain reached Japan, a bonus for arriving one month later than on previous cruises.

Two stops in Hawaii broke the long trip across the Pacific. At the first, Honolulu, the *Empress of Japan*, one year older than the *Britain* and in some ways a smaller version of the company's flagship, docked next to the *Empress of Britain*. She was on a routine passage from the Far East to Vancouver.

At San Francisco and Los Angeles, enterprising reporters and photographers went out in chartered launches to meet the *Empress of Britain* so that her arrival would be widely covered, often on the front pages of newspapers, while the ship was still in port. Two cameramen from Metro-Goldwyn-Mayer embarked with 5,000 feet of film at Los Angeles on April 29 for the passage to Havana. They spent the next 11 days filming backgrounds for scenes in Eddie Cantor's next movie *Kid Millions*; some 50 passengers and crew were enlisted as extras.

The *Empress of Britain* reached New York on May 14 with 346 passengers, the cruise over for all except the hundred or so who had embarked at Monte Carlo and were now returning to Cherbourg and Southampton. The ship had visited 33 ports in 21 countries and in almost every port she was the largest ship ever seen.

The Mayfair was very much in the Grand Hotel tradition of lounges ashore and afloat and made no concessions to contemporary trends in design. Author's Collection

CHAPTER 13

HALF FULL, HALF EMPTY

Rumours of Captain Latta's retirement from the sea had been circulating since mid-May and, in spite of denials by Canadian Pacific, the stories proved to be true. When the *Empress of Britain* left Québec on June 30, 1934, the 60-year-old captain was on the bridge for the last time, although he took up a shore appointment with the company the following year. Before leaving Wolfe's Cove, he reminisced about his 40 years at sea, 30 with Canadian Pacific. Not loquacious at the best of times, he nevertheless had a few remarks for reporters: "You can't get me to say goodbye to Canada. I'll be back before long to have a real look at the Dominion. One doesn't see much of the country in the short time between arrival and departure of the *Empress of Britain*." He added some words about his colleagues and his successor, Captain Ronald N. Stuart, V.C., D.S.O.: "There is no one I would rather see in command of my ship. I call her mine for no matter who is on the bridge of the *Empress of Britain*, she will always be my ship. Captain Stuart's record is so well known that there is little I can say except that I wish him every success. He inherits with his command a staff of officers in all departments and a crew who are second to none. You reporters pick on the captain to interview and the men behind him seem to be left in the shadow. Usually people who follow the sea have little to say about themselves—just for once I want to make an exception. So, please, whatever else you write, don't overlook this much of Jock Latta's farewell, that he wants to pay a tribute to the stout, loyal and willing friends who have served with him in the *Empress of Britain*."

Captain Stuart, 47 years old, came from a seafaring family. He went to sea at 16 in the barque *Kirkhill*. Like many of his contemporaries, he transferred to steamships after it became apparent that the age of sailing ships was nearly over. He was awarded the Victoria Cross in the First World War for his courageous action when the ship he commanded, the *Pargust*, actually a decoy known as a "Q" ship, had allowed herself to be torpedoed off Ireland by a German submarine. A trained "panic party" seemed to be on the point of abandoning the ship and lured the submarine closer to investigate. When she was at point-blank range, the hidden guns of the *Pargust* suddenly appeared and shelled the submarine, which sank in minutes. Lt. Stuart, R.N., then brought his disabled ship back to port.

On completing his first Atlantic crossing as master of the *Britain*, Captain Stuart met the press. A reporter described him as "jovially unwilling to talk about himself" but he was ready enough to speak about his ship. Although outdrawing her competitors on the St. Lawrence route, the ship was far from full on any crossing. She arrived at Québec on August 2 with 776 passengers and on August 30 with 875, her highest numbers for the season. The best eastbound showing came on June 30, when she left Québec with 751 passengers. Fewer than 250 sailed on each of her last three eastbound passages in October and November.

Whether the *Empress of Britain* was nearly full or almost empty did not affect the standard of service or the variety of amenities. The sea-water Olympian Pool remained a great attraction; it stayed open until late evening, then on the midnight to 4 a.m. watch an engineer had to drain and refill the pool and heat the water to a comfortable temperature. A young engineer officer one night thought it would be a fine opportunity to take a swim. After filling the pool and adjusting

FIRST CLASS FARES — From and to Quebec

Line No.	Deck	EMPRESS OF BRITAIN Tonnage 42500		SOUTHAMPTON	OFF SEASON EAST July 10 to June 10 WEST Sept 11 to Aug 12			SUMMER SEASON EAST June 11 to July 9 WEST Aug 13 to Sep 10			Line No.
		Capacity	Fitted with	Apartments	Per Bed	1 in Room	2 in Room	Per Bed	1 in Room	2 in Room	
1	SPORTS	1-Outside	1 Bed	1, 4, 6, 9, 12, 18		$220			$231		1
2		1-Outside	1 Bed with Bath	4, 6, 12, 18		242			255		2
3		2-Outside	2 Beds	21, 24	$228	251	$456	$240	264	$480	3
4		2-Outside	2 Beds	2, 3, 5, 7, 11, 14, 15, 16	220	242	440	231	255	462	4
5		2-Outside	2 Beds with Bath	8, 10, 17, 19, 20, 21, 22, 24	251	277	502	264	291	528	5
6		2-Outside	2 Beds with Bath	2, 3, 5, 7, 11, 15	242	267	484	255	281	510	6
7	A	1-Outside	1 Bed	124, 127, 130, 132, 133, 135, 150, 153, 168, ①170, 171, 172, ①173, 175, 178, 181		241			254		7
8		1-Outside	1 Bed with Bath	124, 127, 130, 132, 133, 135, 150, 153, 168, ①170, 171, 172, ①173, 175, 178, 181		272			286		8
9		1-Outside	1 Bed with Shower and Toilet	180, 182, 183, 185		257			270		9
10		2-Outside	2 Beds	100, 101, 102, 103, 104, 105, 106, 107, 108, 109, 110, 111, 112, 114, 115, 116, 117, 118, 119, 121, 122, 125, ①126, ①129, ①134, 136, ①137, ①138, 139, 140, ①141, 142, 143, 145, ①152, 154, ①155, 156, 157, 158, 159, 161, 162, 165, 166, 169, 174, 176, 177, 179	241	266	482	254	280	508	10
11		2-Outside	2 Beds with Bath	100, 101, 102, 103, 104, 105, 106, 107, 108, 109, 110, 111, 112, 114, 115, 116, 117, 118, 119, 120, 121, 123, ①126, 128, ①129, 131, ①134, 136, ①137, ①138, 139, 140, ①141, 142, 143, 145, ①152, 154, ①155, 156, 157, 158, 159, 160, 161, 163, 164, 166, 167, 169, 174, 176, 177, 179	272	300	544	286	315	572	11
12		Suites — Bed, Bath and Sitting Room		120-122, 123-125, 160-162, 163-165 For three passengers For four passengers		566 841 1088	597 884 1143		595 884 1143	627	12
13		Suites—Bed, Bath, Sitting Room and Verandah		144-146-148, 147-149-151 For three passengers For four passengers		699 868 1113	730 912 1169		734 912 1169	767	13
14	B	1-Outside	1 Bed	210, 211, 221, 223, 232, 248, 249, 256, 257, 260, 261, 273, 277		220			231		14
15		1-Outside	1 Bed	226, 231, 285		231			243		15
16		1-Outside	1 Bed with Shower and Toilet	230		231			243		16
17		1-Outside	1 Bed with Bath	210, 211, 232, 248, 249, 256, 257, 260, 261, 277		242			255		17
18		1-Outside	1 Bed with Bath	285		255			268		18
19		2-Outside	2 Beds	200, 201, 202, 203, 204, 205, 206, 207, 208, 209, 212, 214, 215, ①216, 217, 218, 219, 222, ①224, 227, ①229	220	242	440	231	255	462	19
20		2-Outside	2 Beds	①220, 225, 228, 233, 234, 235, 236, 237, 238, 239, 242, 243, 244, 245, 246, 247, 250, 251, 252, 253, ①254, ①255, ①262, ①263, 264, 265, 267, 269, ①271, ①275, ①279, 281, 283, 287	231	255	462	243	268	486	20
21		2-Outside	2 Beds with Shower and Toilet	258, 259	243	268	486	256	282	512	21
22		2-Outside	2 Beds with Bath	200, 201, 202, 203, 204, 205, 206, 207, 208, 209, 212, 214, 215, ①216, 217, 218, 219, 222, ①224, 227, ①229	242	267	484	255	281	510	22
23		2-Outside	2 Beds with Bath	①220, 225, 228, 233, 234, 235, 236, 237, 238, 239, 240, 241, 242, 243, 244, 245, 246, 247, 250, 251, 252, 253, ①254, ①255, ①262, ①263, 264, 267, 269, ①271, ①275, ①279, 281, 283, 287	255	281	510	268	295	536	23
24	C	1-Outside	1 Bed	310, 311, 321, 323, 326, 331, 334, 336, 339, 341, 348, 350, 352, 353, 354, 355, 356, 357, 358, 359, 360, 361, 362, 363, 365, 367		220			231		24
25		1-Outside	1 Bed with Shower and Toilet	350, 352, 355, 357, 358, 360, 363, 365		231			243		25
26		1-Outside	1 Bed with Bath	310, 311, 336, 341, 348, 353, 354, 356, 359, 361, 362, 367		242			255		26
27		2-Outside	2 Beds	300, 301, 302, 303, 304, 305, 306, 307, 308, 309, 312, 314, 315, ①316, 317, 318, 319, ①320, 322, ①324, 325, 327, 328, ①329, 330, 332, 333, 335, 337, ①338, 342, ①343, 344, ①346, 347, 349, ①351, ①369	220	242	440	231	255	462	27
28		2-Outside	2 Beds with Bath	300, 301, 302, 303, 304, 305, 306, 307, 308, 309, 312, 314, 315, 317, 318, 319, ①320, 322, ①324, 325, 327, 328, ①329, 333, ①338, 340, 342, ①343, 344, 345, ①346, 347, 349, ①351, ①369	242	267	484	255	281	510	28

①An additional bedstead may be placed in rooms 170 and 173.
①An additional bedstead may be placed in these rooms; when used for two passengers the charge for the third passenger will be half the two-in-room rate.
For sailings of Empress of Britain from or to Quebec above fares include Canadian Pacific Railway ticket between Montreal and Quebec.
The Company reserves the right to decline the sale of a room for less than full capacity.
SERVANTS—FIRST CLASS, $140 Off Season; $147 Summer Season.   CHILDREN—For basis for computing fares for children, see page 10.
See page 10 for French Port Tax which must be collected at time of booking from passengers embarking or debarking at Cherbourg.
SEE PAGE 3 FOR REDUCED ROUND TRIP FARES

Early in January, Canadian Pacific supplied ticket agents with a booklet listing the fare structure for the 1934 Atlantic season.
Author's Collection

If the number of dishes on the right side of the menu proved too daunting, the selected menu on the left removed the need to make any choice at all. Author's Collection

In 1934, Cabin 247 on a five-day summer crossing to Southampton could be booked for $536 for two people, the price including the adjoining bathroom, and for $486 without the bathroom.
CP Rail Corporate Archives

the temperature gauge, he waited until he believed the water would be warm enough. He plunged in with the intention of swimming a length or two before returning to his watch, but scarcely had he hit the water than he was scrambling out, his teeth chattering and body shivering. He had forgotten that the *Britain* had been making her way through the ice track off Newfoundland. The freezing Atlantic water was still far from heated when he leaped into the pool.

Fares between Southampton and Québec in 1934 increased slightly over 1933 prices. The minimum one-way summer rates were now $231 in First Class, $127.50 in Tourist, with a discount of about five percent on round-trip tickets. A one-way Third Class passage started at $85.50 westbound, $87 eastbound; round-trip tickets cost about ten percent less than the combined one-way fares. The most expensive accommodation was, naturally, the lavish suites on A Deck. Larger ones cost $767 for two people, smaller ones $627. A servant's fare was $147. In the passenger lists, servants were not identified by name. When the Luden family sailed from Québec on June 30, the entry read: "Mr. William H. Luden, Mrs. Luden, Mr. William H. Luden Jr., maid, valet and chauffeur."

Pets were not forgotten; dogs, whether St. Bernards or Chihuahuas, cost a flat $20 one-way; cats were $5 each and birds $5 a cage, the price including an attendant's fee because owners were forbidden to keep pets in their cabins.

The periodic need to make detours to avoid icebergs affected passage times, but there was nothing to hinder the *Empress of Britain* on the eastbound trip that began on August 4. From Father Point to Cherbourg she took 4 days, 6 hours, 58 minutes, a record crossing at an average speed of 25.08 knots. It remained the fastest passage of her career.

When the *Britain* arrived at Québec on September 27, she set no records for speed, although many passengers had hoped, or even prayed, for the journey to end quickly. It was the stormiest passage the ship had made. Fog, rain, snow, heavy seas, high winds and cold weather all combined to extend the duration of the trip. But even with the 500 passengers in sight of Québec, their ordeal was not over. It took four tugs one and a half hours to dock the ship.

As the season came to an end, passenger totals tapered off, but Canadian Pacific found consolation in the fact that postal authorities made greater use of the *Britain*. She arrived at Québec on October 11 with 6,600 bags for Canada, the United States and New Zealand. Mail for the United States

The bedroom of a suite on A Deck opened on to a sitting room with an electric fire. For an Atlantic crossing in the summer of 1934 the suite cost $627 for two people.
CP Rail Corporate Archives

The sitting room of the suite had a connecting door to the cabin at the left, useful if a family of four wanted two bedrooms with an adjoining sitting room.
CP Rail Corporate Archives

A group of ticket agents, mostly from France, left Cherbourg on July 7, 1934, to see for themselves what kind of ship the Empress of Britain *was.* CP Rail Corporate Archives

was allocated to ships on the basis of their speed and sailing dates, and the company's flagship scored a coup when she was chosen over a ship heading directly to New York.

One of the better-known passengers on the last westbound sailing was Noel Coward. A reporter asked the playwright if he had done any work during the trip. "I did a few notes on my autobiography," was all that he said. It was Mr. Coward's second Atlantic crossing in the ship. Two years earlier he had sailed in her from Southampton to New York. On that passage, George, a bartender in the Knickerbocker Bar, was asked how the writer had spent his time. "He had a little piano wheeled in here and played the accompaniments for a group who gathered round every evening. We got so interested that Eddie, the barkeeper, forgot to collect for some of the drinks he had served to the onlookers and had to pay for them out of his own pocket."

While Noel Coward was an occasional passenger, the Storey family of Vancouver were among the ship's most regular clients. Alfred Storey and his mother were on the final eastbound passage, the seventh time in two years that members of this family had sailed between Canada and Europe in the Empress of Britain. They were two of the 242 passengers who left Québec on November 8 for Cherbourg and Southampton. The ship ran aground shortly after leaving Québec but was refloated without damage in half an hour.

Seventy-five passenger ships sailed the North Atlantic in 1934, and although the *Empress of Britain* ranked about 15th in the average number of passengers per trip (470), it was an indisputable fact that on most crossings the ship was less than half full.

One more Atlantic sailing had to be made, a trip leaving Southampton on December 16 for New York, where two short cruises to the West Indies were to take place before the world cruise began on January 10, 1935. Certainly 1934 had not been a successful year financially for Canadian Pacific. After the figures for its rail, ship and hotel operations, together with its other business concerns, had been added up, shareholders received no dividends. Trying to put as good a front as possible on events, the company's annual report, in speaking of the *Empress of Britain*, said, "The service afforded by this ship has enabled the Company, in the face of most severe competition, to maintain a position in the shipping world which otherwise would not have been possible." It was a statement that could mean as much or as little as the reader wanted to make of it. The program for the 1935 world cruise, however, was as ambitious as ever.

For the golf addict, the Britain*'s entertainment staff could arrange a round at many cruise ports, in addition to providing practice facilities on board.* CP Rail Corporate Archives

CHAPTER 14

THE VOYAGE OF A LIFETIME

Few passengers, if any, booked a world cruise on a whim. They needed plenty of time to make up their minds before leaving home for more than four months. Therefore, the first public announcement of the *Britain*'s fourth cruise came as early as April 11, 1934, while the third was under way.

The worst of the Depression seemed to be over and reservations were up 25 percent by mid-November compared with the year before. William Baird, Canadian Pacific's passenger traffic manager, stated, "Cruise business is good. The travelling public has money to spend, and is spending it." All six suites in the ship were booked and the more expensive cabins were outselling the cheaper ones. He noted also that tickets for the *Empress of Australia*'s 96-day cruise to the Mediterranean, Africa and South America were selling well.

Competition remained as keen as ever. The *Franconia* of Cunard Line and the *Resolute* of Hamburg-American Line both offered world cruises from New York, as did the 6,000-ton *Stella Polaris*. With the lines of a large private yacht rather than a passenger liner, the *Stella Polaris* advertised a westbound 98-day trip, not quite a complete circuit of the globe, that ended in Monte Carlo. Rates for her began at $985, while the *Franconia*'s and *Resolute*'s started at $1,750. The *Empress of Britain*, though, charged a minimum of $2,150 per passenger. In addition, British, Swedish, German, French, Italian and American ships announced short cruises from New York to the West Indies and, in some cases, long trips to the Mediterranean and South Seas.

An innovation for the *Britain*'s fourth world cruise was the appointment of two chaplains, Rev. Stanley Clapham and Father J. Charles Beaudin. Mass would be held in the ship's Writing Room and other services in the Mayfair Lounge. On earlier cruises, the captain usually conducted a service each Sunday, particularly when the ship was at sea, although if a clergyman were aboard he might ask him to take over.

The crossing from Southampton and Cherbourg to New York was a stormy one, and the ship docked at 8:40 a.m. on December 22, a day late. She carried only 180 passengers, but 6,075 bags of mail lay in her holds. In addition, she had $1 million in gold, which had been loaded in Southampton under the scrutiny of one police constable. But New York was different. A large number of well-armed policemen stood conspicuously on guard as 22 cases of gold were placed in armoured trucks at the West 18th Street Pier and delivered to the Federal Reserve Bank.

Late arrival in New York meant that a four-day cruise to Nassau had to begin almost at once. As disembarking passengers left the ship by one gangway, cruise passengers boarded by another. Security measures surrounding the transfer of the gold, together with time needed to unload the large number of mail bags, along with preparing cabins for new passengers—while simultaneously loading provisions and refuelling—led to the crew working in a kind of controlled frenzy for several hours. Obviously the published departure time of 10 a.m. could not be kept, but the ship finally sailed for the Bahamas at 12:34 p.m., just 3 hours, 54 minutes after arriving from England.

The Nassau trip was followed by an 11-day cruise with 500 passengers from New York to the West Indies, calling at Kingston, Havana and Nassau, with a minimum rate of $145. Many Canadians took the short cruises and were enjoying summer temperatures 12 hours after the ship left New York.

The German-built Empress of Australia, *615 feet long, the* Britain's *running mate during the 1930s, was by no means a sister ship. Launched in 1913, she had a long career as a transpacific and transatlantic liner, cruise ship and troopship. She was sold for demolition in 1952.*
Author's Collection

The Sports Deck of the Empress of Britain *was the location of several cabins with bow windows. The nearest bow shown above was an upward continuation of an alcove in the Mayfair Lounge.*
Steamship Historical Society Collection, University of Baltimore Library

Holy Mass was observed in the Tourist Class lounge, which could easily be converted to a chapel. This was one occasion when passengers and crew met on an equal footing. Two crew members can be identified by their jacket collars. Author's Collection

The *Empress of Britain* returned to New York on January 7, 1935, and in contrast to her speedy turnaround two weeks before, she had three days to make final arrangements for the 130-day cruise. Among the items taken aboard were driving nets, putting boards and targets for ardent golfers wanting to practise at sea. At 18 ports Canadian Pacific had arranged for passengers to obtain temporary memberships at local golf clubs, entitling them to a round or two of their favourite sport.

Heavy fog, which had delayed ships entering and leaving New York for four days, lifted on January 10 and the *Empress of Britain*, with more than 400 passengers, slipped away from Pier 59 at 2:32 p.m. Six days later she arrived at Funchal, the first of 32 ports on her itinerary. After calling at Gibraltar and Algiers, she reached Monte Carlo, where the European cruise members joined the ship. Most travellers held tickets for the complete cruise, but some came and left at ports en route.

At Haifa, nearly everyone disembarked for seven days ashore in the Holy Land and Egypt, the remaining 28 leaving at Port Said a day later and travelling to Cairo. The one-week break gave the crew time to clean, polish and paint the ship, make repairs and adjustments, take stock of supplies, and also to have a rest from some of their normal duties. The *Britain*'s crew had an active Social and Athletic Club which arranged shore excursions and sporting events, usually soccer games. Informal diversions for the crew often consisted of card games, and large sums of money sometimes changed hands. Passengers rejoined the ship on February 6 at the southern end of the Suez Canal. The next port was Bombay, seven days away.

The Red Sea and Indian Ocean were as hot on the fourth cruise as they had been previously; passengers endured high temperatures with frequent comments but few complaints. No place on board was more popular all day in the sweltering heat than the open-air swimming pool. The *Britain* reached Bombay with 450 passengers for an eight-day stay.

The passenger list recorded everyone alphabetically, but it also gave clues about some passengers' social standing. Most had a simple "Mr.," "Mrs." or "Miss" in front of their names; a handful boasted titles, none on the 1935 cruise more distinguished than Her Royal Highness Princess Joachim Albrecht of Prussia. From the French aristocracy came the Marquis and Marquise de Falces, and the Comte and Comtesse de Lambertye. One member of the British peerage was aboard, Lord Tennyson, along with Lady Tennyson. Four British passengers, each travelling with his wife, were knights, thus adding eight titles (Sirs and Ladies) to the list, while one knight travelled alone. Three passengers were listed by their military rank, one of whom also possessed a knighthood. Thirteen servants accompanied their employers, only one of them in the service of a titled passenger. Servants, as usual, went unnamed in the passenger list, but their roles were stated precisely: seven maids, three valets, two amahs (or children's nurses) and one nurse.

Until a year or two earlier Penang, an island just off the Malayan peninsula, had not been on the track of the few cruise ships in the East, although George Town, the port, had a harbour deep enough for the largest ships to dock. During the *Britain*'s 11-hour stop, about a hundred passengers crossed to the mainland and went off by private diesel-electric train for a tour of Siam and Cambodia, their main objective a visit to the ruins of the famous temple of Angkor Wat. They re-embarked at Bangkok five days later.

Calls at Batavia and Semarang let passengers combine culture with agriculture. They visited rice fields and tea plantations, as well as Buddhist and Hindu temples. Excursions always allowed time for shopping, and Java was famous for the intricate designs and appealing colours of its batiks.

Following visits to Bali and two Philippine ports, the *Empress of Britain* sailed to Hong Kong then to Shanghai. At Chinwangtao, the large passenger list meant that two trains had to be chartered to take cruise members to Peking. In Japan, the ship's first port was again Beppu and, for the fourth consecutive year, local officials declared a school holiday to mark the *Britain*'s arrival. A choir of 150 little black-haired, brown-eyed children sang "Good Morning to You" in English and presented flowers to the delighted visitors. A fireworks display enlivened the evening ashore. When the ship reached Yokohama, regular sightseeing programs in Tokyo were abandoned because many passengers

The funnels, surrounded by large ventilators, were floodlit at night when the ship was in port.
CP Rail Corporate Archives

The Panama Canal gave photographers a fine opportunity when the Empress of Britain *made her annual passage.*
Les Carson

When passengers required information, needed to exchange traveller's cheques for cash, or wanted to mail a letter, the Bureau on B Deck was always ready to assist. Jay Bascom Collection

attended a public appearance of Emperor Hirohito as he bade farewell to Kang Teh, former Emperor of China and now Emperor of Manchuria.

The seven-day passage from Yokohama to Honolulu was a time to savour shipboard life at its best. Each evening, a bugle call half an hour before dinner broke the quiet, relaxed atmosphere. Apart from the normal diversions of the cruise, one passenger, Mrs. Whittall, travelling with her three children, looked forward to each Sunday she spent in the *Empress of Britain*, knowing that her husband, a Chicago businessman, would try to telephone her. He promised he would call once a week from home, expecting it would take no more than 15 minutes to complete the connection. When the ship cruised between New York and Colombo, calls were routed by New York; after Colombo, they were transmitted through San Francisco.

Reporters in Los Angeles showed more interest in the master than his ship. As well as the Victoria Cross, Captain Stuart held the United States Navy Cross for his work in aiding a crippled American destroyer in the First World War, and the press converged on him eagerly for interviews about his wartime experiences, which he gave reluctantly, downplaying his own role.

On May 13 the *Britain* made her fourth transit of the Panama Canal, followed by a short stop at Cristobal and a full day at Havana, then reached New York on May 20. A day later, 250 passengers on a regular Atlantic crossing joined the remaining cruise passengers. The hundred or so who had been aboard since Monte Carlo began to feel the emotions that Miss Bridie had experienced three years earlier. Camaraderie, which had flourished during the cruise, was becoming less apparent and memories of the past four months were contending with a sense of anticipation at seeing home, families and friends again.

The *Britain* reached Cherbourg on April 27 and Southampton later that day. Another world cruise was over, but in Montréal arrangements for the next one were almost concluded, while plans for the 1935 North Atlantic season had long since been completed.

The Duchess of York, *a 20,000-ton Canadian Pacific ship with accommodation for 1,570 passengers, sailed between Montréal and Liverpool, with calls at Glasgow and Belfast. In winter, when the St. Lawrence was frozen, she left from Saint John, New Brunswick.* Author's Collection

CHAPTER 15

ONLY 3 TO 4 DAYS OPEN SEA

Thick fog blanketed the Gulf of St. Lawrence as the *Empress of Britain* entered Canadian waters on her first trip in 1935. Only 318 passengers were aboard; businessmen formed the majority of the 125 in First Class, with a sprinkling of politicians and a few titled names. Almost 7,000 bags of mail were in the holds, enough to fill six railway mail cars when the ship reached Wolfe's Cove.

The fog seemed reluctant to lift; cargo ships and passenger liners were either at a standstill or barely moving. The Cunard ships *Andania* and *Alaunia* were behind schedule; Canadian Pacific's *Duchess of York* was due in Montréal a day late. Shore staff at Québec, knowing that the *Britain* would be two days late, planned a quick turnaround so her departure would not be unduly delayed. The *Britain* reached Québec at 7:45 a.m. on June 15 and left at 2:30 in the afternoon with about 550 passengers, including the president of Canadian Pacific, recently knighted and now known as Sir Edward Beatty.

But fog persisted in the St. Lawrence and during the morning of June 16, between the easternmost point of the island of Anticosti and the northern tip of the Magdalen Islands, the 42,348-ton *Empress of Britain* and the 5,193-ton British cargo ship *Kafiristan* collided. The *Kafiristan*, carrying 8,000 tons of coal from the Cape Breton port of Sydney to Montréal, was the more seriously damaged. Captain Stuart's collision report gave a terse account:

> S.S. *Empress of Britain* proceeding down Gulf of St. Lawrence at 10.43 a.m. in Lat. 48.13N, Long. 61.38W in fog. Could not have been avoided. Point of impact a few feet from the stern of the *Empress of Britain*. Plate 27Q strake torn and several frames and rivets started.

What this meant was that a steel plate, forming part of the hull, together with some beams of the ship's skeleton, suffered damage and a number of rivets were dislodged. A quick inspection revealed that the *Britain* was in no immediate danger.

The *Kafiristan* was less fortunate. Eight crew members were asleep in her forecastle and three lost their lives. A fire broke out forward but was quickly extinguished. Fred Sammé, still serving as an Able-Bodied Seaman in the *Britain*, recalled the collision: "I was in my cabin, fairly close to where the collision happened. The *Britain*'s whistle sounded, ordering the crew to get to the lifeboat stations. There was fog, and at first the other ship could not be located. Finally she was found and one of our motor lifeboats went over to the ship, bringing back five injured sailors. The three others fell directly into the water and were drowned."

For more than five hours the *Empress of Britain* stood by the *Kafiristan*. As other ships better able to assist the *Kafiristan* arrived at the scene, the *Britain* resumed her passage to Cherbourg and Southampton. The cargo ship could not continue her voyage to Montréal, and one of the first ships to reach the area, the *Beaverford*, took her in tow, stern first because of the damaged bow, and set off for Sydney at four knots.

On hearing of the collision, the salvage tug *Foundation Franklin* left Halifax and the tug *Cruizer* put out from Sydney, each hoping to find the *Kafiristan*. The persistent fog made contact difficult,

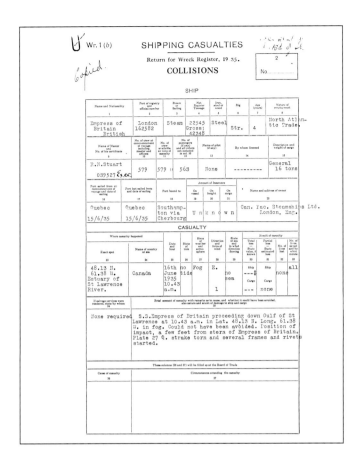

Wr. 1 (b)

Copied.

SHIPPING CASUALTIES

Return for Wreck Register, 19 35.

COLLISIONS

No. 2

SHIP

Name and Nationality	Port of registry and official number	Steam or Sailing	Net Register Tonnage	Iron, steel or wood	Rig	Age (years)	Nature of employment
1	2	3	4	5	6	7	8
Empress of Britain British	London 162582	Steam	22545 Gross: 42348	Steel	Str.	4	North Atlantic Trade.

Name of Master and No. of his certificate	No. of crew at commencement of voyage including master and officers	No. of crew available at time of casualty	No. of passengers (if any) and all others not included in col. 10	Name of pilot (if any)	By whom licensed	Description and weight of cargo
9	10	11	12	13	14	15
R.N.Stuart 039527 £.00	579	579	563	None	---------	General 16 tons

Port sailed from at commencement of voyage and date of sailing	Port last sailed from and date of sailing	Port bound to	Amount of Insurance				Name and address of owner
			On vessel	On freight	On cargo		
16	17	18	19	20	21		22
Quebec 15/6/35	Quebec 15/6/35	Southampton via Cherbourg	U n k n o w n				Can. Pac. Steamships Ltd. London, Eng.

CASUALTY

Where casualty happened		Date and hour	State of tide	State of weather and atmosphere	Direction and force of wind	State of sea and in what direction flowing	Result of casualty					
Exact spot	Name of country or sea						Total loss		Partial loss		No. of lives lost	No. of lives saved and by what means
							State value, if known		State estimated loss			
23	24	25	26	27	28	29	30		31	32	33	
48.13 N. 61.38 W. Estuary of St Lawrence River.	Canada	16th June 1935 10.43 a.m.	no tide	Fog	E. 1	no sea	Ship ---$ Cargo ---		Ship none Cargo none		all none	

If salvage services were rendered, state by whom	Brief account of casualty with remarks as to cause, and whether it could have been avoided, also nature and extent of damage to ship and cargo
34	35
None required	S.S.Empress of Britain proceeding down Gulf of St Lawrence at 10.43 a.m. in Lat. 48.13 N. Long. 61.38 W. in fog. Could not have been avoided. Position of impact, a few feet from stern of Empress of Britain. Plate 27 Q. strake torn and several frames and rivets started.

These columns (36 and 37) will be filled up at the Board of Trade.

Cause of casualty	Circumstances attending the casualty
36	37

The collision between the Empress of Britain *and the* Kafiristan *required the completion of a form setting out the details.* National Archives of Canada

Shuffleboard, a time-honoured game on passenger ships, had fairly simple rules, was not too strenuous and required no special clothing. The ship's radio officer appears to be indifferent to the player's shot. CP Rail Corporate Archives

but the tugs finally located the damaged ship, took over from the *Beaverford* and towed the *Kafiristan* into Sydney, arriving just before nightfall on June 18. She was later repaired and returned to service.

A fine point in maritime law arose when the owner of the *Beaverford*, Canadian Pacific, submitted a claim for helping save the *Kafiristan*. The inquiry following the collision stated that the *Britain* was 75 percent accountable and the *Kafiristan* 25 percent. The fact that one Canadian Pacific ship, the *Beaverford*, had assisted the stricken *Kafiristan*, while another, the *Empress of Britain*, was held largely to blame for the collision, raised the question of whether the company was eligible for any salvage money at all. An arbitration committee ruled against Canadian Pacific, as did a Court of Appeal. The company was unwilling to accept these verdicts and two years after the incident a further appeal reached the House of Lords in London, where five learned law lords finally ruled that the owner, master and crew of the *Beaverford* were indeed entitled to a salvage award.

When the *Empress of Britain* arrived at Southampton at the conclusion of the unfortunate voyage, workmen from Harland & Wolff's local yard spent 22 hours carrying out repairs, and the ship began her next crossing less than a day behind schedule.

Several weeks later, fog again delayed her on a westbound trip, but after disembarking her 400 passengers, unloading a large number of mail bags and taking on food, fuel, water and supplies, the *Britain* left Québec within hours with more than 700 passengers. Among them was Douglas Fairbanks, who had been on the first crossing in 1931. Since then he had parted from his wife, Mary Pickford, and was now travelling with his companion, Sylvia Ashley. Another notable passenger was the Honourable David Croll, Minister of Welfare in the Government of Ontario, but better known in the 1930s as the official guardian of the Dionne quintuplets. A news item in the Montréal *Gazette* was headed "Quints' God-Pop Sailing." More than 50 years later, Senator Croll (as he had then become) reminisced about the voyage: "Mrs. Croll and I were passengers on the July 12 sailing. We boarded at Québec and disembarked at Southampton. The crossing was, for us, a leisurely sort of holiday. The captain invited us to his cabin and poured me a drink that contained rum and cream, a mixture I had not tasted before. It was a smooth, misleading and powerful drink. While we were getting near to Southampton, I was impressed by the huge number of naval vessels off Spithead."

On nearly all crossings the captain entertained the most prominent passengers at cocktail parties in the sitting room of his suite. The *Britain*, like other ships in the Canadian Pacific fleet, carried a good supply of alcoholic drinks. Her wine list included 13 kinds of champagne, 6 red and 2 white Burgundies, 4 red and 4 white clarets, 9 kinds of Scotch whisky, and several brands of rye whisky and bourbon, as well as a wide choice of sherry, port, vermouth, gin, brandy, liqueurs, ale and stout, all at duty-free prices. Most champagnes cost $4.80 a bottle, wines ranged from 80 cents to $2.15, whisky was 15 cents a single and 30 cents a double, liqueurs were 20 cents a glass, while cocktails were between 15 and 55 cents each. Beer and most soft drinks were priced at 15 cents a bottle. Tobacco products were also listed; cigars varied from 5 to 50 cents apiece and cigarettes were 20 cents for American brands in packages of 20, and 55 cents for British and Canadian brands in boxes of 50. The wine list provided advice as well as drinks:

> Sound champagne in sparkling condition is sold by the glass. Passengers, particularly ladies, who may be feeling indisposed will find a glass with or before lunch or dinner very beneficial. Dry ginger ale with a slice of lemon is recommended to those who do not take alcohol.

"Indisposed" meant, of course, seasick, a word that was never seen in the publicity material of any shipping line. One phrase, stating that an Atlantic crossing on the St. Lawrence route entailed less time on the broad ocean and hinting, therefore, that the trip was subject to fewer days on rough

Every afternoon, tea was served in the Mayfair Lounge, usually to the accompaniment of orchestral music.
Author's Collection

The commanding and resonant tone of the Britain's triple-chime whistle left no doubt that the ship was about to leave port.
CP Rail Corporate Archives

seas than the New York to Europe route, appeared frequently in Canadian Pacific's advertising. It read, "Only 3 to 4 Days Open Sea."

Most passengers considered trips in the *Empress of Britain* a splendid time to relax and enjoy themselves, and except when heavy seas swept the Atlantic they succeeded in doing so. One who did not—in fact, could not—was Mary Shiman, an 11-year-old girl who came aboard with her parents at Cherbourg on September 7, leaning heavily on her mother's arm and hardly able to walk. Her illness had not been diagnosed, but when one of the *Britain*'s doctors examined her after the ship was under way he informed her parents that she had diphtheria. Mary was placed in the isolation hospital on A Deck for the remainder of the crossing. Although her illness was highly contagious, her mother insisted on sharing her room. When the ship reached Québec, Mary was taken ashore and kept in another hospital for several weeks. Many years later she spoke about the devoted attention she received from the medical staff of the *Britain*, who visited her day and night. The care she was given by the ship's doctors and nurses, she insisted, had saved her life.

A passenger with a much happier experience was Eleanor Thomas, a teenager returning from a visit to Europe with her parents. Occupying a First Class cabin that adjoined her parents', she was thrilled to be chosen to toss the dice in the traditional ship's game of horse racing, where six wooden horses were moved around a course according to the roll of the dice, with 25-cent tickets sold on each horse. Her delight continued when, later in the crossing, she wore her first evening dress, bought that summer in Paris, and a young man asked her to dance. She had never danced with a male before, however, and her pleasure in accepting the invitation was marred somewhat because, quite overcome by the occasion, she could only stumble awkwardly around the floor. With the resilience of the young, though, she recovered from her embarrassment and managed to enjoy the rest of the trip.

The *Empress of Britain*'s 1935 passenger lists shrank late in the season, particularly on eastbound crossings. On September 12, 710 passengers disembarked at Québec, but only 287 went aboard for the trip to Cherbourg and Southampton. One month later the respective figures were 450 and 184. For the final voyage, 285 passengers came ashore on November 6 at Québec and 269 embarked the next day on the eastbound passage. Although numbers were low, there was no lack of distinction among late-season names. The Earl of Bessborough, completing a four-year term as Governor General, returned to England with his family on the September 28 sailing. Vincent Massey left on the last crossing of 1935 to take up his new duties as Canada's High Commissioner to Britain.

After reaching Southampton, the *Britain* entered dry dock to have her hull cleaned and painted and the outer propellers removed before leaving on her next world cruise. She had carried 10,604 passengers in 1935, compared with 10,264 the year before, making 22 crossings each year. First Class passengers numbered 3,364, Tourist 3,191 and Third 4,049. Once again, the ship had sailed at less than half capacity on average from June to November. Regardless of this, it was the best financial year for the *Empress of Britain* since she had entered service four and a half years earlier.

The Empress of Britain *at Wilmington, a suburb of Los Angeles, showed the inevitable paintwork blemishes that occurred on long passages.* Steamship Historical Society Collection, University of Baltimore Library

CHAPTER 16

THE SUPREME TRAVEL EXPERIENCE

Italian soldiers crossed the Abyssinian border on October 3, 1935, an act that led to the declaration of war. This event was the unlikely cause of Canadian Pacific revising the *Empress of Britain*'s 1936 world cruise itinerary. Back in July, a route similar to the previous year's had been announced, but within three months it had to be radically altered. The company, wanting to avoid the unsettled conditions in the Mediterranean and Red Sea regions, resolved to send its flagship around southern Africa for the first time then, resume the regular itinerary when she reached Bombay. This led in turn to cancelling the *Empress of Australia*'s plan to make a long cruise from New York to South Africa and South America, and replacing it with five shorter ones from New York to the West Indies.

Intending to send the *Franconia* on her tenth world cruise, Cunard anticipated that the long-standing tension between Italy and Abyssinia would not disappear quickly and had from the start advertised a route that took in South America and South Africa. Hamburg-American Line now decided to send its ship, the *Reliance*, around the world by way of South Africa, but, like Canadian Pacific, did not announce the new itinerary until late October. As a result, the *Franconia* had about 300 bookings and the *Reliance* only 220. The *Empress of Britain*, expecting more than 400 passengers before her route was changed, settled for 240 when the ship left New York.

But before the world cruise began, the *Britain* fitted in a nine-day trip from New York to the Caribbean. While 400 passengers were desirable for a globe-circling cruise, on a short journey to the West Indies the ship could accommodate more than 600 in comfort. Prices for the nine days ranged from $132.50 to $550.00 per person. Children between one and ten paid half fare; for babies below the age of one, a flat rate of $20.00 was charged. The most expensive cabins were sold out long before the sailing date and, in all, 610 people took the cruise. Although it lasted just over a week, the passenger information folder made pointed recommendations about baggage:

> Although there is practically no limit to the amount of personal baggage which may be carried on the steamship, it is inadvisable for members to burden themselves with too many trunks and bags. Large trunks or other baggage not regularly needed or which cannot be conveniently accommodated in the cabin, will be placed in the baggage room, which will be accessible throughout the cruise.

Fog and snow yielded to sunshine as the *Empress of Britain* withdrew from her berth at the Chelsea pier at noon on January 7, 1936, to begin the first leg of the world cruise, a 2,800-mile passage to Funchal. Here 100 British and Continental passengers came aboard from the *Empress of Australia*, which had been diverted to the Madeiran port rather than sailing directly from Southampton and Cherbourg to New York.

The *Britain* made a day-long stop at Las Palmas in the Canary Islands then reached Cape Town after ten days on the high seas. Although passenger numbers were down from the previous world cruise, fares stayed about the same. The two most expensive suites cost $12,500 per person for

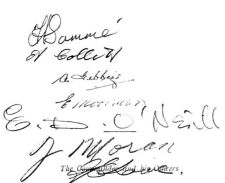

Hammé
A. Collett
a. Gibbs
E. Moorman
E. D. O'Neill
J. Moran

The Commodore and his Officers,

wish all Ratings

the Compliments of the Season.

A. Work

W. Marwell

Empress of Britain   December 25, 1935

Xmas Dinner

———

Tomato Soup

Grilled Cod Steak

Roast Sirloin of Beef
Boiled and Browned Potatoes
Peas au Sucre

Roast Turkey, Cranberry Sauce

Xmas Pudding
Mince Pie

Dessert
Coffee

On December 25, 1935, the crew sat down to a traditional Christmas Dinner, then autographed the menu. Fred Sammé

For the 1936 world cruise, two people could book Cabin 128 for $5,550 each. The price for single occupancy was $6,200.
CP Rail Corporate Archives

Cabin 253 was priced at $3,950 per person for two passengers, or about $30 a day each, for the world cruise of 1936. CP Rail Corporate Archives

the 132-day voyage. Most cabins with private bathrooms were priced between $4,000 and $5,000 per person. A passenger travelling alone could have an inside cabin on E Deck, close to the stern, with no porthole and no private bathroom, for $2,150. Fares included sightseeing tours at all ports. Maids and valets accompanying their employers were carried at $1,750 when occupying servants' cabins, but this amount excluded sightseeing excursions. For these, it cost another $400, with the stipulation that all shore trips must be done in the company of their employers or with other servants.

When the *Empress of Britain* steamed into Cape Town harbour, her size and commanding appearance brought huge crowds down to the Duncan Dock. She was the largest passenger ship to call at 24 of the 26 ports during the 1936 cruise, and because this was her first trip to South Africa, the press covered her arrival thoroughly. One reporter, George Young, who spent many years writing about ships, had no reservations about the *Britain*. Forty years later he wrote, "The *Empress of Britain* was the most beautiful ship I ever saw."

Beautiful or not, the *Britain* faced serious difficulties when she tried to leave Cape Town. A strong southeast wind held her fast against the quay, and it took more than an ordinary struggle by the ship, assisted by tugs, to get away, finally succeeding 24 hours behind schedule. Most passengers were not on board to see her depart. They had left on a special train for a four-day journey to Durban with stopovers at Kimberley, Johannesburg and Pretoria. The *Britain* sailed around the Cape of Good Hope to Durban, where passengers rejoined her on February 3.

The ship's stay in Durban was a major event for many residents and a big headache for the local public transit system. On the Sunday she arrived, 22,000 of the company's 31,000 passengers

INCLUDED SHORE EXCURSIONS

THE CRUISE FARE INCLUDES THE FOLLOWING COMPREHENSIVE PROGRAMME OF SHORE EXCURSIONS:

MADEIRA—Evening of arrival: Ball at Casino, including transportation to and from Casino; admission to Casino and dancing. Full-day sightseeing, including transfer by bullock carroe or motor car from pier to railway station, special train to top of mountain, Terreiro da Lucta, 3,285 feet; luncheon at Chalet Restaurant or Reid's Palace Hotel; descent by toboggan or train.

LAS PALMAS—Full-day trip by motor car; luncheon at hotel.

CAPE TOWN—Full-day drive to Cape Point with luncheon enroute; half-day drive around Cape Town. Four-day trip by special train from Cape Town to Durban with stop-overs at:

KIMBERLEY—Half-day drive around city and to Diamond Mine.

JOHANNESBURG—Morning drive to Gold Mine; luncheon at hotel; afternoon drive around the city and to the zoo. Dinner at hotel.

PRETORIA—Half-day city drive.

DURBAN—Half-day Marine Drive; luncheon at hotel. Half-day Circular Drive; visit Zulu Kraals. Half-day drive around the city and to the Valley of a Thousand Hills.

BOMBAY—Five-day trip by special train from Bombay to Delhi, Agra, the Taj Mahal, and Fatephur Sikri, with meals and sleeping compartment on train, including sightseeing by motor car or carriage at all places and meals at hotels. Full-day motor trip around Bombay; luncheon at Taj Mahal Hotel, Bombay.

COLOMBO—Morning motor drive around Colombo; luncheon at Galle Face Hotel; afternoon motor trip to Mt. Lavinia for tea. Full-day trip to Peradeniya and Kandy with luncheon at hotel in Kandy; motor to Elephant Park.

PENANG—Full-day motor trip around the Island and to points of interest in Penang, including Snake Temple at Sungei Glugor, Botanical Gardens and Aier Itam Temple; luncheon at hotel.

SINGAPORE—Morning motor trip to the independent State of Johore, via Seletar Village, and the Johore Causeway, including drive around the town of Johore Bahru. Afternoon motor trip in and around Singapore.

BANGKOK—Full-day trip by special electric train from Paknam to Bangkok; sightseeing by motor car; launch to Wat Arun; luncheon at hotel; motor to the Grand Palace, Temple of the Emerald Buddha and Wat Poh; tea and exhibition of Siamese Classical Dancing at Bangkok Riding and Polo Club.

BATAVIA—Afternoon drive by motor car to Weltevreden and new suburbs; full-day trip by motor car to Buitenzorg with luncheon at hotel; morning drive by motor car to Old Batavia, Aquarium and Museum with luncheon at hotel.

SEMARANG—Full-day trip by motor car to Boroboedoer, passing through old and new parts of Semarang; motor to Kopeng; luncheon at hotel.

BALI—Full-day motor trip in the Island of Bali, including the Bats' Cave, Penelokan and Kintamani. Luncheon at The Bali Hotel in Den Pasar; Balinese music and dance performance at the Poera Satrya.

MANILA—Half-day drive by motor car around Manila. including Fort Santiago and Fort McKinley. Dinner dance at Manila Hotel.

HONG KONG—Dinner Dance at Peninsula Hotel, Kowloon; Three half-day motor trips around New Territory, Victoria Peak and to Repulse Bay, where tea will be served at the famous Repulse Bay Hotel.

SHANGHAI—Morning motor trip around Shanghai and Chapei and to the Native City; luncheon and Thé Dansant at the Cathay Hotel.

PEIPING—Special train from Chinwangtao to Peiping and return via Tientsin; accommodation and meals at Peiping hotels for 3½ days; sightseeing by motor car and ricksha, including Summer Palace, Forbidden City and Temple of Heaven; special train to Great Wall of China at Ching-lungchiao.

As transfer between the ship and pier at Chinwangtao takes place from the ship at anchorage some three miles from shore and as the weather is fresh in late March and early April, members are advised to wrap themselves warmly.

BEPPU—Morning: sightseeing by motor car, including Hot Springs and Japanese Garden; luncheon at Kamenoi Hotel; afternoon: Geisha Dance performance at City Auditorium.

KOBE—Full-day ricksha drive around Kobe; two-day trip by special train to Kyoto and Nara, with hotel accommodation at Kyoto. Sightseeing by motor car in Kyoto and by ricksha in Nara.

YOKOHAMA—Morning motor trip around Yokohama; full-day trip by special train to Tokyo, sightseeing by motor car and luncheon at Imperial Hotel in Tokyo.

HONOLULU—Morning motor drive through Honolulu and around the Island, including Nuuanu Pali, Pearl Harbour and Kahuku Point; afternoon: visit Waikiki Beach; luncheon and dinner at Royal Hawaiian Hotel. Transfers to and from hotel.

HILO—Full-day motor trip from Hilo to Rainbow Falls, Hawaii National Park, Kilauea Volcano, Lava Tubes and Fern Forest; luncheon at Volcano House Hotel.

SAN FRANCISCO—Morning motor trip around San Francisco, to Golden Gate Park, the Presidio and Twin Peaks; luncheon at hotel.

LOS ANGELES—Full-day trip by motor car from San Pedro to Los Angeles, Santa Monica, Beverley Hills and Hollywood; luncheon at the Ambassador Hotel.

PANAMA CANAL ZONE—Morning motor trip around Balboa, Ancon and Panama City, also to historic ruins of Old Panama. Sail through Panama Canal by daylight.

HAVANA—Morning motor trip around Havana and to Marianao.

Long before they stepped on board, passengers on world cruises knew what sights to anticipate on shore excursions. Author's Collection

headed for the harbour. Overcrowded trolley buses fell far behind schedule, and even when all available motor buses were added to the route, reports continued to mention congestion and delays.

There was no overcrowding aboard the *Empress of Britain*, however, because some of the already small number of passengers had ended their journey at Cape Town. Another group disembarked at Bombay, but as well as losing passengers the *Britain* also acquired new ones, some travelling only from one port to the next and others taking longer trips.

After India came ports of earlier cruises, Colombo, Penang, Singapore, Bangkok, Batavia, Semarang and then the island of Bali before the ship continued to Manila and Hong Kong. The *Britain*'s size did not allow her to reach Shanghai. At Woosung, about 10 miles downriver from the city centre, the ship anchored and passengers travelled in two large steam tenders to the city itself. On disembarking at the Bund, they found 150 maroon Canadian-made automobiles waiting to take them on their sightseeing tour.

Following a stop in Chinwangtao, where the passengers left for a four-day visit to Peking, the *Empress of Britain* sailed for Beppu. On earlier cruises the small Japanese port had always given a warm reception to the ship, and this time was no different. But a problem regarding photography had occurred during the 1935 call, when some passengers, perhaps thoughtlessly, took snapshots of military locations, leading to the confiscation of their films. To prevent a recurrence, the water police came aboard and distributed maps showing the fortified zones and warning crew and passengers not to approach the forbidden areas. Some crewmen who had been on past cruises saw this action as evidence of Japan's growing military strength. For passengers, though, the pleasures of sight-seeing in cherry blossom time outweighed less agreeable matters.

The *Britain* reached Hawaii on April 22, and after calling at Honolulu and Hilo, she arrived at San Francisco on the last day of the month. There and at Los Angeles many passengers left the ship and returned home, and a smaller number came aboard. Those boarding in California had to disembark at Havana rather than New York because United States law forbade a non-American ship to embark passengers at one American port and disembark them at another. For most, this meant going from Havana to Miami by ferry before travelling to their final destinations.

After a 33,632-mile journey, the *Empress of Britain* docked at New York early on May 18 with over 300 passengers, and for 173 of them the cruise was over. Newsmen interviewed Captain Stuart shortly after the ship arrived. Hoping for at least one colourful story, a reporter asked the ship's master if he had any amusing incidents to relate. There was, said Captain Stuart, an event at Bali which stuck in his mind. As was their habit, natives came out to the ship in small canoes, beseeching passengers for small presents and sometimes offering local handicrafts in exchange. According to the Captain, one passenger looked out his porthole, saw a native wringing his hands, and took for granted that the man was soliciting laundry. He lowered two white tropical suits through the porthole and never saw them again. He discovered his error on complaining to the Purser that his laundry had not been returned. The reporter dutifully wrote down the anecdote and it was published the following day. What he did not know was that the tale of the missing laundry, with minor variations, had been circulating throughout the Far East for many years.

In May 1937, Canadian Pacific issued its annual report for the year ending December 31, 1936. Page 8 stated, "Net earnings of cruise services decreased substantially, due primarily to the itinerary of the world cruise of the *Empress of Britain* made necessary by the disturbed conditions in the Mediterranean."

Competition for Canadian Pacific came mostly from Cunard Line. The 14,000-ton Ascania, *shown leaving Montréal, was one of six near sisters.* Author's Collection

CHAPTER 17

39 PERCENT LESS OCEAN

Early in 1936 the words "First Class" were abolished. The North Atlantic Passenger Conference, to which Canadian Pacific and most other shipping companies belonged, resolved to amend the terminology. First Class was now designated Cabin Class, Tourist Third Cabin became simply Tourist—the name by which it was popularly known—and Third stayed Third. Renaming the classes made little difference in fares, except for a $5 one-way reduction in the newly named Cabin Class. Service and amenities did not change, no matter what label was attached to the best accommodation (which in the following pages will continue to be called First Class, a more fitting term and one used by most passengers).

Canadian Pacific remained the leader in passenger travel between Canada and Europe, but its ships still had to share the market with the Cunard Line's *Alaunia, Andania, Antonia, Ascania, Aurania* and *Ausonia* and Donaldson Line's *Athenia* and *Letitia*, all with Montréal as their Canadian terminal for most of the year.

The *Britain* left Southampton and Cherbourg on June 6, 1939, her first voyage of the season, under a new master, Captain George Parry, a native of Beaver River, Nova Scotia. A veteran of the First World War, in which he served at the Battle of Jutland, George Parry went to sea at the age of 16. He joined Canadian Pacific as a junior officer in 1911 and after the war worked his way up the promotion ladder in the company's ships until he received his first command, the cargo ship *Beaverhill*. In quick succession, Captain Parry became master of the passenger ships *Melita, Duchess of York* and *Duchess of Bedford*. Now in his early fifties, the tall, big-boned Maritimer was chosen to succeed Captain Stuart, who had been named general superintendent of the company in Montréal in succession to Captain Latta, promoted to general manager in London. Although the *Empress of Britain* had her third master in five years, two senior officers who had served in the ship since her maiden voyage remained, Purser Stanley Pearch and Chief Engineer H.G. Donald.

On her first eastbound sailing, the *Britain* took 4 days, 10 hours, 25 minutes between Father Point and Cherbourg, three and a half hours more than the record between these points, but still very satisfactory. It was not always possible to set records or even to adhere to published times. Fog, gales and ice fields intermittently detained the ship from a few minutes to many hours. Her 2 p.m. departure time from Québec depended on the prompt arrival of the special train which left Windsor Station, Montréal, at 9 a.m., and while there was seldom a delay between these cities, occasionally the transcontinental train from Vancouver ran late, causing the boat train to be held at Montréal until passengers from Western Canada arrived. For nearly all passengers, the train trip was an intrinsic part of the journey; on board the *Britain* they could buy rail tickets and make sleeper reservations to Canadian and United States destinations from two Canadian Pacific Railway representatives with an office on B Deck.

The military-sounding bugle, which for five years had warned First Class passengers each evening that dinner would commence in 30 minutes, was discarded in 1936 and replaced by the softer tones of chimes. Eating in the Salle Jacques Cartier was not compulsory. Apart from cabin service for meals, passengers could arrange private dinner parties in the Salle Montcalm or the Salle Wolfe, small rooms adjoining the main dining saloon. All it required was a discussion about the menu

Smoke belched from the funnels of the tugs when they assisted the Empress of Britain *at Québec.*
CP Rail Corporate Archives

Looking aft from the starboard wing of the bridge, the officer of the watch could see passengers exploring the Sun Deck as the ship left Québec.
CP Rail Corporate Archives

Donald and Peggy McCuaig, neatly dressed for their first Atlantic crossing, greeted their mother on deck during a 1936 crossing. Donald McCuaig

with the Chief Steward or Head Waiter; there was no additional cost for the party. Young children did not share their elders' dining tables. They had their own meal times and sat with adults only if they paid adult fares. Below the age of one, a child's fare was $16 in First Class and $10 in Tourist; from one to ten years it was half the adult fare; and when the child passed his tenth birthday full adult fare applied.

Children crossing the Atlantic in the *Britain* saw it as an adventure, a long-remembered highlight in their lives. One girl, Peggy McCuaig, left Québec on August 15, 1936. Many years later she wrote about her trip:

> One reason we travelled in the *Empress of Britain* was because of the colourful brochures. The whole family pored over a number of brochures for months before making up our minds and the *Britain* was the number one choice of everyone. There were movies to see, sumptuous meals to eat and music to listen to—after we recovered from seasickness with the help of a kind Scottish nurse. My most vivid memory is of the swimming pool with its surrounding marble changing rooms and their thick, warm towels. The crew were friendly and very patient. They introduced my brother and me to other youngsters and taught us to play ring toss and ping pong. It was the most fabulous trip of my life. Nothing I've done since is as bright in my memory.

A constant reminder to passengers that the sea imposed its own discipline was the presence of lifebelts in every cabin. Instructions for emergency stations were specific:

> An exercise will be carried out the day after sailing, weather permitting. Passengers will don lifebelts and proceed to muster station, in accordance with arrow direction signs and framed plans in alleyways.

Salle Wolfe and its counterpart on the port side, Salle Montcalm, could be reserved for private dinner parties.
CP Rail Corporate Archives

The ventilation louvre could be freely adjusted to send a flow of fresh air in any direction. CP Rail Corporate Archives

Lifeboat drill was taken seriously, and irrespective of the number of times old hands among the passengers had crossed the Atlantic, they were expected to take part, even though some good-natured grumbling inevitably accompanied their appearance at the muster station. Sickness, however, might prevent a few from attending the drill. To care for the ills and injuries of a crew greater than 600, together with a passenger list that could run from 200 to 1,000, the *Britain* carried two doctors, the Senior Surgeon and the Second Surgeon, in addition to a nursing staff. Doctors wore the same navy-blue uniforms as other officers; they could be distinguished by the red velvet between the gold stripes on their cuffs. As a rule, they charged passengers a fee for their services, unless they were treating an illness that originated on board, usually seasickness.

On three of the *Britain*'s westbound sailings in 1936 the number of passengers disembarking at Wolfe's Cove exceeded a thousand: 1,043 on August 13, 1,052 on August 27, and 1,030 on September 10. The eastbound traffic was higher earlier in the season. On June 12, June 27 and July 11, passenger numbers were 677, 957 and 955 respectively.

The final crossing from Québec began on November 7. The *Empress of Britain* had arrived the day before from Southampton and Cherbourg with 278 passengers and left with 318. This was more than Canadian Pacific expected, but a strike in the port of New York compelled 50 travellers to journey north by train to Québec. To their surprise, they discovered that even with the overnight trip, they would arrive at Southampton a day earlier than if they had sailed from New York. Not only that, their crossing would include 39 percent less ocean, according to the often-used slogan on the front of Canadian Pacific's sailing schedules.

Statistics for the North Atlantic route published some months later showed that the *Empress of Britain* had maintained a very creditable average of 24 knots for the season. The *Normandie*, *Queen Mary*, *Bremen* and *Europa*, all of which had at various times held the Blue Riband of the Atlantic, exceeded her speed with averages of 28.29, 28.27, 26.71 and 26.40 knots respectively. Two fast Italian ships, the *Rex* and *Conte di Savoia*, in service between Mediteranean ports and New York, also had higher speeds than the *Britain*.

The waiting room of the First Class beauty saloon on A Deck was both spacious and comfortable.
Glasgow University Archives / Scottish Record Office

CHAPTER 18

TRAVELLING IN STYLE

For most passengers, a world cruise represented a once-in-a-lifetime experience, but the *Empress of Britain* attracted a core of repeat clients who made the trip year after year. For them, the ship was their winter home, a place to escape the cold of the northern hemisphere and renew old friendships. They knew the ropes, so to speak, but Canadian Pacific wanted to ensure that first-timers also got the most out of their cruise, and to help them it issued comprehensive pamphlets on clothing and shopping. On the subject of clothing, Gladys M. Gowlland, an Assistant Cruise Director, wrote in chatty style:

> First and foremost, the fur coat question! A fur coat on a world cruise is not a real necessity; life is quite livable without one, but if you are one of those "chilly" mortals, better pack your furs. Indispensable is a heavy travelling coat, preferably inter-lined with chamois to keep out the wind, and trimmed with fur to look cosy. Nothing unusual about it—just the type you would choose to wear at home when the weather is nippy... To match this coat should be a small "comfortable" hat in felt—one that will wear well and retain its shape and smartness—one that can be used on land and sea—in train or motor.

After discussing the merits of silk and cotton in warmer climates, Miss Gowlland offered guidance on how ladies should dress in the evening:

> For the many delightful evenings which abound on the cruise, let your frocks follow your own fancy, for no woman knows what another likes in the way of dress for the gala evenings on board and ashore. Be sure, however, to include some which are of the lightest weight, for even in the tropics one trips the "light fantastic" and filmy chiffons, organdies and organzas are in demand. Lace is really priceless for travelling; it always comes up fresh and smiling from your wardrobe trunk... And remember that more light than dark evening dresses will be required on your cruises. Every year I hear women cry, "Why didn't I bring more light things?" So take warning.

Recommendations for women filled two closely printed pages, but for men two paragraphs were considered enough. Gladys Gowlland's words were to the point:

> What one wears at home one wears on a world cruise; the only difference being that an adequate supply of cool clothing for the tropics should be included; the thinnest of underwear and plenty of shirts. Full dress is not required— a dinner jacket is considered sufficiently formal for all occasions, while in the tropics men find comfort in the evenings by donning a white dinner jacket of linen, drill, or other cool-looking material or a "mess" jacket—a short, neatly-fitting coat, such as is worn by army and naval officers for formal affairs in hot countries. These and light-weight tropical suits may, if necessary, be purchased in Bombay and Colombo—the native tailors are usually reliable and their prices quite low.

Cabin 240, like most in the ship, had a length that greatly exceeded its width. The fabrics came in several different patterns.
Jay Bascom Collection

Shortly after the Britain left Colombo, five passengers posed for the camera with a large collection of model elephants.
Author's Collection

Bookings for the 1937 world cruise were up from the year before. The route through the Mediterranean, Suez Canal and Red Sea had been restored; South Africa had been dropped. The only question mark was Barcelona, where the Spanish Civil War might force cancellation of the *Britain*'s visit. Fares for the 125-day journey began at $2,300 per person, an increase of $150 from the previous year. Top price was $12,850 for each person in the best suites. For passengers who disembarked at San Francisco or Los Angeles and missed the last two weeks of the cruise, fares were reduced by $125.

About three dozen Canadians were among more than 400 passengers aboard the *Britain* when she left Pier 59 on the Hudson River at noon on January 9, 1937. For the third successive year her departure was marked by sun-dispelling fog. Just before the ship sailed, the stop at Barcelona was cancelled and Algiers substituted.

Perhaps typical of the calls the ship made on a world cruise was the visit to Ceylon. The Canadian Pacific brochure came close to effusion:

> Glittering jewel of an island—basking in the sunshine—quivering in the breeze. Elephants and bullock bandies, coconut groves and and coffee, tree-fringed roads, happy natives, laughing brown babies, yellow-and orange-robed Buddhist priests, a riot of flowers. . .everything green and smiling. Yes. . .this tropic "Isle of Spices" is certainly the greenest place we've ever seen. Such a medley of races— Tamils, Moors, Malays, Parsees. Graceful Singhalese men striding along in ankle-length sarongs.
>
> Fine shops line Colombo streets. Particularly attractive are the jewellers' stores, where precious and semi-precious stones are displayed in exotic profusion— satiny pearls, gleaming rubies, sapphires, cat's-eyes, amethysts, topaz and limpid zircons. And the stores showing really fashionable dresses, as well as the native shops where one may purchase exquisite materials and have them made up in a couple of days, will delight all feminine cruise members.

The *Britain* reached Colombo at 7 a.m. on February 22 and anchored in the harbour for a four-day stay. Between 8:30 and 9 that morning, 200 passengers left by automobile for a full-day excursion to Peradeniya Gardens and the Brahman and Buddhist temples of Kandy, the former capital. Others went by car to the Mount Lavinia Hotel and its palm-fringed beach, where one passenger described the swimming as intoxicating, with the water as buoyant as champagne.

Miss Gowlland was familiar with Ceylon and offered shopping hints with the confidence that came from experience:

> Ceylon is famous for its tailors and dressmakers. The speed with which these men work is amazing. They can copy anything. Just pick out the material, give them a favourite dress and in a few hours the reproduction is ready, complete down to the very last button and tuck.

As if to put her words to the test, on the last day of her visit she entered a shop at 11 in the morning, saw some material she liked and contemplated ordering two dresses. She planned to leave for the *Britain* in the 2 o'clock tender but did not know if the dresses could be finished in three hours. "Plenty time," said the merchant and, sure enough, the dresses were ready at 1:45. On the other hand, she cautioned against buying bargain-priced carved elephants. After two days, their tusks began to fall out and in a week cracks covered their entire bodies.

The alternating periods of leisure and sightseeing that passengers enjoyed differed sharply from the working day of the crew. One waiter recalled the long hours of work by saying that table service was only one facet of the job. Three times a day he set the tables before each meal and tidied up after the last diners had left. After breakfast, he might be ordered to clean the brass portholes of the dining saloon or wash the stairways. Following an hour or so of free time in the morning, he

After a day of sight-seeing ashore, the privacy and comfort of one's own cabin were always appealing.
CP Rail Corporate Archives

When the Britain *sailed under the Golden Gate Bridge in San Francisco, her masts were well clear of the safety nets.*
Wellington Harbour Board

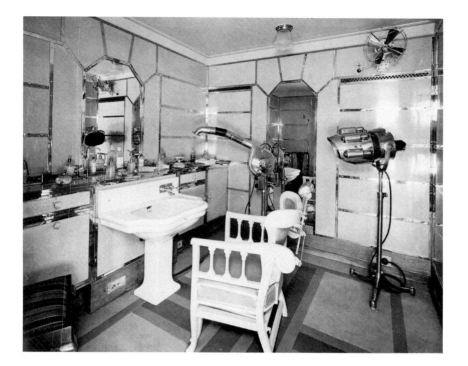

reported to the Salle Jacques Cartier 30 minutes before lunch. The waiter then stood beside one of his tables while the dining saloon steward and an assistant selected tables at random and inspected linen, cutlery, chinaware and glassware. It was then time to study the menu. Some dishes were listed in French and the waiter had to know the English translation. When a new dish was introduced, it was not enough for the waiter to recite its contents and method of cooking to the diners; he also had to learn the correct serving procedure. He followed the same routine before dinner.

Waiters had their quarters on E Deck, almost directly below the Salle Jacques Cartier, with 6 to 18 sharing different-sized but always crowded cabins. The large numbers were common, a simple fact of seagoing life in the 1930s. Showers and baths were few but cleanliness was essential for all crew members in direct contact with passengers. A partial solution when the regular facilities were in use was to fill three adjoining hand basins with water and rinse oneself down in a standing position. On cruises, and when it was warm on the St. Lawrence, waiters wore white jackets rather than dark blue. Smoking on duty was, of course, forbidden. Cigarette lighters and sulphur-ignited matches were prohibited, as they were considered fire hazards. The company supplied safety matches instead.

Since the *Britain*'s visit to San Francisco a year before, the Golden Gate bridge had been all but completed. Captain Parry was not certain about the ship's ability to pass unharmed beneath the bridge, so 2 feet had been lopped off each of the *Britain*'s masts. The difficulty was not the structure itself but the safety nets strung beneath. They tended to hang loose in dry weather and to tighten up in the rain. The ship arrived on April 29, a damp day, and there was sufficient clearance for her to sail under the bridge without incident.

The cruise ended for most North American passengers on May 14, when the *Britain* docked at New York, and a week later for European passengers, when she reached Cherbourg and Southampton. Financial returns for the cruise had far exceeded those of 1936, and Canadian Pacific planners hoped to repeat the itinerary in 1938. When the accountants totalled the figures, they found that the cost of provisioning the ship for the cruise came to about $135,000, or just over $1,000 a day. Fresh water taken aboard from shore installations and water tenders at 19 ports en route came to $12,645.81.

When the Empress of Britain *was on the North Atlantic, the exposed decks were often deserted. At least one lifeboat on each side was always ready to be launched when the ship was under way.*
CP Rail Corporate Archives

CHAPTER 19

A SEASON OF
STEADY SERVICE

P assengers in Third Class often speculated about occupants of First Class cabins and wondered about the state of luxury in which they spent their time on an Atlantic crossing. Although the *Britain* was a three-class ship, with each class confined to its own territory, equality existed for a period on Sunday mornings when a religious service, open to all passengers, was held in the Empress Room. Joan Davis, one of a group of English schoolgirls who boarded at Québec on August 28, 1937, after a three-week visit to Canada, discovered that the well-known Hollywood star Maureen O'Sullivan was travelling—in First Class, of course—with her husband John Farrow, a film director. Keen to obtain Miss O'Sullivan's autograph, Joan and her friends attended the service, and when it was over she encountered the actress, who obligingly signed her name. The delighted girls then returned to their more modest accommodation.

At the start of the 1937 season, Canadian Pacific was cautiously optimistic about passenger bookings for the *Empress of Britain*. The first westbound crossing had 486 passengers, compared to 332 the year before and 318 in 1935. Fog, however, the nemesis of shipping on the North Atlantic and in the Gulf of St. Lawrence, was particularly dense around Cape Race and delayed the ship's arrival at Wolfe's Cove by one day.

In three successive midsummer westbound crossings the *Empress of Britain* carried more than 1,000 passengers, but her best eastbound trips did not reach four figures, with 925 embarking on June 26 and 856 on July 10. These were busy trips for dining saloon staff, who carried out their duties with calm assurance, particularly in First Class, which employed the best waiters. There, tips ran ran about $5 per passenger for an Atlantic crossing, but a waiter with exceptional skill often exceeded this amount. Celebrities nearly always tipped more than other passengers.

Between crossings, the ship spent two days in Québec, where the waiters usually worked from 8 a.m. to 5 p.m. There were no passengers, of course, but waiters cleaned the dining saloons and lounges and carried out assorted other tasks, not all directly related to their job. The *Britain* had her own laundry, but on some crossings it could not keep up with demand, so waiters had to carry bags of soiled linen ashore and bring clean linen aboard. Canadian Pacific owned the city's largest hotel, the Chateau Frontenac, and occasionally waiters from the ship were ordered to assist on busy evenings. When off duty, crewmen visited their favourite bars, played soccer, attended movies or looked up friends they had met on past visits to the city. Delays in arriving, resulting from fog or rough seas, cut into free time at Québec, since it was imperative not only to meet the date of sailing but the hour of departure as well. The ship left for Cherbourg and Southampton every second Saturday afternoon, reaching her destinations the following Thursday.

Canadian Pacific reminded crews that a satisfied passenger was the best and cheapest form of advertisement, but the company left nothing to chance. A steady stream of folders and booklets poured out of the advertising offices in Montréal, informing the traveller what to expect:

Two of Canadian Pacific's proudest possessions were the Chateau Frontenac *at Québec and the* Empress of Britain.
Jay Bascom Collection

The laundry at the after end of C Deck handled the requirements of the ship and passengers without difficulty on most occasions.
Glasgow University Archives / Scottish Record Office

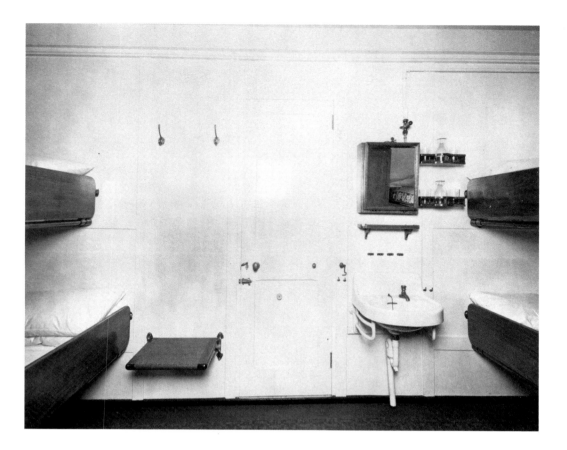

A Third Class passenger had little privacy and a minimum of furniture, but the bunks were comfortable and the cabin clean.
CP Rail Corporate Archives

One of the distinctive things about cuisine on Canadian Pacific liners is its cosmopolitanism... English chefs, yes, French chefs also, American chefs, too, and Scandinavian chefs. And every chef is a specialist. One does only breads, another only roasts, his compeer only steaks and chops...

Few hotels on earth present a menu so vast, so varied, so elaborately served. Each liner carries some six hundred different items of food; about three hundred tons of the world's choicest delicacies. All yours; not a price mark in sight.

Tourist cuisine comes out of the same kitchen as First Class, although it is served less elaborately. Third Class has its own kitchen from which comes a surprising variety of food, wonderfully well cooked and seasoned, all that you can eat... Everything concerning the preparation of your food is the last word in cleanliness and freshness. And, as a final precaution, travelling Canadian Pacific chefs pop aboard frequently to ascertain that service, variety and excellence are being kept up to Canadian Pacific's inviolable standards.

Passengers had more than eating to occupy them on an Atlantic crossing. The tennis court, available at no charge and floodlit after dark, had not lost any of its popularity. Rackets could be hired for 25 cents an hour or purchased outright from the shop. Players were limited to one hour unless no one was waiting. The same conditions applied to the squash court. Stewards in the Cathay Lounge and the Mayfair kept a supply of indoor games, including chess, checkers, backgammon, dice and poker chips.

Captain W.G. Busk-Wood took over as master from Captain Parry in October 1937. He was already familiar with the ship, having served in her as staff captain several years earlier. Like his predecessors, he had gone to sea as a youth in a sailing ship before joining Canadian Pacific as

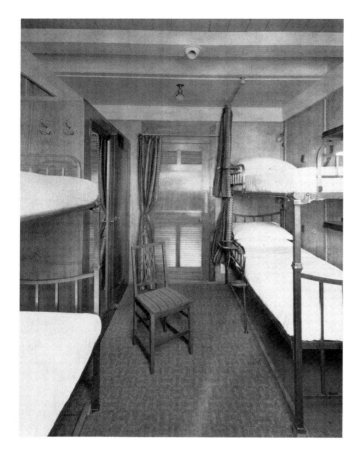

Cabin 454 accommodated four Tourist Class passengers, but on a world cruise the upper berths were removed. The long floor rail below the bunks prevented suitcases from sliding out when the sea was rough. CP Rail Corporate Archives

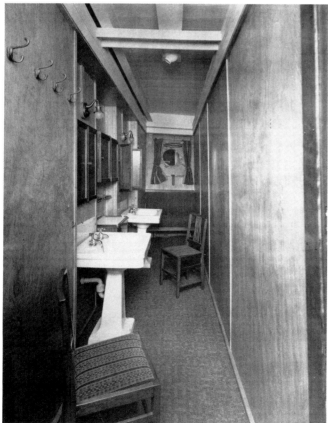

The narrow corridor allowed natural light to reach the bedroom area and thus the cabin could be classified as an outside one and command a higher price. CP Rail Corporate Archives

Table VIII

CANADIAN PACIFIC STEAMSHIPS

MONTREAL, QUEBEC ⎫
SAINT JOHN, HALIFAX ⎬ CHERBOURG, HAVRE, SOUTHAMPTON

WESTBOUND				SHIP	EASTBOUND			III Total	III Divided							
Arrival	Cabin	Tourist	III		Departure	Cabin	Tourist		Brit.	Scan.	Finn.	Cont.	Ital.	Grk Or'l	Cns.	Dp
				Empress of Australia	Apr. 24	252	197	170	121	..	2	39	8	.. ..		1
Apr. 25	34	51	201	Montcalm.........												
May 15	35	65	75	Montclare.........	May 15	63	56	148	100	9	1	35	1	2 1		2
				Duchess of Atholl...	" 28	141	130	148	95	9	..	44	..	.. ..		..
" 26	141	116	103	Empress of Australia	" 29	149	194	191	89	..	65	37	..	.. ..		1
June 3	169	168	165	Montclare.........	June 5	70	51	156	97	2	4	53	..	.. 3		4
" 11	158	151	177	Empress of Britain.	" 12	159	134	363	226	19	14	91	11	2 ..		
" 15	98	122	110	Empress of Australia	" 16	140	228	184	93	8	4	55	21	.. 1		..
" 24	143	112	165	Empress of Britain.	" 26	302	234	389	278	43	2	63	3	.. 1		..
" 30	127	98	267	Empress of Australia	July 2	184	212	253	130	10	..	104	9	.. ..		1
				Montcalm.........	" 3	186	125	185	125	5	..	53	2	.. 2		4
July 8	243	172	212	Empress of Britain.	" 10	250	202	404	226	28	..	142	8	.. 2		..
" 22	103	99	193	Montcalm.........												
" 29	321	244	302	Empress of Britain..	" 31	154	168	210	144	3	..	49	14	.. 4		..
Aug. 13	330	257	418	Empress of Britain.	Aug. 14	122	144	187	129	5	..	50	3	.. ..		1
" 24	244	255	363	Duchess of Richmond	" 25	34	36	82	52	1	..	29	..	.. ..		2
" 26	389	248	418	Empress of Britain.	" 28	124	107	233	185	6	..	42	..	.. 2		..
" 31	334	264	206	Empress of Australia	Sept. 1	57	90	65	41	2	..	21	1	.. ..		1
				Montrose.........	" 10	53	38	70	44	2	..	24	..	.. 3		..
Sept. 9	296	220	290	Duchess of Richmond												
" 9	389	241	423	Empress of Britain.	" 11	110	91	118	96	..	..	17	5	.. ..		1
" 16	303	192	196	Empress of Australia	" 16	70	91	50	22	..	..	26	2	.. ..		2
" 23	281	166	304	Empress of Britain.	" 25	109	188	198	135	..	..	62	1	.. 2		1
" 30	79	83	166	Montrose.........	Oct. 2	29	37	77	67	4	..	6	..	.. 2		..
Oct. 7	172	137	250	Empress of Britain.	" 9	91	96	139	96	1	2	33	7	.. ..		1
" 21	150	142	130	Empress of Britain.	" 23	120	76	83	62	..	..	21	..	.. ..		4
" 28	29	15	116	Montrose.........												
Nov. 4	99	81	148	Empress of Britain.	Nov. 6	82	55	87	60	1	..	24	2	.. ..		3
				Duchess of Richmond	" 25	38	46	256	125	28	4	94	4	1 1		3
Dec. 12	29	33	131	Duchess of Richmond	Dec. 11	20	29	222	90	2	3	121	6	.. 5		1
25 Trips	4696	3732	5529	Totals	26 Trips	3109	3055	4668	2928	188	101	1335	111	5 29		33

NEW YORK — CHERBOURG, SOUTHAMPTON

Arrival	Cabin	Tourist	III	SHIP	Departure	Cabin	Tourist								
Jan. 5	41	26	24	Empress of Australia											
				Empress of Britain.	May 15	226	40	..	..	..	..	..	..	.. ..	
Dec. 23	41	23	38	Empress of Britain..											
2 Trips	82	49	62	Totals	1 Trip	226	40	..	..	..	..	..	..	.. ..	

Carefully compiled statistics were recorded for Atlantic crossings. Figures for 1937 showed that the Empress of Britain *was again Canadian Pacific's leading ship on the Québec-Southampton run. The column at the extreme right gave the number of deportees carried on each crossing.* CP Rail Corporate Archives

a junior officer, then had risen to command of a cargo ship and eventually passenger liners. The company did not look beyond its own officers when it came to filling the senior positions in its ships. Junior officers in the lowest ranks were selected not only for their qualifications and experience but also for their character, appearance, manners and general deportment.

The final 1937 eastbound crossing began on November 6 with a mere 224 passengers. When the *Britain* left Québec, Wolfe's Cove was closed down for the winter as a passenger terminal. The season had been the *Britain*'s best, in numbers of passengers carried, exceeding 13,000 for the first time, but it was still only an average of about 600 for each Atlantic crossing. Just 42 percent of First Class berths had been filled, 60 percent of Tourist Class and 52 percent of Third Class. The leading North Atlantic ships on the New York to Europe route had fared better. Between June and November, the load factors for the principal ships were:

Queen Mary	74 percent
Bremen and *Europa*	64 percent
Rex and *Conte di Savoia*	60 percent
Normandie	56 percent

One possible reason for the low figures of the *Empress of Britain* was that Québec was still considered by many travellers as too remote from the main cities of North America. Another was the lack of a balanced weekly service between Southampton and Québec, which an identical sister ship to the *Britain* would have provided. These perceptions blunted the impact that Canadian Pacific wanted to make on the market. The *Empress of Australia,* which shared the Southampton-Québec service with the Britain, was older and considerably slower. Sometimes the two ships left Québec 4 days apart and sometimes 14 days apart. Stories circulated about building a new ship as a running mate for the *Empress of Britain*, but they faded to idle rumours when faced with economic reality.

The Empress of Britain *attracted the attention of an Australian family as the ship entered Sydney Heads.* Jay Bascom Collection

CHAPTER 20

CIRCLING THE GLOBE AGAIN

Canadian Pacific announced the 1938 world cruise itinerary with a mixture of confidence and uncertainty. The confidence came from knowledge that the *Empress of Britain* had established herself as the leading long-distance cruise ship, the uncertainty from qualms about the itinerary.

With the improving economic situation, the number of Atlantic liners spending the winter months on cruises around the world, to South America, the Mediterranean and the West Indies was greater than ever. Again the *Franconia* and *Reliance* advertised world cruises, but the *Empress of Britain* was newer, larger and more luxurious than either; her crew and staff equalled or surpassed the service British and German ships provided. The *Reliance* suffered also from growing unease that people felt about travelling under the German flag when there was a risk of war in Europe. Some, however, were willing to take a lengthy journey in a German ship and, in addition to Hamburg-American's *Reliance*, North German Lloyd had for the first time scheduled a world cruise in its 52,000-ton *Bremen*, nine years old and former Blue Riband holder.

No cruise appeared more alluring than the *Normandie*'s trip from New York to Rio de Janeiro and back. It was the ship rather than the itinerary that commanded attention. French Line's much-heralded 83,000-ton ship, less than three years old, had wrested the Blue Riband from the *Queen Mary*, albeit temporarily. Like nearly all North Atlantic liners, she had not been designed for cruises, but the publicity surrounding her three-week South American trip attracted almost a thousand passengers.

The *Empress of Britain*'s itinerary was published well in advance and followed the most popular route, although doubts arose about including China and Japan. When the conflict between these countries made a visit unsafe, or at least undesirable, an alternative had to be found; in October 1937 a new itinerary was drawn up, substituting Australia and New Zealand. Hong Kong, a British colony, was retained because it was not embroiled in the Japanese-Chinese war. Owners of the *Bremen*, *Reliance* and *Franconia* rerouted their ships and added Australia and New Zealand, too, at the expense of the two Oriental lands.

After a successful 12-day cruise to the West Indies, the *Empress of Britain*, with Captain Busk-Wood in command, left New York's Pier 61 on January 8, 1938, at 11 in the morning, a bright winter sun adding to the holiday atmosphere. Only 20 Canadian passengers were on board, half taking the complete cruise and others bound mostly for Mediterranean ports. Passenger totals, American and Canadian, were down from the 1937 figures. Despite the reduced numbers, the ship carried $150,000 in United States currency and £20,000 (about $100,000) to meet passengers' needs.

Only one untoward incident occurred in the voyage. In Bombay, while most passengers were ashore, the *Britain* sustained slight damage to her side in a minor collision with the 6,000-ton British tanker *Pellicula*.

Australia was observing the 150th anniversary of the arrival of the first European settlers, with celebrations planned in cities and towns throughout the country. Visits by four large cruise ships in quick succession provided a bonus organizers had not expected. A radio broadcast from the *Britain* on March 31 was relayed across the country. The next day, Australian newspapers published accounts of ship-to-shore telephone interviews with prominent passengers.

The position of the sofa against the folding door suggested that the bedroom had been booked but not the adjoining sitting room. CP Rail Corporate Archives

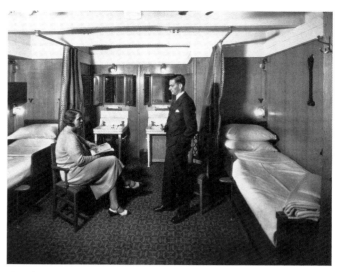

Reading lights near the top of the wood panelling indicated that the upper berths of the Tourist Class cabin had been removed for a world cruise. CP Rail Corporate Archives

Silhouetted against sea, land and sky, the Britain *sailed through Cook Strait on her only peacetime visit to New Zealand.* Wellington Harbour Board

Tugs were in attendance but were hardly needed when the Britain *reached Wellington on April 10, 1938.* Wellington Harbour Board

The *Empress of Britain* reached Sydney on Saturday, April 2, docking at Wooloomooloo because her masts were too high to let her pass under the Sydney Harbour bridge. An estimated 30,000 people lined the shores to greet her, while the harbour and nearby waters were alive with hundreds of yachts, motorboats and chartered ferries. Hotels advertised rooftop cocktail parties, the sites chosen, of course, to give patrons the best view of the biggest ship ever to steam into the harbour. Planes circled overhead and dipped their wings in salute. Newspapers issued special supplements with their regular editions. During the *Britain*'s three-day stay, several luncheons and dinners were held in the Salle Jacques Cartier for eminent Australians, the Governor General the most distinguished among them.

While passengers were ashore shopping and sightseeing, thousands of Australians inspected the ship. It was not a matter of just walking aboard casually and strolling around at will. Permits had to be obtained. Applications had been pouring into the Canadian Pacific agent's office in Sydney at the rate of 1,500 a day for three weeks and most had to be rejected.

Many passengers travelled by train to Melbourne, where they rejoined the ship. Her next stop was Wellington, the New Zealand capital, for a one-day stay. Newspapers began coverage several days before the *Britain*'s arrival. Not content simply to repeat the usual information about the ship's size and luxury, they tried to put her in a context that would carry meaning for local readers. For example, each of her funnels was wider than the Mount Victoria traffic tunnel in Wellington; the ship's breadth was more than twice that of Willis Street.

On Sunday, April 10, as the *Britain* neared Wellington, thousands of spectators, in cars and on foot, watched her arrival from positions along the marine drive and on the waterfront. Fourteen traffic officers were on duty. "The combination of the visit of the superliner, a wonderful autumn day and public interest were almost too much for Wellington streets," said Inspector T. Broughton.

When the ship appeared off Point Halswell shortly before eight in the morning, the Harbourmaster left the pilot launch, climbed up a rope ladder and boarded the *Empress of Britain* through a door on F Deck. Moments later, the Port Health officer, Customs officers and Tourist Bureau staff came aboard from the *Janie Seddon*, so that most formalities could be completed before the *Britain* docked at Pipitea Wharf. The tugs *Terawhiti* and *Toia* were in attendance, but there was little need of their services; the 42,000-ton ship docked with evident ease.

Apart from the cost of tugs and the fee for a local pilot, port expenses often reached a substantial amount. For example, harbour charges for the *Britain*'s stay in Wellington came to £329 1s. 9d. (about $1,645), with an additional fee of £46 19s. 5d. (about $235) for berthage. Light dues amounting to £658 3s. 6d. (about $3,290) were also assessed, the money used to defray the expense of building and maintaining lighthouses around the New Zealand coast. The charge for the Harbourmaster's services in bringing the ship in from Point Halswell and taking her out that evening came to £281 16s. 3d. (about $1,410).

Passengers thronged ashore almost as soon as the gangway was lowered, then climbed into cars to tour Wellington and the neighbouring countryside. Some travelled overland, planning to rejoin the *Britain* at Auckland five days later. Five hundred local residents had been invited by Canadian Pacific to tour the ship, among them William Essex, the company's New Zealand traffic agent. While Mr. Essex was eating with the Chief Officer, a seaman approached the table and informed his superior that the ship was flooded with visitors and that an irate passenger who had not gone ashore was threatening to send off a cable of complaint to Sir Edward Beatty. The Chief Officer went off immediately to investigate and soon found the cause of the unexpected influx. A Harbour Board employee was collecting passes from invited guests when they arrived at the foot of the gangway, then selling them to eager citizens who had come down to the harbour to see the largest and finest ship ever to enter New Zealand waters and now had an unanticipated chance to come aboard. His money-making scheme came to a quick end, but not before he had made a neat profit.

A few weeks before the *Britain*'s arrival, Mr. Essex placed an advertisement stating that cabins were available for passages to Honolulu, San Francisco, New York or Southampton. The morning

The Britain, *in the process of anchoring at Sydney on April 2, 1938, during her first visit to Australia. The passengers' swimming pool is directly aft of the foremast, while the crew's pool is forward on the port side of A Deck. Note the flags on the top of the cabs of the Navigating Bridge.*
Jay Bascom Collection

Powerful little locomotives on both sides were ready to assist the Empress of Britain *through a lock of the Panama Canal.*
Reg Lucas

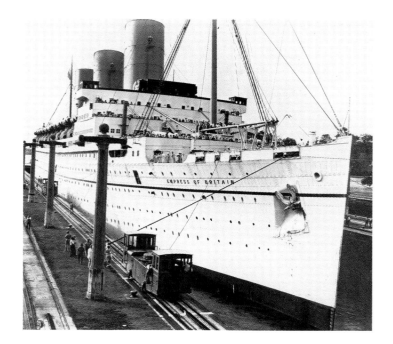

The foredecks were popular viewing points for passengers when the Britain *sailed through the Panama Canal locks.* Reg Lucas

after the announcement appeared in the newspapers, a business acquaintance burst into his office at nine o'clock sharp. He wanted to book a cabin. "Who for?" asked Mr. Essex. "Myself and a certain lady," the businessman said, then he gave the lady's name. "Marry the woman," advised Mr. Essex, "and you can have a cabin." His visitor rose without a word and left. A few days later he returned to the office, stood in the doorway and exclaimed, "I've married her!"

At Auckland, dredges had been working for several weeks to deepen the harbour for the *Britain*, with her 32-foot draft, to dock. Residents of the North Island submitted several thousand requests for permits to visit the ship, but only a few hundred were issued. And this time there was no black market in passes. After a four-day stay in New Zealand's largest city, the *Britain* left for Fiji, Honolulu and San Francisco.

One newspaper in New Zealand did not share the enthusiasm for the *Empress of Britain*. A reporter for *N.Z. Truth* was more interested in the crew's quarters than the opulence several decks above. He found a handful of disaffected crew members and soon had a story of unpleasant odours, cockroaches, cramped and dingy living accommodation, a lack of washbasins and a shortage of space to hang clothes up to dry. His informants admitted that towels and bedding were above average and food was reasonably good, although they alleged there was a lack of green vegetables. By the time the story reached print, however, the ship was somewhere between Fiji and Honolulu.

For some crewmen, the sea was an opportunity to get away from home for a year or two and see the world; for others it represented a career with a chance for advancement; for many it was a steady job that would, they hoped, last a lifetime. Most passengers were unaware of the lives and working conditions of the crew, except for those they met regularly such as dining saloon staff, bedroom and deck stewards, barmen and the purser's staff, and officers who dined with passengers in the Salle Jacques Cartier.

For passengers disembarking at New York and Southampton in May, the cruise had been an adventure, an achievement or simply an agreeable way of spending four months in the sun. For Canadian Pacific, it had been a disappointing year; cruise earnings were down from 1937. Australia and New Zealand were interesting countries but lacked the drawing power of China and Japan. The war between those two nations showed no signs of abating, but an itinerary had to be drawn up for 1939. And the first of 22 crossings between England and Canada was only 11 days away. It was time for the *Empress of Britain* to return to dry dock and have her outer propellers reinstalled before resuming five months of demanding service on the North Atlantic.

The two days the Britain *spent at Québec between crossings were a time to refuel the ship and touch up the paintwork. A lifeboat remained on duty when men were painting the ship's sides.* CP Rail Corporate Archives

CHAPTER 21

THE PREMIER SHIP OF THE ST. LAWRENCE

I f, comparatively speaking, 1937 had been a good year for the *Empress of Britain* on the North Atlantic, signs for 1938 were discouraging from the start. The number of businessmen crossing the Atlantic by ship might remain constant, but tourists were becoming more reluctant to visit continental Europe. Fear of war grew steadily and bookings dropped. Attempting to make the best of the situation, Canadian Pacific and its competitors reduced Tourist and Third Class fares by 25 percent on many sailings, the cheaper fares applying to travellers from both sides of the Atlantic.

Package tours from Southampton were also available, starting at £54 17s. 6d. (about $270) in Tourist Class, a price that let a passenger enjoy a crossing to Québec, spend two busy days of sightseeing with overnight stays at the Chateau Frontenac in Québec and the Windsor Hotel in Montréal, together with parlour-car seats in the train between these cities, and arrive home on Thursday of the second week. Variations of this basic plan provided for tourists wanting a longer stay. Unfortunately, there were few takers.

Third Class excursion fares began at about two-thirds of the Tourist Class rate. Like most space in the ship, Third Class was seldom filled to capacity. A Canadian Pacific folder extolled its advantages:

> Solid comfort at low cost is the keynote of Third Class, Canadian Pacific style. Whether you travel in the blue-ribbon ship of the Atlantic, the *Empress of Britain*, the Regal *Duchesses*, or on one of the popular *"Mont"* ships, your cabin is brightly lighted, well ventilated and spotlessly clean, with comfortable sleep-giving beds. Bathrooms are in close proximity with a steward in attendance... For rest, reading, cards, dancing, movies, concerts, there are large, bright and cheerfully furnished Public Rooms. There is ample deck space for games and sports and your companions are real home folks, economically inclined but sociable and friendly. And that's why there's "never a dull moment" when you travel in this outstanding Third Class to Europe.

Notwithstanding the advertised attractions, only 4,261 passengers travelled Third Class in the *Britain* in 1938 and, of these, 2,455 were westbound.

The most prominent passenger aboard when the *Empress of Britain* left Québec on July 9 was Sir Edward Beatty. He was on a ten-day business trip to Britain, and on arriving at Southampton he announced that if world conditions were favourable, Canadian Pacific would order five new passenger ships from British builders in the next three years. "Late in 1940 we shall probably build a sister ship to the *Empress of Britain*. The new Empress will probably be faster than the *Britain*," he stated. None of the five ships was built. The uncertainty of the times forced Sir Edward to put his plans aside.

The *Britain* no longer broke Atlantic speed records, nor was there any need for her to try. She remained the fastest ship between Canada and Europe, others not even approaching her speed. Rival companies placed no new liners on the route, leaving the *Empress of Britain* as the premier ship of the St. Lawrence for the eighth successive season.

Patrick Campbell, making his first trip aboard a ship, posed for a snapshot beside one of the Britain's *bells on a 1938 crossing.*
Patrick Campbell

No cruise was complete without its official photographers. During the 1931-1932 cruise, Les Carson (extreme right) and his colleagues were for once in front of the camera.
Les Carson

The occupants of the sitting room of a suite chatted while a bellboy waited patiently for instructions.
CP Rail Corporate Archives

To passenger Patrick Campbell there was no doubt of the *Britain*'s position as Canada's finest ship. As he left the shed at Wolfe's Cove and walked towards the gangway, he saw a gigantic white hull towering far above him and stretching as far as the eye could see, or so it seemed to the Manitoba teenager on his first ocean crossing. Much as he enjoyed the trip, he became dreadfully seasick when the ship reached open seas. On this crossing she pitched and rolled a great deal, causing Patrick to suffer with every motion the ship made. Nonetheless he managed to take his place in the dining saloon with commendable regularity and obtain double helpings of lamb with mint sauce whenever this dish appeared on the menu.

Patrick travelled Third Class, whose dining saloon was on D Deck. Three round tables stood on either side of the saloon, each seating eight people. Long tables in the centre of the room could be extended to link up with adjacent ones, so that two for six people each could be combined into one for 14, with two diners seated at opposite sides of the central extension. In waiters' jargon, tables were referred to as "long sixes," "round eights" and so on.

John Jones was a crew member serving his first season on the North Atlantic in 1938. One of a dozen or more bellboys in the ship, he signed on at Southampton at the monthly wage of £3 7s. 6d. (about $16) and looked forward to seeing the world. Wearing his chocolate-brown velveteen uniform, he felt privileged to be working in the ship and hoped that some opportunity would arise to allow him to "improve my station in life," as he later expressed it. His living quarters in the ship soon brought home to him that his present station was a lowly one. Many years afterwards he wrote:

> The "glory hole" where we lived was a large room, with two tiers of metal bunks around the walls, or bulkheads, to give them their correct name, several portholes and a battery of small lockers just large enough to contain a few small personal possessions such as books and toilet gear, odds and ends, that was all. There was no table or chairs; we just used to sit on our bunks, or on the deck if we were playing cards.
>
> There was nowhere to put our clothes except in our suitcases under our bunks, and we had to hang our uniforms on lines of string, or place them around our bunks. We

NAME MISS ESTHER BYRNES
S.S. EMPRESS OF BRITAIN
SAILING DATE SEPT. 3RD 1938 SUITE 144
ROOM 146
To QUEBEC 148
FINAL DESTINATION

Red and gold baggage tags arrived with the tickets. Miss Byrnes occupied one of the two best suites in the ship. Author's Collection

TRANS-ATLANTIC PASSENGER MOVEMENT, 1938

Table VIII

CANADIAN PACIFIC STEAMSHIPS

MONTREAL, QUEBEC ⎫
SAINT JOHN, HALIFAX ⎬ CHERBOURG, HAVRE, SOUTHAMPTON

WESTBOUND					EASTBOUND				III Divided								
Arrival	Cabin	Tourist	III	SHIP	Departure	Cabin	Tourist	III Total	Brit.	Scan.	Finn.	Cont.	Ital.	Gr'k Or't.	Cns.	Dep.
				Empress of Australia	Apr. 30	111	125	94	53	..	11	30	..	..	..	1
			—	Montcalm..........	May 20	76	82	97	87	3	1	6	..	..	7	..
May 25	68	75	89	Empress of Australia	" 28	166	207	255	135	8	63	43	6	..	..	..
June 10	71	106	130	Empress of Britain..	June 11	128	86	168	134	6	5	21	..	2	2	..
" 13	71	68	111	Empress of Australia	" 15	111	121	130	69	5	7	43	3	3	..	..
" 23	62	125	137	Empress of Britain..	" 25	181	192	358	205	13	1	133	3	3	..	..
July 1	83	117	164	Empress of Australia	July 1	165	212	133	106	1	3	22	1	..	1	..
				Montclare..........	" 2	125	108	362	314	11	2	35	..	..	..	..
" 7	98	117	159	Empress of Britain..	" 9	134	135	284	211	8	7	53	1	4	..	1
" 16	103	152	133	Empress of Australia	" 19	170	186	156	98	4	4	46	4	..	5	..
" 21	50	47	115	Montclare..........												
" 28	269	245	219	Empress of Britain..	" 30	149	164	222	153	5	8	52	3	1	9	..
Aug. 4	123	132	244	Empress of Australia	Aug. 4	67	79	67	47	..	6	14	..	..	..	..
" 11	148	115	170	Empress of Britain..	" 13	73	106	131	92	2	6	27	2	2	..	..
" 19	159	116	81	Empress of Australia	" 19	64	46	47	38	2	5	2	..	..	..	1
" 24	131	111	195	Duchess of Richmond	" 24	27	34	30	19	..	4	7	..	..	..	..
" 25	255	248	424	Empress of Britain..	" 27	103	92	89	66	..	3	20	..	..	1	1
Sept. 3	262	215	210	Empress of Australia	Sept. 3	100	84	51	41	3	1	4	2	..	..	..
" 8	176	96	312	Duchess of Richmond												
" 8	231	178	392	Empress of Britain..	" 10	113	117	151	129	..	1	20	1	..	..	..
" 17	171	121	145	Empress of Australia	" 17	80	100	85	64	..	1	18	2	..	..	..
" 22	251	167	248	Empress of Britain..	" 24	86	64	109	94	..	6	9	..	..	..	..
Oct. 7	305	193	281	Empress of Britain..	Oct. 8	81	61	85	66	..	1	18	..	..	1	..
" 20	140	158	170	Empress of Britain..	" 22	55	48	89	66	4	6	11	1	1	3	..
Nov. 3	98	62	125	Empress of Britain..	Nov. 5	40	70	120	53	1	4	59	3	..	..	..
				Duchess of Richmond	" 24	29	50	197	92	1	11	88	3	2	1	2
Dec. 13	37	33	108	Duchess of Richmond												
23 Trips	3362	2997	4362	Totals	24 Trips	2434	2569	3510	2432	77	167	781	35	18	30	6

NEW YORK — CHERBOURG, SOUTHAMPTON

Jan. 1	21	17	10	Empress of Australia	Apr. 24	23	28	3	3	..	..	..	..	..	..	1*
				Empress of Britain..	May 17	382	..	..	..	..	..	..	..	..	..	..
Dec. 22	54	64	43	Empress of Britain..												
2 Trips	75	81	53	Totals	2 Trips	405	28	3	3	..	..	..	..	..	..	1*

*Stowaway.

The 1938 totals showed that the Empress of Britain *carried more passengers than any other Canadian Pacific ship between Québec and Southampton.* CP Rail Corporate Archives

had sheets and pillowcases but they tended to get a bit grubby. There were blankets and a patterned counterpane with the words "Canadian Pacific" on them. The bunks had detachable lee rails on the side to prevent one from rolling out in rough weather. When you were tucked up in your bunk, you were in your own private, warm and cozy world.

Bellboys' duties included opening doors, running errands, giving directions to passengers unsure of the ship's layout, and generally making themselves useful to First Class passengers and officers. Passengers tipped them for their efforts but, according to Mr. Jones, he and his young fellow workers had to share their tips with the steward in charge of bellboys.

One-way fares during the 1938 summer season began at $251 in First Class, $149.50 in Tourist and $96.50 in Third, prices including rail fare between Montréal and Québec. Almost every year fares had risen, but in 1938 the cost of sending an urn with human remains across the Atlantic dropped to $25, compared with $50 only four years earlier. The price of shipping a casket was $150, the same as in 1934.

The *Empress of Britain* made 22 crossings on the North Atlantic in 1938, but the ship was never full. Her best performance for the year was on August 28, when 927 passengers disembarked at Québec. On eastbound sailings, 731 boarded at Wolfe's Cove on June 25, but there were only two other trips when eastbound passengers exceeded 500. As in earlier years, bookings dropped off abruptly for eastbound trips in October and early November. One westbound crossing had more passengers than might be expected. With the German invasion of Czechoslovakia imminent and a full-scale war involving the major powers of Europe appearing likely, some Canadians in Europe felt it was time to return home. The October 1 sailing from Southampton and Cherbourg included people who had booked at the last moment on hearing the unsettling news. On the *Britain*'s arrival at Québec on October 7, 779 came ashore, 305 in First Class, 193 in Tourist and 281 in Third.

When the season's figures were added up, only 10,181 passengers had sailed in the *Britain*. There was no thought, however, to altering her 1939 transatlantic schedule. But before she returned to her Southampton-Québec service, there was another world cruise, this time with an itinerary greatly changed from former years.

Funchal, the capital of Madeira, was the first port on world cruises after the Empress of Britain *left New York, but the big ship had to anchor outside the harbour.* Reg Lucas Collection

CHAPTER 22

THE BRITAIN'S FINAL CRUISE

The final world cruise was not a circumnavigation of the globe. In April 1938 Canadian Pacific announced that the 1939 route would include both China and Japan because the danger from war had diminished, at least for visiting cruise ships. Three months later, visits to China and Japan were cancelled when hostilities intensified. An amended itinerary was issued.

The *Empress of Britain* was to follow her customary route as far as Hong Kong, then call at Manila, Bali and Batavia before making the long westward passage across the Indian Ocean to South Africa. After visiting Durban and Cape Town, she would stop at St. Helena for a day, then cross the Atlantic for two calls in South America. Her final stops were to be in the West Indies before returning to New York on May 14. This imaginative route, with its many fascinating ports, afforded full scope for tourists to expand their knowledge, enjoy the sunshine and shop the stores, stalls and bazaars. There would be 77 days at sea, 50 in port.

Passengers, though, were reluctant to book. War was a reality in the Far East and a growing possibility in Europe. Pros and cons of making a 127-day voyage had to be weighed thoroughly before purchasing tickets. If further consideration were needed, it soon arrived. Because of what Canadian Pacific called "upset political conditions," the Holy Land was omitted and a visit to Beirut substituted.

There had been few alterations in the structure of the *Empress of Britain* in her more than seven years but for the 1939 cruise there was one major improvement, welcomed by passengers and crew alike. Air conditioning, capable of circulating 2 million cubic feet an hour, was installed in the Salle Jacques Cartier. Elsewhere, the ship still had the ball-louvre type of ventilation, which passengers could adjust in their cabins to suit themselves.

The outer propellers were removed at the King George V Dry Dock in Southampton, and the ship crossed to New York, arriving on December 22, 1938, a day late because of strong westerly gales on the Atlantic. Next day, she left with 650 passengers on a four-day Christmas cruise to Bermuda. This was followed by an eight-day journey to Havana, Nassau and Bermuda, again with more than 600 people. While these two trips attracted passengers quite easily, the world cruise was a different matter. Only 164 boarded before the ship left New York on January 7, 1939. True, more would join at Monte Carlo, but there would still be far fewer than the ideal number of just over 400.

Making his first cruise in command of the *Empress of Britain* was Captain C.H. Sapsworth. Like Captain Latta, he was Scottish by birth and, like all previous masters, he had served in sailing ships before transferring to steamships. Charles Sapsworth, a quiet, self-effacing man, had also spent time ashore as manager of a nautical school, but when the call of the sea became too strong he returned to his first love. He joined Canadian Pacific in 1912 as a second officer and within a year was promoted to first officer. It was not until 1934, however, that he received his first command, the cargo ship *Beaverburn*, after which he became master of five of the company's passenger ships in quick succession before his promotion to the *Britain*.

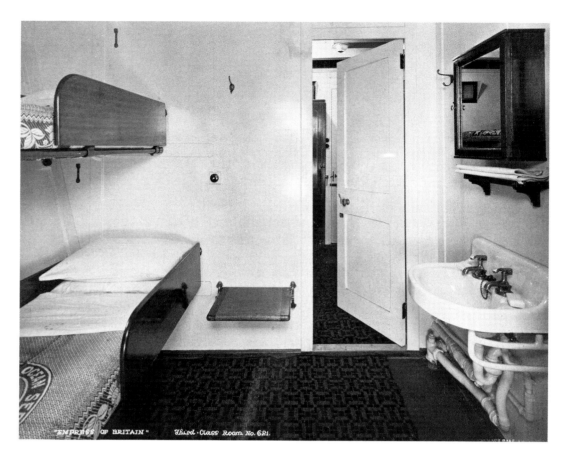

Cabin 621, a Third Class room, accommodated only one person on a world cruise. It cost $2,625 for the 1939 cruise.
Glasgow University Archives / Scottish Record Office

Potted trees were not essential for tennis matches but added a decorative touch when the court was used for moonlight dances while the Britain was in tropical waters.
CP Rail Corporate Archives

A trio of passengers had not started dinner when the ship's photographer reached the table. The waiter at the right, Reg Lucas, eventually became a Chief Purser and finally Catering Superintendent for Canadian Pacific.
Reg Lucas Collection

Shore excursions on this cruise, as on earlier ones, were nearly always by automobile and train. Buses were seldom used. The spacious automobiles were never filled to capacity and a few spare cars followed the tourists in case of mechanical problems or a collision. Cruise staff, ready to purchase tickets, deal with guides and smooth out complications, accompanied the cars. At certain ports, police supplied an escort to alleviate traffic problems and, in some countries, keep beggars and touts away from the visitors.

Passage through the Suez Canal from Port Said to Port Tewfik was invariably a slow procedure, the ship making about four knots. A canal boat and three men were normally taken aboard at Port Said. If a sandstorm blew up, reducing visibility to nil, the boat would be lowered into the water to take the heaving lines ashore. These light ropes were secured to the mooring lines, which would be placed over the bollards, and the ship would then pull herself over to the embankment and remain there until the weather cleared.

A week-long stop at Bombay gave off-duty crew time for sports and sightseeing. The Social and Athletic Club held a swimming gala at Breach Kandy with seven races and a diving competition. Making its first appearance of the season, the ship's cricket team lost to a British army side through slow fielding. The soccer team played three games, two against army teams and one against a naval side, winning only one. In addition to sports, a picnic was held at Jehu, with the ship's Catering Department providing food. Before the *Britain* left Bombay, the Social and Athletic Club donated £5 10s. (about $26) to the Bombay Mission to Seamen.

Since the first visit in 1934, Bali had become a regular stop on world cruises. A crew member recalled that soon after the ship anchored at Padang Bay in Bali, local people arrived in outrigger canoes. The men indicated that they would dive for money, and passengers began throwing coins into the sparkling water, watching them shimmer and spin as they sank, and photographing the brown bodies diving to retrieve these prizes. The women were of even greater interest than the men, at least to the males aboard. They indicated by pantomime that they wanted to wash themselves, and the crew started throwing bars of soap to them. They would then open their blouses and wash their upper bodies while the sailors watched with undiminished attention. Some crew members tossed Lifebuoy soap overboard, but the Balinese women threw it into the sea after sniffing it. All

When a world cruise ended, the Empress of Britain *entered the King George V dry dock at Southampton to have her outer propellers restored.* Associated British Ports Collection / Southampton City Museums

Teak was the wood with the best qualities for open decks. On most occasions, passengers preferred to have cushions on their deck chairs.
CP Rail Corporate Archives

they wanted was scented soap. By the time the women left, the ship's supply of soap had been considerably depleted.

Batavia was the last port of call in Asia before a ten-day, 4,500-mile uninterrupted passage to South Africa. The ship spent four days in Durban and six in Cape Town, not because these cities offered so many tourist attractions, but to give passengers time to travel through South Africa in special trains before rejoining the ship at Cape Town. The *Britain* left Cape Town on April 16 with her passenger list substantially increased. Well over a hundred South Africans had boarded for the trip to New York. Regular service between Cape Town and New York was by much more unassuming ships, but on this one occasion a luxury ship, the *Britain*, connected both ports, although with five calls en route.

The stop at the small, isolated island of St. Helena was brief, only seven hours. Passengers went by car to inspect Napoleon's house at Longwood, four miles from Jamestown, the main settlement. The limited number of cars required the visitors to travel out to Longwood in relays. Rio de Janeiro, the next port, was all that St. Helena was not—large, bustling and animated. Two days in the Brazilian capital were hardly enough for passengers or crew. Organized excursions left the tourists with very little time to explore the city on their own. The printed sheet they received was concise if not abrupt:

> Motor drive around Rio de Janeiro, thence to Petropolis; luncheon at Petropolis; return via Tijuca. Motor car and aerial railway to Sugar Loaf; luncheon at hotel; motor car and rack railway to Corcovado. Dinner Dance at hotel.

Bahia, the second call in Brazil, was more subdued. Port of Spain, Trinidad, and Havana were the last two stops before the *Empress of Britain* returned to New York on May 14, where most passengers disembarked. The 50 mainly British cruise members who remained on board were joined by another 50 people making a routine Atlantic crossing. It was an exceptionally small passenger list but not unexpected now that war in Europe appeared inevitable.

A formal photograph of the Empress of Britain's *officers and nursing sisters was taken before the royal party came aboard. The front row, from left to right, consisted of an unidentified officer, Purser W.S. Pearch, Chief Officer H.H. Davies, Staff Captain B.B. Grant, Captain C.H. Sapsworth, Chief Engineer E. Redmond, Assistant Chief Engineer P. McKillop, Dr. E.F.D. Owen and Chief Steward L.F. Moss.* CP Rail Corporate Archives

CHAPTER 23

UNDER ROYAL PATRONAGE

Whether war was unavoidable or not, the *Empress of Britain*'s sailing schedule for 1939, published in mid-February, confidently listed 22 crossings between Europe and Canada. Two events forced alterations. One was the royal voyage, the other the outbreak of the Second World War. The season began typically, with the ship returning from dry dock and making her first crossing from Southampton and Cherbourg. After the 299 passengers disembarked at Québec, the *Britain* was chartered to take King George VI and Queen Elizabeth from Halifax to Newfoundland, thence to Southampton, at the conclusion of their extensive tour of Canada.

For the crew, preparations for the royal journey began in a cloak of mystery. Chief Catering Superintendent D.H. Allan came aboard at New York on May 16, and during the crossing to Southampton he assembled groups of selected waiters in the Salle Jacques Cartier. He interviewed each man individually, asking his age, length of time in the *Empress of Britain* and with Canadian Pacific, and posing a few questions on proper methods of service in a first-class restaurant. As he listened to the responses, he scrutinized each waiter carefully, noting his manner and appearance. Some were called back later for further questioning and by the time the ship reached Southampton their numbers had been reduced to 15. From this group, ten were selected and were informed that they had been chosen as waiters for the royal voyage.

With her hull freshly painted, the *Britain* left Québec for Halifax on June 11. Aboard was an exclusive group of invited passengers, headed by Governor General Lord Tweedsmuir, three aides-de-camp, Lady Tweedsmuir, Sir Edward Beatty and some Canadian Pacific executives. The two-day trip gave the ten waiters an opportunity to practise the skills needed to serve the royal party, although their experience in dealing with celebrities on the Atlantic and on cruises was already ample guarantee of their ability.

One of the hand-picked waiters was Reg Lucas, and nearly 50 years later he recalled the voyage from Québec to Halifax:

> The Governor General and his lady occupied the royal chairs in the restaurant and we served them and the official party under the supervision of our Catering Superintendent and our travelling chef. At Halifax I seem to remember that we anchored for a while but owing to adverse weather reports the ship was moved alongside the quay and because there was some movement the ship's gangway became damaged. Their Majesties arrived the following day, June 15. The Royal Standard was lowered from the train as they got off and when they came aboard the *Empress of Britain*, our own Royal Standard was broken at the masthead. The ten waiters stood five at each side of the gangway, now repaired, with linked arms so that no one could move in and touch the King and Queen.

When the journey to Halifax ended, the royal chairs Mr. Lucas mentioned were placed in an alcove of the Salle Jacques Cartier. The dining saloon was clearly much too large for the King and Queen and their retinue. Two alcoves were screened off, the first as a reception room, the second a dining room. Stained-glass windows were set into the screen panels and beside the portholes.

The royal table was located in an alcove of the Salle Jacques Cartier. Chairs for the King and Queen were slightly higher than the others and had seats covered with a different fabric. Reg Lucas

GRE

SOUND PICTURE

in the

EMPRESS ROOM

at 9.30 p.m.

"KEEP YOUR SEATS, PLEASE"

featuring George Formby and
Florence Desmond

EMPRESS OF BRITAIN   FRIDAY, JUNE 16, 1939

MENU

Suprême of Grape Fruit

Potage Gombo

Butterfish Meunière

Chump Chop Grillé
Wax Beans au Beurre
Lyonnaise Potatoes

Lettuce Salad

Apple Pie
Coffee

EMPRESS OF BRITAIN   SATURDAY JUNE 17 1939

The menu for the royal couple and their retinue was simple and it offered no choice of dishes. The film Keep Your Seats, Please *was a broad comedy starring George Formby, one of Britain's leading comedians.*
Jay Bascom Collection

A long table was installed in the newly created intimate restaurant. It seated 16 people, 7 on each side and 1 at each end. King George VI sat in the centre of one side of the table, with Queen Elizabeth opposite him; the backs of their chairs rose slightly higher than the others.

To accommodate the royal couple and staff, only a few alterations had been made in the cabins. The King occupied the deluxe suite on the port side of A Deck, Cabins 147, 149 and 151, while the Queen had the corresponding one on the starboard side. The King's bedroom was decorated mainly in green and gold, the Queen's in rose, silver, grey and gold. Except for new beds, the regular furniture occupied the rooms.

The *Britain* left Halifax at 6:32 p.m. on June 15, proudly flying the Canadian Pacific flag from the jackstaff, the Admiralty flag on the foremast, the Royal Standard on the mainmast and the Red Ensign on the ensign staff. The passenger list named only 40 people. Apart from the King and Queen, the royal party of 13 consisted of ladies-in-waiting, equerries, a lord-in-waiting, private secretaries and medical officers. The 22-strong household staff that came aboard included maids, dressers, stewards, valets, footmen, a hairdresser, a page, a clerk and police officers, in addition to a photographer and two reporters, one Canadian and one British.

In just over 25 hours the *Britain* arrived at Conception Bay, Newfoundland, where she anchored for the night. The King and Queen went ashore on June 17 and returned late that afternoon for a five-day passage to Southampton. Three ships of the Royal Navy, the *Southampton*, *Glasgow* and *Berwick*, and two of the Royal Canadian Navy, the *Saguenay* and *Skeena*, escorted the *Britain* across the Atlantic.

The Canadian reporter, R.K. Carnegie, wrote that shipboard routine was casual and unhurried and everyone appeared to enjoy the prospect of relaxing after the strenuous royal tour. They played tennis, watched movies, strolled around the Lounge Deck promenade, attended a religious service and called friends on the ship-to-shore telephones. The King made a 40-minute tour of the engine room.

Preparing and serving meals presented no difficulties to the dining saloon staff. Chefs and First Class waiters carried out their duties with customary skill. Reg Lucas later wrote:

> A proof copy of the meals for the day was printed in royal blue and on one occasion I was detailed to proceed to the Royal Suite with this copy, where it was handed to the Queen who approved it. I then returned it to the chef who passed it on to the chief printer, who would print it on a card with the Royal crest embossed in gold.
>
> Serving the meals was simplicity itself and they were never long and drawn out. I am sure they never exceeded one hour and were often less. I remember the first dinner and when it was nearly over we were standing well back from the table. The Queen half turned in her seat and remarked, "You boys need not wait; we can let ourselves out." As for the food, I believe the chickens came from their own farms. They also had fresh strawberries and a special blend of tea from Twinings. We served a rack of fresh Melba toast with each course.
>
> The cleaning of the ship was carried out at night and any unnecessary movement of staff was taboo. Normally one would see staff moving up and down and forward to aft but on this occasion they were instructed to use service stairways only. The huge ship seemed so quiet and even the Queen one day remarked that it was like a ghost ship.

The *Empress of Britain* steamed up the Solent, the approach to Southampton, on June 22. Princess Elizabeth and Princess Margaret came aboard from the Royal Navy destroyer *Kempenfelt* and joined their parents for the last few miles. The royal children spent several minutes at the shop on the Lounge Deck, where they bought two Mountie dolls, two sailor dolls and six penknives engraved with the ship's name.

For the passage to Southampton, the two beds in Cabin 144 were replaced with a single bed when Queen Elizabeth occupied the room. The cabin was part of a deluxe suite. CP Rail Corporate Archives

Because of the royal charter, Canadian Pacific cancelled three of the *Britain*'s scheduled Atlantic crossings. She resumed regular service when she left Southampton and Cherbourg with 435 passengers on July 1, the first of eight sailings before war broke out. With July 22, a regular Saturday departure, approaching, one family found itself in a quandary. Mrs. Therese Zwetschkenbaum, with her husband and little daughter, had fled Czechoslovakia and after living for some months in England received permission to come to Canada. She wished to observe the Jewish practice of not starting a journey on a Saturday and with some trepidation asked if the family could come aboard on Friday. "Of course you can," a Canadian Pacific representative in London informed her, and the Zwetschkenbaums embarked a day early with a distinct feeling of relief. There was even kosher food available in the dining saloon.

On the next westbound trip, one passenger who felt no misgivings at all was 16-year-old Jim Scandrett, returning to Canada as a member of the Canadian Schoolboys XI cricket team, which had just completed a tour of England. He and three teammates were travelling Third Class in Cabin 671 on D Deck. With unbounded confidence he made his way to First Class where he explored the public rooms and had a long conversation with a passenger, then went off for a game of ping-pong, still in First Class. Jim's good fortune did not last, though. He expressed himself with some indignation in his diary: "Was kicked out of 1st Class. Boy, they are strict here and even lock the doors on this ship." This was, however, only a temporary setback, and for the remainder of the crossing he succeeded in returning regularly to First Class to meet a young lady who had caught his attention.

Early in August 1939, the 1940 world cruise was called off and a six-week journey around South America announced in its place. Financial returns from the 1939 cruise had been unsatisfactory and the planning staff knew that without China and Japan the ship was unlikely to attract the numbers needed to make the trip successful. The South American cruise was to be made with the ship using all four propellers in order to complete the 14,000-mile trip within 42 days and still include 14 ports. Fares beginning at $692.50 were advertised and travel agents were advised to start accepting bookings. In addition, there were to be three short trips to the West Indies before the South American voyage and four after the *Britain* returned to New York. When war began, the plans evaporated and none of the cruises materialized.

The *Empress of Britain*'s final scheduled westbound sailing of 1939 began on September 2. It was not a typical passage. The German army had crossed the Polish border; a declaration of war between Britain and Germany was only a day away. Bookings for the ship had poured into the London office of Canadian Pacific in record numbers, not only from Canadians and Americans, but also from Australians who had decided that the safest way home was via Canada. For a while, it was uncertain if the British Admiralty would allow the ship to sail. Rumours were followed by more rumours. Finally, permission was granted, but even then the *Britain* was some hours late in leaving Southampton. A large quantity of baggage had to be taken on board and the crew had been reduced by the general mobilization in Britain.

The *Britain* was filled beyond her capacity. Makeshift cots were erected in several of the public rooms. Portholes in the cabins were boarded up and windows of the public rooms heavily curtained. The thick drapes could be pushed aside by thoughtless people, however, so Captain Sapsworth ordered the windows painted over in black. He also gave strict instructions that passengers were to carry their lifejackets at all times. Taking the warnings a step farther, some passengers slept fully clothed every night.

On the second day, Sunday, September 3, passengers heard over the ship's radio the news they had been expecting—that war between Britain and Germany had been declared. The radio was then turned off, and for the next four days they read only the barest outline of war news in the ship's daily paper. Not until they were well into the St. Lawrence did they receive the official announcement about the sinking of the British passenger ship *Athenia* in the Atlantic on the first day of the war, although reports had been circulating throughout the *Britain* for several days.

The Britain *had an unofficial yet inevitable escort when she left Halifax on June 15, 1939. The royal standard on the mainmast indicates that King George VI and Queen Elizabeth are aboard.* Private Collection of Everett E. Viez

King George VI and Queen Elizabeth stood on the port bridge wing as the ship left Halifax.
Author's Collection

The *Britain* followed a zigzag course across the Atlantic to avoid any German submarines that might be lying in wait. It was a sensible precaution but it lengthened the journey. One day, when passengers were having luncheon, the ship took an extremely sudden and heavy list. Chairs, people, tablecloths, food, cutlery and glassware all slid across the Salle Jacques Cartier as a result and a few passengers suffered minor injuries. An explanation came shortly afterwards. The *Britain* was enveloped in fog and refrained from using her whistle in case it betrayed her location. Without warning, a tanker had loomed up, so close that the passenger ship had to take immediate evasive action. The helm was thrown hard over to starboard in order to prevent the *Britain* from slicing right through the tanker. Tension filled the air for the entire crossing and did not dissipate until the 1,140 passengers finally stepped ashore at Québec on September 8.

There was no thought of the *Britain* making the return journey to England right away. Plans existed for the ship's role in time of war, but in the meantime she remained tied up at Wolfe's Cove, patiently awaiting instructions.

In December 1939, when the Britain *made her first wartime crossing as a troopship from Halifax to the Clyde, there was no reserved accommodation and soldiers arriving early were fortunate to get cabins like this one.* CP Rail Corporate Archives

CHAPTER 24

A TROOPSHIP IN WARTIME

In November 1939 the *Empress of Britain*, her hull and upperworks painted drab grey, left Québec and sailed to Halifax. On the 25th she was requisitioned by the British Ministry of War Transport for one month as a troop transport. Units of the First Canadian Division, mostly from Ontario and the Prairies, began to arrive by train at Halifax in December for a passage to an unnamed destination. Accommodation was allotted on a first-come, first-served basis, and the early arrivals commandeered the best cabins. When many luxury liners were being refitted as troopships, with cabins for two and four persons transformed to hold six, eight, ten or more, the *Britain* retained her peacetime configuration for the time being.

William Simcock, in 1939 a lance-bombardier in the Royal Canadian Horse Artillery, wrote later:

> In particular, the *Empress of Britain* still gleamed with her magnificence. . . It would seem doubtful that, in the entire history of warfare, any other troops could have travelled overseas in such luxury as that enjoyed by those of Convoy TC1 sailing out of Halifax that December.
>
> Between gourmet meals served by properly attentive stewards in dining saloons resplendent with shining silverware, gleaming crystal and white linen, time was spent in such activities as P.T., lifeboat drills and lectures which helped to familiarize officers with their men and vice versa. After whiling away the evening hours in the cinema, the bar, the library and other public rooms, we would retire to our white and gold-trimmed cabins, made immaculate during the day by cabin stewards who betrayed nary a trace of rebellion or resentment at having to serve passengers so unlike the gentry to whom they were accustomed.

Convoy TC1, consisting of the *Empress of Britain*, *Empress of Australia*, *Duchess of Bedford*, *Aquitania* and *Monarch of Bermuda*, left Halifax on December 10. For the first two days the Royal Canadian Navy destroyers *Ottawa*, *Fraser*, *Restigouche* and *St. Laurent* provided a local escort before returning to Halifax. Remaining with the convoy for the entire crossing were the Royal Navy ships *Resolution*, *Repulse*, *Furious*, *Emerald*, *Hyperion* and *Hunter*.

Security precautions started with lifeboat drill before the *Britain* left port; soldiers were ordered to carry life jackets at all times. Early in the crossing a routine of physical training, marches around the Lounge Deck promenade, and more lifeboat drill was established, interspersed with concerts, bingo games, lectures on poison gas and talks on the need for secrecy.

The *Britain* could do very little to protect herself if attacked. Her limited armament consisted of a 6-inch naval gun, a 3-inch anti-aircraft gun at the stern, four Lewis machine guns on the bridge and one Lewis gun on either side of the second funnel. Artillery units took turns manning the anti-aircraft gun, and extra lookouts were ordered to be on the alert at all times.

The convoy altered course regularly during the crossing, but the *Empress of Australia* became separated from the other ships in foggy weather on December 13. Her disappearance, which caused a great deal of speculation, was the result of misreading instructions from the *Resolution*. Three

The daily menu was limited when the Britain *was a troopship, but soldiers spoke highly of the food and the service.*
Gordon Collinson

Instructions regarding preparation of War Diaries: (which will be kept from first day of mobilization or embodiment) are contained in F.S. Regs. Vol. 1.

(Title pages will be prepared)

WAR DIARY

(erase heading not required)

Duplicate
Triplicate

M.F.M. 11.
A.F.C. 2118

Original, duplicate and triplicate to be forwarded to O.1/c 2nd Echelon for disposal.

IST CORPS AMMUNITION PARK   RCASC   CASF

Place	Date	Hour	Summary of Events and Information	Remarks, references to Append. & Initials.
ABOARD TRANSPORT E.22 (Empress of Britain)	3Feb 40	0800hrs 1200hrs 1400hrs 1630 hrs	Slight running sea. Sea getting heavy. With heavy seas more personnel sick. High wind turning sea quite rough. Ship rolling a little. Boat Drill now held morning and afternoon alternate days. Ships Training continued. Towards evening or dusk sea easing off noticeably. Darkening ships rounds.	A.D.
Aboard Transport E.22 (Empress of Britain)	4Feb 40	1015hrs 1630hrs	Weather - Overcast - traces of fog. Strong N.E.wind 20 miles. Medium running seas. Divine service for all denominations. R.C.'s separate. All others together. R.C.Communion 0600 hrs. O.C. Troops & Staff & Ship's Officer attend Anglican service. Boat Drill Training only to-day. Darkening ships rounds. No complaints. Everthing generally satisfactory.	A.D.
Aboard Transport E.22. (Empress of Britain)	5Feb 40	1000hrs 1400hrs 1630hrs	Weather - Cloudy & foggy - strong N.E.wind about 35 miles. high seas, but ship today riding steady. Speed approx. 14 k.p.h. Test of emergency boat drill - only 8 troops Officers knew of such. For first test gave troops 20 minutes to man stations. From results only 10 minutes required. Results of Drill - Allowing for sick in Hospital 99.2% of troops were standing to at boat stations within 10 minutes. Troops mustered in a steady manner. No rushing or stampeding. Officers were placed at certain locations on the ship to observe troop movements to Boat Stations. Report very favourable. Ship's Officers very pleased with result. Gave them data to go on for succeeding trips. No injuries occurred. Reissuing of rifles began on account nearing land. Paybooks completed, issued troops. Medical short arm inspection carried out by 15Gen. Hospital Officers. 12 or 14 H.M.Ships (Destroyers) came out to convoy us safely in. This a very cheering sight. Troops quite excited. Darkening ships rounds. No complaints.	A.D.

The War Diary of a unit of the Royal Canadian Army Service Corps gave a factual, unembroidered account of life aboard a troopship. National Archives of Canada

days later she rejoined the convoy unharmed. The *Resolution* welcomed her back with the signal "Luke 15:6." A Bible was found in the *Australia* and an officer looked up the verse. It read, "Rejoice with me; for I have found my sheep which was lost." The danger of sailing in convoy in poor weather was again emphasized when the westbound Cunard passenger ship *Samaria* passed down the centre line of the convoy at night off the coast of Ireland and struck the *Furious* and *Aquitania* with glancing blows.

Nevertheless, all ships arrived safely at their destination, the Firth of Clyde, on December 17, and the soldiers disembarked at Gourock the next day. The *Empress of Britain* was only a few miles from her birthplace, her first visit to Scotland since she left John Brown's yard more than eight years earlier.

After a stay in British waters, including an overhaul in dry dock at Southampton, the *Britain* returned to Halifax and was again taken up as a troop transport, her charter lasting from January 16 to February 22, 1940. Soldiers started coming aboard two days before the January 30 sailing date. To preserve some degree of secrecy, their orders simply stated that they were to join Transport E22 at Halifax. As on the earlier crossing, boat drill began before the ship left the harbour.

This convoy, TC3, was identical with the previous one, except that the Polish ship *Chrobry* replaced the *Duchess of Bedford*. When the ships sailed from Halifax, the same four Royal Canadian Navy destroyers of TC1 accompanied them for the first two days. Again the Royal Navy supplied an escort for the complete crossing, the number of warships increasing as the convoy neared the British Isles. The passage, once more to the Firth of Clyde, was uneventful. A typical day was February 2, for which this entry was made in the war diary of No. 4 Casualty Clearing Station, Unit 137:

> There was lifeboat drill at 0900 hours and Unit drill at 1000 hours and 1500 hours. No. 4 C.C.S. has been made responsible for the fire picquet on the ship. . . At 1520 hours we sighted an oil tanker going in the opposite direction. A destroyer from our convoy went over to investigate it and let it pass. As far as we know this was the only ship we passed thus far. At 2030 there was another concert in the main dining room with No. 4 C.C.S. well represented among the entertainers and we discovered that Capt. M. Weinlos has talent as a song leader. Father Malone acted as chairman. The weather was practically unchanged from yesterday. A few men are sick with colds but there is practically no seasickness.

The troops left the ship on February 8, the day after she arrived in Scotland. This time the *Britain* did not return to Canada and was never again seen in Canadian waters. She was chartered for a third time on March 1, without an expiry date to the agreement. The ship left the Clyde, called at Southampton, then sailed by way of the Mediterranean to Wellington, reaching the New Zealand capital on April 14.

Sharing the port of Wellington with the *Britain* were the *Aquitania* and *Empress of Japan*. They took aboard the Second Echelon of the 2nd New Zealand Expeditionary Force and left on May 2 as part of Convoy US3, along with the *Andes*, the four troopships sailing with a naval escort. When the convoy was off Sydney, it was joined by the *Queen Mary, Mauretania* and *Empress of Canada*. They all proceeded to Fremantle, Western Australia, arriving on May 10, where the three Canadian Pacific ships lay end to end in the harbour. The ships sailed two days later, bound for Cape Town, one of the mightiest troopship convoys of the Second World War. Various warships came and went as escorts. It took two weeks to reach Cape Town, where the *Britain* remained for five days. After a short stop at Freetown in West Africa, she reached the Clyde on June 16.

The *Empress of Britain*'s next trip began on August 6, when she left Liverpool for Suez. Once again she was part of a convoy, this one including the large passenger ships *Empress of Canada, Strathaird, Stratheden, Monarch of Bermuda, Andes* and *Batory*. Italy's entry into the Second World

The Britain *arrived at Wellington in April 1940 with her hull, upperworks and funnels painted grey. Wartime conditions made it impossible to obtain the same shade of grey to touch up the paint.*
Wellington Harbour Board

NOTICE.

Empty bottles must not be thrown overboard as floating bottles may be a source of information to the enemy.

Bottle boxes are provided in all Troop quarters where empty bottles can be placed.

A reminder of the constant need for caution in wartime was this notice, displayed prominently throughout the ship.
Gordon Collinson

War as an ally of Germany meant that the Mediterranean was unsafe, and the ships had to take the long route around South Africa. Convoy WS2 contained a few cargo ships at the start of the journey, thus making it slower than an entirely passenger-ship convoy until divided after a few days into fast and slow sections.

The *Britain*'s capacity as a troopship had been enlarged after her first wartime crossing and there were now up to 12 bunk beds in larger cabins. Three thousand or more soldiers were aboard. Most were assigned four hours of duty each day, their tasks including night or day lookout duty, helping in the kitchens, cleaning toilets and assisting the medical personnel. Three sittings were necessary for each meal, but the food continued to be better than typical army fare. Although the ship carried a four-month stock of food, water was available for only two hours in the morning, one hour at lunchtime and three hours in the evening.

Soldiers were not allowed to disembark when the *Britain* called at Freetown to replenish her water supply, but they had shore leave at the next stop, Cape Town. Passage from Freetown took nine days, longer than expected, because one ship was limping and the rest had to reduce speed to keep her in the convoy.

One change that troops on the lower decks welcomed was the rotation of cabins when the ship reached the Indian Ocean. Percy Mansell of the South Staffordshire Regiment, who had occupied a cabin on C Deck, was highly pleased when he moved up to A Deck, the location of the best of the First Class cabins, for the remainder of the trip. It was almost as good as the time he won £15 (about $75) playing bingo one evening. He also recollected Captain Sapsworth announcing the latest war news each day over the ship's public address system.

There were no ports of call for the *Britain* between Cape Town and Suez, a long, hot two-week journey. Soldiers left the ship on September 16 and she remained at the Egyptian port until the 24th, when she joined Convoy SW1 for the trip to Durban. Instead of transporting several thousand soldiers on the return passage, only a small number embarked, along with families of Army and Royal Air Force personnel.

One of those leaving was Ronald Light. His father was a soldier, and when Italian planes began to bomb Egypt, military authorities resolved to evacuate wives and children. Ronald, ten years old, travelled with his mother in an ambulance to Suez, where they were assigned to the *Empress of Britain*. Many years afterwards he remembered that quite a number of children were aboard. An attempt was made to start a school for them, but it somehow petered out. On one occasion, a plane was spotted and passengers were ordered to lie in the corridors. When it came close, it was identified as British. Ronald and his mother disembarked at Durban and the *Britain* sailed to Cape Town, where she took on a cargo of 300 tons of sugar. She left Cape Town on October 11 and was expected back in Britain before the end of October. There were 643 people in the ship, 224 military personnel and civilians, and a crew of 419.

Oberleutnant Bernhard Jope (left), the German pilot who bombed the Empress of Britain *on October 26, 1940, received congratulations when he returned to his base in Occupied France.* CP Rail Corporate Archives

CHAPTER 25

THE END OF THE EMPRESS

The attack came unexpectedly. About 9 o'clock in the morning of Saturday, October 26, the *Empress of Britain* was 60 miles off the northwest coast of Ireland, travelling without an escort because of her speed. Zigzagging at 22 knots, she was expected to reach her destination within a day. The weather was fine, with some clouds, a moderate wind, and a slight swell on the sea. At 9:20 a lookout spotted a four-engined plane as it approached the ship. It began to circle the *Britain*.

Captain Sapsworth, who was on the bridge, described the attack later in his report:

> (The plane) was at first thought to be friendly until getting closer it suddenly turned directly towards us at a height of about 2,000 feet and released a bomb. At this moment our 3-inch high-angle gun came into action and continued firing until put out of action by a direct hit. Four Lewis guns also kept up a continuous fire and several hits by tracer bullets were observed on the plane. The engines were put to full speed (24 knots) and helm used to keep plane in arc of the high-angle gun fire.

The German aircraft, a long-range four-engined Focke-Wulf Condor 200 with a crew of seven, probably carried six 550-lb. high-explosive bombs. Like much of the story about the last few days of the *Empress of Britain*, it is impossible to relate each detail with absolute certainty. Contemporary accounts, along with official reports made shortly after the attack and the subsequent sinking, are frequently contradictory. Recollections of the *Britain*'s survivors, crew members of the rescue ships, the captain and the second-in-command of the German submarine *U-32*, and the pilot of the attack plane, often given many years later, provide different perceptions, sometimes inconsistent, about the events of October 26 and the following two days.

According to the British official account, the plane made its first approach from the *Britain*'s stern, dropped two bombs and machine-gunned the ship. One bomb penetrated to the Mayfair Lounge, and within moments thick black smoke filled most of the *Britain*. Firefighting parties responded at once, but their efforts were in vain, as the entire midships area was well ablaze in minutes.

Now the plane made a second attack, again from the stern, and released two more bombs, neither doing any damage. Changing tactics, the pilot returned for a third run, this time from the bow, raking the *Britain* with machine-gun fire and dropping another two bombs. One struck the Sun Deck, crippling several lifeboats and setting more fires, while the other hit the ship near the stern, putting the anti-aircraft gun out of action and starting a serious fire which caused stored ammunition to explode. The enemy had not finished his work, however. Again the plane attacked from forward, spraying the bridge with machine-gun fire, then disappeared to the south, but not before sending out signals indicating the stricken ship's position.

Oberleutnant Bernhard Jope, pilot of the Condor, was making his first operational flight. Writing more than 40 years later, he recalled the attack somewhat differently from the British account. He confirmed the four attacks, but stated that the successful ones were the second and fourth, adding that he released his bombs at a height of about 200 feet to hit the target. Bullets from the *Britain*'s

Raymond Davis, a signalman in the Royal Canadian Navy Volunteer Reserve serving aboard the Britain, *photographed the burning vessel from a lifeboat after he was forced to abandon ship.* Raymond Davis

Alexander Sosnkowski, a crewman in the Burza, *had his camera ready as his ship approached the* Britain. *Barely visible are the lifeboat (left), to which some survivors are clinging, and an overturned raft (right).* Alexander Sosnkowski

Lewis guns struck his plane, rupturing oil lines and putting one engine out of action, but it landed safely at Brest on the west coast of Occupied France.

Captain Sapsworth quickly assessed the situation. He was unhurt, although Chief Officer Henry Davies sustained injuries. The engine-room staff were still at their posts, but smoke forced them to put on gas masks. Fires, which had spread to several decks, were too severe to be brought under control and, moreover, much of the firefighting apparatus had been damaged. In addition, flames and smoke cut off communication between the aft and forward areas. Captain Sapsworth, reluctantly yet realistically, ordered the engines stopped and gave the "Abandon ship" signal. The radio operator sent out SOS messages, which were immediately acknowledged. From the time the lookout observed the plane until "Abandon ship" was sounded, only about 30 minutes had elapsed.

Apprehension gripped everyone on board, and there were, in fact, signs of panic among a handful of passengers, who had been ordered to remain below until the attack ended. When it was obvious that the German plane would not return, the crew began lowering lifeboats. Although the engines had been stopped, the ship had not yet come to standstill, thus adding to the difficulty of taking off survivors. Some lifeboats on the starboard side were badly damaged, but enough undamaged ones remained for everyone. It became essential to launch these boats from the still moving ship before the midships fire rendered them inaccessible or burned them beyond use.

Casualties were comparatively few, considering the ferocity of the attack and the rapid spread of the fires. About 300 people assembled forward on the open space of A Deck at the bow. They were safe at least temporarily, but from this position fires placed the lifeboats beyond reach. Other passengers and crew gathered near the stern, where they had to face the alarming prospect of exploding ammunition. Some boats were lowered with only a handful of sailors in them, the objective being to get the boats away from the burning part of the ship and bring them close to the bow or stern to take off the survivors. This manoeuvre was quickly successful with some boats, but a few did not have enough crewmen to control them and began to drift away from the *Britain*. Finally, a motor lifeboat was lowered to take the drifting boats in tow, but its engine could not be started until a Royal Air Force officer brought it to life.

The difficult task of getting passengers to descend by rope ladders from the ship's bow into lifeboats commenced. No one had a more demanding job than Able Seaman James McKever, who had suffered a deep gash in his head when hit by a piece of flying metal after the first bomb exploded. He noticed a young mother on deck carrying a baby and realized that she needed both hands free to grasp the ladder. Taking the baby from her, he fetched a blanket and wrapped it around his body, tucked the little boy inside and began his 60-foot descent. Years afterwards he wrote:

> It was a terrible strain as I knew I had charge of another life. I held on grimly to that baby as I went down that swinging Jacob's ladder to shouts of encouragement from both people above and those in the bobbing lifeboat below.
> Painfully, I reached the half-way mark and thought I would not make it, but at last I did and passed the baby to the willing hands stretched out from the boat.

Thus 11-month-old Neville Hart reached safety and he, along with others in the lifeboat, was picked up later by a Royal Navy destroyer. The people left on the fo'c'sle, unsure if more lifeboats would appear, started to make three large rafts from cabin doors and awning supports under the direction of Lieutenant-Commander Charles Garrett, a naval officer travelling in the *Britain* as a passenger.

Other stories of courage emerged. Second Steward Arthur Street had left the ship but noticed that some sailors on deck needed help in lowering a lifeboat. He climbed back aboard to assist his fellow crew members, and as a result the boat was lowered and 30 men who had been trapped by flames were saved.

Most of the Empress of Britain*'s lifeboats had been launched and survivors had been taken off when a boat from a rescue ship went over to examine the damaged liner. The bridge had collapsed, paint had peeled from the ship's side, she was listing to starboard and smoke continued to seep out of her; nevertheless, an attempt was made to tow the* Empress of Britain *to port.* Imperial War Museum

The Polish destroyer Burza *sped to the rescue of survivors on hearing that the* Britain *had been bombed.*
Victor Mordasiewicz

Great clouds of smoke poured from the Britain *as the* Burza *drew near.* Alexander Sosnkowski

Captain Sapsworth, still on the blazing bridge, decided to leave the ship, an act that later aroused some criticism because there were a number of passengers and crew left on the forward section of A Deck, waiting anxiously for rescue. His defenders, however, stated that the intensity of the fires left him no option. In any event, the survivors on the fo'c'sle, towards which the fires were steadily spreading, were finally taken off by lifeboat.

Nearly six hours after the attack ended, the last of the survivors left the *Britain*. Relatively few of them suffered from injuries, although some of the wounded died later aboard the resuce ships. When the final casualty list was published, only 45 people were unaccounted for, 25 of them crewmen, all presumed either killed outright, dead from wounds, or drowned.

About 4:30 in the afternoon the first rescue ships, the Polish destroyer *Burza* and the Royal Navy destroyer *Echo*, arrived at the scene, followed an hour later by the trawlers *Cape Agona*, *Drangey* and *Paynter*.

The *Burza* had been on convoy duty when she was called away and ordered to proceed at full speed in a new direction. Her crew were given no information, but when thick smoke appeared on the horizon they guessed correctly that a ship was burning and that the *Burza* would be involved in searching for survivors. Victor Mordasiewicz, a member of the destroyer's crew, wrote many years later about the rescue:

> As we came closer, huge flames began to shoot up from the *Britain*. We began to see bodies in the water, scattered over a wide area, some hanging on to debris, others to the sides of an overturned lifeboat. We received orders to man our small boats and they were lowered into the sea. As the small boats picked up the survivors, they came alongside. Some of the people clambered up rope ladders but those who could not were hauled over the *Burza*'s side by ropes tied around their bodies.

Sailors on deck were waiting to assist the survivors. We had alcohol with which to rub down those who were frozen and rum to give them to drink. Temptation proved too strong for some sailors who began to sample the rum but this did not stop the rubbing process. In fact it gave the process more vigour!

We picked up 250 people and as we were fully loaded we left for a Scottish port. I remember one man, an Australian. I gave him my extra suit of overalls. Several months later, I received a parcel. Astonished, I opened it and found my suit of overalls, cleaned, pressed and returned to me by the Australian crewman. Later, when I got around to wearing the suit, I discovered that each of the six pockets had a one-pound note in it!

The trawlers picked up about 250 survivors and transferred them to the *Echo* and *Burza*, which had, of course, been fully occupied themselves in the rescue work. Both naval ships then received orders to proceed to the River Clyde, where the survivors were taken ashore. The destroyers *Broke* and *Sardonyx* took their places.

Although the *Britain* had been dealt a dreadful blow, her hull was intact and she was listing only slightly; seemingly she was not in immediate danger of sinking. Vigorous efforts to save her began. On Sunday, October 27, a boarding party from the *Broke* went aboard just long enough to attach hawsers, or strong ropes, from the ocean-going tugs *Marauder* and *Thames*, which took the still burning ship in tow, intending to bring her into port. It looked for a while as if they might succeed, and the *Broke* and *Sardonyx* started escorting the immense hulk which moved along sluggishly at 4 knots. Unknown to anyone in the tugs or destroyers, however, was the presence of the German submarine *U-32*, which had been about 60 miles to the southwest when Jope's plane had attacked the *Britain*.

Oberleutnant Hans Jenisch, *U-32*'s commander, had been notified that the *Britain* had been bombed but was still afloat. By midday on October 27, he spotted the ship. A patrolling plane forced the submarine to dive, and when she resurfaced the *Britain* was nowhere to be seen. Because the visual search was unsuccessful, the U-boat submerged and by using passive sonar located the *Britain* that night and began to close in on her.

The U-boat commander was not to be hurried. His submarine crept surreptitiously between the *Britain* and her zigzagging escorts and placed herself on the ship's port side. When the opportunity came, *U-32*, now in the position 55.16N, 9.50W, fired two torpedoes from between 500 and 600 yards. The first, which was meant to hit the *Britain* in line with her foremast, detonated prematurely, making the submarine shudder from stem to stern. *U-32*'s second torpedo was aimed to strike the hull directly below the third funnel position. There was no malfunctioning this time. The torpedo struck the *Britain* squarely, causing a tremendous explosion.

By now the destroyers were fully alert. They fired star shells and flares, but evidently believed that the blasts were the result of internal detonations in the *Britain*, perhaps caused by fire reaching the fuel tanks. They did not consider that *U-32* had infiltrated between the escorts and the *Britain*. Time was running short if the submarine hoped to escape undetected. But not knowing if one torpedo was sufficient to sink a 42,000-ton ship, Oberleutnant Jenisch swung *U-32* round and fired another, which pierced the hull aft of where the second torpedo exploded, tearing open another gaping hole. The submarine now sneaked off in the wake of her victim and resumed her patrol.

It was obvious that the end was only moments away, less than half a day's sailing time from the yard where the *Britain* had been launched a mere ten years earlier. To save themselves, the tugs hurriedly released their hawsers. The great ship began immediately to list heavily to port, and within ten minutes she capsized. At 2:05 in the morning of Monday, October 28, 1940, the *Empress of Britain* slipped beneath the surface of the North Atlantic.

EPILOGUE

The 598 survivors landed at Gourock and Belfast. After a period ashore to recuperate from their ordeal, military personnel rejoined their units, and most of the *Britain's* crew returned to duty in other ships.

Captain Sapsworth had to complete the official papers concerning the loss of his ship. He used the form that applied to the death of a sailor. It began, "Relating to the death of _____ I do solemnly and sincerely declare." In the blank space he typed *"Empress of Britain,"* then gave a succinct account of the attack.

Sir Edward Beatty issued a statement shortly after he learned of the sinking of his company's flagship:

> News of the loss of the *Empress of Britain* will come to the great army of people who have travelled aboard her very much as would that of the loss of a personal friend, while all Canadians will hear with a feeling of deep regret that the gallant ship which for nine years proudly represented Canada in all the world's great ports has met her fate at the hands of the enemy.
>
> The *Empress of Britain* was designed and built to help maintain for the St. Lawrence gateway of Canada a position of high importance among the world's ocean ports, and splendidly she accomplished that duty. She had many proud moments in her all too short career. Those who saw her first entry into Québec harbour will not forget the tremendous demonstration that greeted her. This was an event second only in interest to the day the ship bore Their Majesties the King and Queen from Halifax on their way home.
>
> To the Canadian Pacific Steamships Limited her loss brings an especially keen regret. We were proud of her beauty and of her consistently fine performance, and we had reason also to be gratified by the fact that while her building might have been termed a bold experiment, it was seen to be thoroughly justified very early in her career. The ship has met her end gallantly in the service of the country, as have many others, but when the war is finished and won, still others equally as fine will be built to take their places and carry on the work of maintaining our British supremacy on the seas.
>
> Of the loss of forty-five of her crew one can only speak with sorrow, which may be somewhat mitigated by pride in the fact that they went to their death with their faces bravely turned to their duty as is the manner of British seamen. To their relatives and friends will go the country's heartfelt sympathy.

Sir Edward's statement that 45 crewmen died was not quite accurate; 20 victims were military personnel and civilians.

Tributes to the *Empress of Britain* appeared in newspapers across Canada, but perhaps the most moving was published in the *New York Times* on October 29:

> No ship ever fitted her name more truly than the *Empress of Britain*. She was, indeed, an empress, with pride and grace and dignity in every inch of her. She had millions of devoted subjects in many countries; for she was primarily a cruise ship, and she had been seen and admired in more out-of-the-way harbors than any other liner. Her white paint was a coat of ermine that set her apart from the throng. It was always a thrill to see her, in the blue Mediterranean or in more distant ports of call; it was always an event in our own harbor when the great white *Empress* came in.

She had many proud moments in her reign of only a decade, notably when she brought the King and Queen home from Canada. But we suspect that the proudest of all were the months when the *Empress* wore her uniform of gray in wartime service. She carried thousands of troops from the free dominions to the Old Country; she played her part in keeping England free. She now lies blackened and twisted on the ocean bottom, the largest of all the ships that have gone down in this war; but she lived up to the traditions of her flag to the very end, for the Admiralty has praised "the resolute and efficient handling" of her anti-aircraft guns in her death struggle. The memory of this fine ship will survive until a new *Empress of Britain* inherits her name.

One might debate the phrase "primarily a cruise ship," but there was no argument about the sincerity of the sentiments the writer expressed. Although the war continued for almost another five years, the *Empress of Britain* remained the largest passenger ship sunk on the high seas during the Second World War.

U-32 was sunk by the British destroyer *Harvester* on October 30, only two days after she torpedoed the *Empress of Britain*. Most of the submarine crew survived the sinking. Some of them arrived in Canada aboard, ironically enough, the Canadian Pacific ship *Duchess of York* to spend the rest of the war in internment camps.

Captain Latta died at his home in England on November 6, 1940.

A memorial service for the ship and those who had died in her was held on November 10, 1940, at the Church of St. Andrew and St. Paul, Montréal.

Late in December 1940, Canadian Pacific printed 10,000 copies of an illustrated eight-page memorial booklet outlining the ship's career. Most were sent, along with a cabin plan of the ship, to former passengers.

Sir Edward Beatty died on March 23, 1943. Friends and business associates felt that he aged almost perceptibly after the loss of the *Empress of Britain*.

A newspaper report on January 3, 1949, stated that a team of divers had located the remains of the *Empress of Britain* in 180 feet of water and that the ship was lying at an angle of 55 degrees. Unsubstantiated rumours of a large number of gold ingots in her strongroom circulated, although plans to recover the alleged gold came to nothing.

When the *Britain* began her wartime service, works of art in the ship were boarded over rather than removed, and all were lost when she sank. However, one preliminary design by Frank Brangwyn for a mural in the Salle Jacques Cartier may still be seen in the Brangwyn Museum in the Belgian city of Bruges.

A new and much smaller *Empress of Britain* was launched in 1955. She entered service between England and Canada the following year and also made cruises, but was sold in 1964. A fine ship in her own right, she was nevertheless only a pale shadow of her illustrious namesake.

APPENDIX I
Glossary

Most people are familiar with port and starboard, meaning left and right respectively, and are aware that the bridge is the structure from which the ship is navigated. They know that the stem is at the opposite end of the ship from the stern. A few less common terms are explained below:

bollard — A vertical metal upright, about 2 feet high and 1 foot in diameter, around which a ship's mooring lines are tied.

draft — The depth of water needed to float a ship.

fathom — Six feet.

forecastle — (Usually shortened to fo'c'sle.) The fore end of a ship.

gross registered tonnage — A measurement of volume, not of weight. One gross registered ton is equal to 100 cubic feet of a ship's internal space.

hawsepipe — A large hole in the bow through which a ship's anchor chain passes.

heaving line — A light rope, weighted at one end as an aid to throwing. A mooring line is usually attached to it.

knot — A measure of speed, one knot being roughly equal to 1.15 miles per hour. A 24-knot ship thus can travel at 27.6 miles per hour.

mooring line — A heavy rope which is hauled ashore and placed over a bollard when a ship docks.

nautical mile — A measure of distance at sea, equal to about 6,080 feet.

shackle — A heavy U-shaped metal bracket with a pin across the open end, used to connect lengths of anchor chain. Patent shackles later replaced the U-shaped type.

tender — A small vessel which ferries passengers and crew ashore from an anchored ship.

voyage — Strictly speaking, a ship's combined outward and homeward passages, although sometimes used informally to refer to a passage from one port to another.

APPENDIX II
The Empress of Britain's Transatlantic Passenger Totals

Southampton and Cherbourg to Québec (westbound)
Québec to Cherbourg and Southampton (eastbound)

Westbound

Year	First	Tourist	Third	Total	Crossings
1931	2113	2216	562	4891	9
1932	1951	1860	2101	5912	10
1933	1894	2023	1993	5910	13
1934	1844	1798	1921	5563	11
1935	2053	1747	2187	5987	11
1936	2273	1865	2941	7079	11
1937	2675	1951	2947	7573	11
1938	1928	1714	2455	6097	11
1939	1151	1232	1520	3903	6
	17882	16406	18627	52915	93

Eastbound

Year	First	Tourist	Third	Total	Crossings
1931	1687	1707	1302	4696	9
1932	1284	1682	2416	5382	10
1933	1314	1753	2474	5541	13
1934	1298	1387	2016	4701	11
1935	1311	1444	1862	4617	11
1936	1746	1400	2428	5574	11
1937	1623	1495	2411	5529	11
1938	1143	1135	1806	4084	11
1939	468	587	633	1688	4
	11874	12590	17348	41812	91

Total number of westbound passengers 52915
Total number of eastbound passengers 41812
Total number of passengers 94727

Southampton and Cherbourg to New York (westbound)
New York to Cherbourg and Southampton (eastbound)

Westbound

Year	First	Tourist	Third	Total	Crossings
1931	247	101	30	378	1
1932	175	67	34	276	1
1933	184	104	31	319	1
1934	102	51	27	180	1
1935	80	46	18	144	1
1936	53	10	7	70	1
1937	41	23	38	102	1
1938	54	64	43	161	1
	936	466	228	1630	8

Eastbound

Year	First	Tourist	Third	Total	Crossings
1932	342	77	57	476	1
1933	300	67		367	1
1934	326	56		382	1
1935	348			348	1
1936	349	78		427	1
1937	226	40		266	1
1938	382			382	1
1939	104			104	1
	2377	318	57	2752	8

Total number of westbound passengers 1630
Total number of eastbound passengers 2752
Total number of passengers 4382

Grand total of westbound passengers, both routes 54545
Grand total of eastbound passengers, both routes 44564
Grand total of passengers, both routes 99109

APPENDIX III
Places Visited by the Empress of Britain

1931-1939

Algiers (Algeria)
Athens (Greece)
Auckland (New Zealand)
Bahia (Brazil)
Balboa (Panama)
Bangkok (Siam)
Batavia (Java)
Beirut (Lebanon)
Beppu (Japan)
Boeleleng (Bali)
Bombay (India)
Cape Town (South Africa)
Cherbourg (France)
Chinwangtao (China)
Colombo (Ceylon)
Conception Bay (Newfoundland)
Cristobal (Panama)
Durban (South Africa)
Funchal (Madeira)

Gibraltar
Haifa (Palestine)
Halifax (Canada)
Hamilton (Bermuda)
Havana (Cuba)
Hilo (Hawaii)
Hong Kong
Honolulu (Hawaii)
Jamestown (St. Helena)
Kingston (Jamaica)
Kobe (Japan)
Las Palmas (Canary Islands)
Los Angeles (United States)
Manila (Philippines)
Melbourne (Australia)
Monte Carlo (Monaco)
Naples (Italy)
Nassau (Bahamas)
New York (United States)

Padang (Sumatra)
Padang Bay (Bali)
Penang (Malaya)
Port of Spain (Trinidad)
Port Said (Egypt)
Port Tewfik (Egypt)
Québec (Canada)
Rio de Janeiro (Brazil)
San Francisco (United States)
Semarang (Java)
Shanghai (China)
Singapore (Malaya)
Southampton (England)
Suva (Fiji)
Sydney (Australia)
Wellington (New Zealand)
Yokohama (Japan)
Zamboanga (Philippines)

Second World War

Aden
Cape Town (South Africa)
Colombo (Ceylon)
Durban (South Africa)
Freetown (Sierra Leone)
Fremantle (Australia)

Gourock (Scotland)
Halifax (Canada)
Liverpool (England)
Melbourne (Australia)
Port Said (Egypt)

Québec (Canada)
Simonstown (South Africa)
Southampton (England)
Suez (Egypt)
Wellington (New Zealand)

APPENDIX IV
Extracts from the Specification Book

Builder: . . . . .John Brown & Co., Ltd., Clydebank, Scotland
Yard Number: 530
Description: . . . . Lloyd's 100 A1 shelter-deck
quadruple-screw steamer with single reduction turbine machinery

Dimensions:

Length between perpendiculars . . . . .730 feet   0 inches
Length overall . . . . .760 feet   6 inches
Breadth moulded . . . . 97 feet   6 inches
Depth moulded to Shelter Deck . . . . 60 feet   9 inches
Depth moulded to Upper Deck . . . . 52 feet   3 inches
Load draft . . . . 32 feet   0 inches

Tonnages:

Gross tonnage 42,348.48
Net tonnage 22,545.46
Displacement tonnage 40,680
Deadweight tonnage 9,530

Capacities:

Holds and lower 'tween decks, permanent . . . . 85,270 cu. ft.
Insulated cargo spaces, permanent . . . . 24,350 cu. ft.
ceserve cargo spaces . . . . 66,450 cu. ft.
Trunked hatchways . . . . 33,600 cu. ft.
Baggage, mail and specie rooms . . . . 41,640 cu. ft.
Insulated stores . . . . 26,010 cu. ft.
Sundries and stores . . . . 33,100 cu. ft.

Total capacity 310,420 cu. ft.

Oil fuel in deep tanks and double bottom tanks . . . . .6,024 tons
Salt water in double bottom . . . . 147 tons
Fresh water in double bottom . . . . .2,386 tons
Salt water in peaks . . . . 367 tons
Fresh water in engine room wing tanks . . . . 834 tons
Salt water in deep tank . . . . .1,050 tons
Salt water in emergency double bottom wing tanks . . . . 556 tons

Total water capacity 5,340 tons

Designation of decks:

Sun Deck . . . . .Sun Deck	Upper Deck . . . . .C Deck
Boat Deck . . . . .Sports Deck	Main Deck . . . . .D Deck
Promenade Deck . . . . .Lounge Deck	Lower Deck. . . . . .E Deck
Bridge Deck . . . . .A Deck	Orlop Deck . . . . .F Deck
Shelter Deck . . . . .B Deck	Lower Orlop Deck . . . . .G Deck

Length of erections:

Shelter Deck . . . . .Full length
Bridge Deck. . . . . .Full length
Lounge Deck. . . . . .648 ft. 3 in.
Sports Deck. . . . . .455 ft. 0 in.
Sun Deck . . . . .191 ft. 9 in.
Captain's Bridge . . . . .91 ft. 0 in.
Navigating Bridge . . . . .32 ft. 6 in.

Lifesaving equipment:

18 lifeboats to carry 89 persons each 1602
6 lifeboats to carry 46 persons each 276
2 motor lifeboats to carry 44 persons each. 88
Total number of persons 1966
Total number of souls aboard (excluding pilot). 1908
Surplus 58

APPENDIX V
Passenger Accommodation

First Class Passengers

On Sports Deck

6 one-berth cabins 6

16 two-berth cabins 32

2 one-berth servant's rooms 2

Total First Class passengers on Sports Deck 40

On A Deck

20 one-berth cabins 20

62 two-berth cabins 124

4 one-berth servant's rooms 4

Total First Class passengers on A Deck 148

On B Deck

17 one-berth cabins 17

59 two-berth cabins 118

3 one-berth servant's rooms 3

Total First Class passengers on B Deck 138

On C Deck

26 one-berth cabins 26

40 two-berth cabins 80

3 one-berth servant's cabins 3

Total First Class passengers on C Deck 109

Grand total First Class passengers
(including 12 passenger servants) 435

Provision for the following additional First Class passengers can be made:

A Deck 10

B Deck 11

C Deck 9

Total additional First Class passengers 30

First Class saloon dines 452

Tourist Cabin (Tourist Third) passengers

On C Deck

19 two-berth cabins 38

11 four-berth cabins 44

Total Tourist Cabin passengers on C Deck 82

On D Deck

15 four-berth cabins 60

Total Tourist Cabin passengers on D Deck 60

On E Deck
      13 two-berth cabins 26
      23 four-berth cabins 92

Total Tourist Cabin passengers on E Deck 118

Grand total Tourist Cabin passengers 260
Tourist Cabin saloon dines 164

Third Class passengers (permanent)
On C Deck
      10 two-berth cabins 20
      14 four-berth cabins 56

Total Third Class passengers on C Deck 76

On D Deck
      22 two-berth cabins 44
      12 four-berth cabins 48

Total Third Class passengers on D Deck 92

On E Deck
      36 two-berth cabins 72
      29 four-berth cabins 116
       1 six-berth cabin 6

Total Third Class passengers on E Deck 192

Total permanent Third Class passengers 362

Third Class passengers (portable)
On E Deck
       2 two-berth cabins 4
       9 four-berth cabins 36

Total Third Class (portable) passengers on E Deck .40

On F Deck
       8 two-berth cabins 16
      13 four-berth cabins 52

Total Third Class (portable) passengers on F Deck 68

Total Third Class (portable) passengers 108
Grand total Third Class passengers 470
Third class saloon dines 234
(From specification book issued by John Brown & Co., Ltd., 1931.)

APPENDIX VI
Crew

Captain	1	Stewards and Waiters	246
Staff Captain	1	Stewardesses	34
Pilot	1	Nurses	2
Officers (Deck)	7	Swimming and Turkish Bath Attendants (Female)	2
Engineers, Electricians and Writer	45	Laundry Staff (Female)	8
Wireless Operators	8	Laundry Staff (Male)	7
Doctors	2	Ship's Police	2
Pursers and Assistants and Ticket Agent	11	Storekeeper and Lamp Trimmer	2
Chief and Second Stewards	8	Storekeeper (Steward's)	1
Writers and Cinema Operator	3	Linen Keepers	3
Stenographers and Lady Hairdressers	8	Head Pantrymen	2
Shop Attendants	4	Ship's Cook and Assistant	2
Carpenter, Bo'sun, Mates, Joiner, Gardener	8	Leading Cooks	8
Quartermasters	6	Senior Cooks	12
Look-out Men and Divers	5	Assistant Cooks	30
Masters-at-Arms, Baggage Master, Interpreter	4	Assistant Pantrymen	18
Chef and Extra Chef	2	Assistant Storekeepers	4
Chief Baker, Pastry Cook and Butcher	3	Printers	3
Head Barman and Assistants	11	Assistant Bakers	6
Gymnastic Instructors	2	Assistant Butchers	8
Swimming and Turkish Bath Attendants (Male)	2	Donkeymen and Storekeepers	3
Dispenser and Hospital Attendants	4	Seamen and Boys	54
Chief Barber and Barbers	4	Refrigerating and Diesel Greasers	6
Bandsmen	14	Greasers	24
Head Waiters	4	Wipers	29
		Boiler Attendants	30

Total 714

(From specification book issued by John Brown & Co., Ltd., 1931.)

APPENDIX VII

The Steamship Empress of Britain's Machinery

The *Empress of Britain*'s hull has been constructed by John Brown & Co. Ltd., Clydebank, Scotland, which company also built and installed the main engines, boilers, etc., under the supervision of Mr. John Johnson, Canadian Pacific's Chief Superintendent Engineer.

The ship is propelled by four screws, each driven by an independent set of single-reduction geared turbines of the Parsons type. To suit the conditions under which she will run, viz., between Great Britain and Canada during the summer and world cruises during the winter, the engines driving the two inboard screws are designed to develop two-thirds of the total power, while the engines driving the two outboard screws develop the remaining one-third. In other words, the power of the outboard engines is only one half that of the inboard engines. Under cruising conditions, if full power is not required, only the inboard engines will be used, and the ship will then be virtually a twin-screw one. The machinery has been designed to develop normally a total output of 62,500 s.h.p. continuously at sea, in order to maintain a normal speed of 24 knots. If an increase of speed is necessary at any time, however, an overload power of 66,500 s.h.p. can be maintained for long periods. Two engine-rooms are necessary for the main propelling machinery, the two inboard sets being arranged in a compartment forward of that in which the two outboard sets are installed; while certain

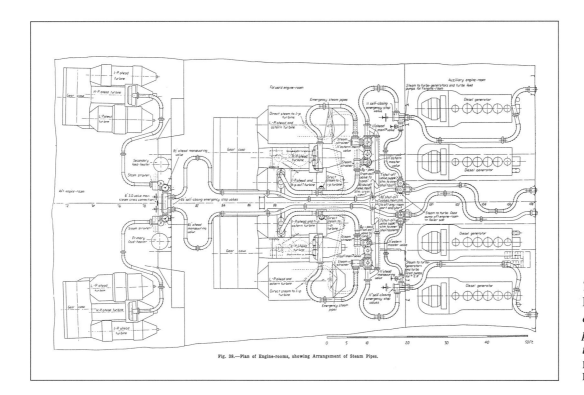

Fig. 38.—Plan of Engine-rooms, showing Arrangement of Steam Pipes.

The plan of the Empress of Britain's engine rooms showed plainly the layout of the steam pipes.
Marine Publications International Ltd.

The intermediate-pressure turbines are clearly visible in an illustration of the forward engine room, looking aft.
CP Rail Corporate Archives

of the auxiliary machinery is situated in a separate auxiliary engine-room immediately forward of the two main engine rooms.

The main turbine sets each comprise one high-pressure, one intermediate-pressure, and one low-pressure turbine, working in series; each turbine drives a separate pinion, which engages with the main gearwheel. For astern running, a high-pressure unit is incorporated in the same casing with each of the two intermediate ahead turbines and a low-pressure unit in the exhaust end of each of the two low-pressure ahead turbines of the inner-shaft machinery only. No provision is made for astern working on the outer shafts, which are employed exclusively for ahead duty. The astern turbines are capable of developing 60 per cent of the aggregate ahead service power.

The high-pressure turbines are all constructed to withstand a maximum working pressure of 425 lb. per sq. in. and an initial steam temperature of 725 deg. F., but they have been designed to develop the service and overload powers when employing steam between the limits of 375 lb. per sq. in. (gauge) and 0.50 lb. per sq. in. (absolute) with an initial steam temperature of 700 deg. F. The high-pressure ahead turbines are of the impulse-reaction type, comprising a 2-row velocity wheel with blades of stainless steel, and a reaction portion fitted with end-tightened blades of Monel metal. Nozzle control valves are fitted to enable a gradual increase of power to be obtained, and at the same time maintain as high a pressure as possible in the control chest for quick operation. The intermediate-pressure ahead turbines are of the reaction type throughout, with end-tightened blades of phosphor-bronze. The low-pressure ahead turbines are also of the reaction type, with phosphor-bronze blades.

The high-pressure astern turbines each consist of a 3-row impulse wheel; the low-presure astern turbines each have 2 impulse wheels with 2 rows each, in which the blades are of stainless steel. To eliminate vibration, all the rotors have been dynamically balanced. The low-pressure ahead turbines are of the double-flow balanced type, and each of the other turbines is fitted with a dummy to reduce the end thrust due to the difference in steam pressure. Michell thrust bearings of the spherical-seated type are fitted to each rotor to take up any remaining axial thrust. Owing to the high steam temperature employed, the turbine casings are of cast steel, with the exception of the low-pressure casings, which are of cast iron. To facilitate the lifting of the upper portions of the turbine casings, the receiver pipes have been connected to the lower halves of the turbines in every case. In each set the high-pressure turbine is fitted with an Aspinall patent governor, combined with a fore-and-aft indicator and control; the intermediate-pressure and low-pressure turbines are fitted with fore-and-aft indicators and controls only. With this arrangement, the steam would be shut off in the event of the turbine speed exceeding a certain limit. The fore-and-aft indicators show any axial movement of the turbine rotors; and should the wear on the thrust pads make this movement excessive, the control would then operate and shut off steam to the turbines. Steam would also be shut off in the event of the oil pressure in the lubricating system dropping unduly or failing entirely.

The main condensers, which are of the Weir 2-flow regenerative type, with a large reservoir at the bottom for storing the water required for the successful operation of the closed-feed system, are slung underneath the low-pressure turbines. Each inboard condenser has a cooling surface of 20,700 sq. ft., the tubes being 3/4 in. diameter and 14 1/2 ft. long; each outboard condenser has a cooling surface of 9,600 sq. ft., with 3/4 in. diameter tubes 11 1/2 ft. long. The tubes for all the condensers are made of cupro-nickel. A particular feature of the condensers is the water doors, which have been designed to facilitate the quick examination of the tubes. Large doors have been fitted in each end, and these are jointed with rubber rings recessed into the casing. The doors are secured by swivel bolts and dogs, which may be removed for inspection purposes in a few minutes.

Gearing, Shafting and Propellers. — The main gearing is of the usual double-helical, single-reduction type, and the main gearwheels of the inner and outer shafts have diameters of 14 1/2 ft. and 11 ft. 3 1/2 in. respectively. All the pinions are connected to their respective rotors by flexible claw-type couplings. The gearwheels and pinions are are enclosed in strong cast-iron gear cases. The thrust of the propellers is transmitted to the ship through Michell thrust bearings of the single-collar type, fitted to the main lines of shafting immediately aft of the gearing. The tunnel shafting is supported by bearings of the Michell pivoted-pad journal type. The propellers, which are of solid bronze, have diameters of 19 1/4 ft. and 14 ft. for the inner and outer shafts respectively. When developing the normal service power of 60,000 s.h.p., the speeds of the propellers are 150 and 200 r.p.m. and the corresponding speeds of the turbines are 1,365 and 1,795 r.p.m. for the inner and outer shafts respectively. The reduction ratio therefore is about 9 to 1.

Steam-generating Installation. — The boiler installation consists of 8 oil-fired water-tube boilers of the Yarrow type and one oil-fired water-tube boiler of the Johnson type. The boilers are arranged in

To the uninitiated, the forward engine room looked intimidating, but the engineers in the Empress of Britain *saw it as, literally, a well-oiled machine. The curved metal casing at the right enclosed the starboard low-pressure turbine.*
Glasgow University Archives/ Scottish Record Office

The upper parts of diesel generators stood out prominently in this view of the ship's machinery.
CP Rail Corporate Archives

2 compartments, and the same principle of division of power has been carried out in the boiler arrangement as with the main engines. Six of the boilers are placed in the after boiler room, normally supplying the forward inboard engines, and 3 boilers are installed in the forward boiler room, supplying the outboard engines in the after engine room. The arrangements are such that any or all of the boilers can supply the ahead and astern turbines in the foward engine room.

The Yarrow boilers are of the double-flow, side-fired type, having one steam drum, 3 water drums, and one superheater drum. The flow of the gases is through both sides of the boiler, after which it passes through a large tubular air heater and thence to the funnel. The boiler and superheater drums are hollow rolled forgings, with ends formed integrally, and represent the latest practice for high-pressure boiler work. The Johnson boiler consists of 2 large diameter drums, placed vertically one above the other, and connected to each other by curved tubes which are arranged longitudinally and across the ends so that the combustion space is almost entirely enclosed by water tubes. In addition there is a wall of water tubes along the center of the boiler, which divides the combustion space into two separate compartments. This arrangement of tubes provides for a considerably larger amount of tube surface exposed to radiant heat than in other types of marine water-tube boilers. The boiler was built at Clydebank and a series of very complete trials showed that it is capable of generating double the amount of steam per square foot of heating surface, while registering the same efficiency, as a Yarrow or other standard type of boiler worked at ordinary mercantile rating.

Supreme Vortex steam dryers have been fitted to the boilers in the after boiler room, and Tangential steam dryers are installed in the boilers in the forward room. Each main boiler is fitted with two automatic feed regulators, one of the Weir and the other of the Mumford type, and Parry soot blowers are provided. In order to give an alarm when the water in the boilers falls below pre-determined level, Mumford low-water alarm gear has been installed. In the forward boiler room there are also two cylindrical boilers of the return-tube type, for domestic and other auxiliary purposes. These boilers are arranged to burn oil fuel with the Howden system of forced draft, and are designed for a working pressure of 200 lb. per sq. in. The oil-fuel pumping and heating installation is of the Wallsend-Howden type.

Electric-generating plant. — In the separate compartment between the forward main engine room and the after boiler room are four Fiat British Diesel engine-driven generators. Each of these generators, which has an output of 450 kw., is driven by a Fiat British single-acting, 2-stroke cycle, 4-cylinder engine developing 660 b.h.p. at 260 r.p.m., and each driving its own double-acting scavenging pump, 3-stage air compressor, circulating water pump and lubricating oil pump. For emergency use, and for supplying the starting air, there is a Reavell electrically-driven compressor, and in the auxiliary engine room there are also 2 fuel-oil transfer pumps. In addition to the Diesel engine-driven generators, there are 2 British Thomson-Houston turbo-driven generators of 800 kw. each, in the forward engine room, which are supplied with high-pressure superheated steam from the main boilers, the exhaust being connected directly to the condensers. The turbo-driven generators are driven at 670 r.p.m. through gearing, the turbines running at 6,000 r.p.m.

Other Engine Room Auxiliaries. — The remaining auxiliaries, which are mostly electrically driven, are arranged in pairs, so that one pair will serve each of the larger main engines and the remaining pair the smaller outboard sets. The Weir closed feed water system comprises electrically-driven centrifugal extraction pumps, feed pumps of the turbo-driven centrifugal type and filters and primary and secondary heaters. The Drysdale main circulating pumps are of the vertical-spindle centrifugal type, driven by electric motors. Nine Drysdale Centrex pumps have been supplied for the forced lubrication system, and Vickers centrifugal separators are installed for the purification of the lubricating oil. Centrex pumps are also provided for the bilge, ballast, sanitary, fire and wash-deck services, a battery of 6 pumps being situated in the forward engine room. Three smaller pumps of a similar type are installed for dealing with fresh water. A well-equipped work shop is situated in the shaft tunnel, the Hall refrigerating machinery being also arranged in the tunnel. A complete Lux CO_2 fire extinguishing system is provided in the boiler rooms and in the auxiliary machinery room.

(From *Canadian Railway and Marine World*, May 1931.)

APPENDIX VIII

Operating an Atlantic Liner

by Captain R.N. Stuart, V.C., D.S.O., U.S.N.C., R.D., R.N.R.
General Superintendent, Canadian Pacific Steamships

Far back in antiquity a primitive man stood on the bank of a river or lake and a desire arose within him to reach the other side by the shortest route. Knowing that wood floated on water, he searched around and found a part of a fallen tree, laid himself prone, and, using both hands and feet, propelled his craft safely to the opposite bank. There and then the first voyage had been completed and transport by water had begun.

Ever since, his descendants have slowly and steadily improved on his original idea, learned how to build ships, voyaged farther and farther from the shore, and from hard experience and disaster imposed by the sea, improved design and built sturdier ships. For many centuries they constructed with wood until they learned to construct with iron and again to change from iron to steel. The primitive man was the crew of his primitive means of water transport, but as the means or ship has developed, so the number required to tend and navigate the ship has had to be increased. A crew of several hundred is needed to do the work that must be done in the great steel liners of to-day in caring for ship and passengers during the ocean voyages which these vessels make safely, swiftly, and with a regularity equal to a train. While one of these great vessels is in port—the crew not yet engaged—shore labour is employed in loading cargo, replenishing fuel, food and fresh water, overhauling and repairing equipment, fittings, and furnishings.

The crew for one of these ships is engaged by the Captain in the presence of a superintendent of the Board of Trade. All are assembled in a convenient place ashore or on the ship, and the terms of the agreement are read over so that all may hear what they agree to do before signing. The Captain signs first and each follows in arranged sequence in the department in which he or she is to work—deck, engine, catering, or medical. In the terms of agreement are included time and date when all are to be aboard to commence work.

Several hours before the time appointed for all to be aboard, engineers have commenced raising steam to the required pressure to start the great turbines rotating when the voyage is to commence, and attending to other machinery that will give power for lighting, heating, ventilating, steering, hoisting, telephones, wireless, cooking, laundry, movie shows and good santitation: in a few words to give life to the ship. For a ship in service is alive, but a ship "laid off" is like a dead thing.

At an early hour on the day when the voyage is to commence, the crew joins. Each reports to the departmental officer under whom he or she agreed to work when signing articles, then changes into uniform, dons a life-belt and a brass badge on which is embossed the number of the lifeboat into which the wearer is to embark should occasion necessitate. The sounding of a bugle is the call for all to muster on the Promenade Deck where the crew "fall in" by departments in the sequence in which each signed articles. In the presence of the Captain, Board of Trade surveyor of life saving appliances and a Board of Trade medical officer, the name of each member of the crew is called and each replies by giving the number of the boat to which he or she has been detailed, walking past the inspecting officers who examine each life-belt and the wearer for fitness. From the muster all take their stations about the ship to combat fire and all appliances are surveyed; then to the lifeboats which are swung out, equipped, and lowered down to the water until all are afloat. The motor lifeboats are sent away under their own power, and each boat's wireless equipment is tested in receiving and repeating back messages sent from the ship's wireless station. Wireless signals sent from these motor boats can be heard at a distance of about a hundred miles. When the inspecting party is satisfied with the efficiency of the crew and equipment, all boats are re-covered and the crew disperses to begin the work which they agreed to do. Water-tight doors, which are operated hydraulically from the navigating bridge and fitted to allow the crew to pass out of one water-tight compartment into the next—all below the water line—are tested. Whistles, steering gear, and mechanical devices for transmitting orders from the navigating bridge to the engine room are tried for good working order.

The ship is now ready to embark the passengers, and the Captain is handed sailing orders from his employers, giving him the date and hour at which he is to proceed on the voyage and directing him to exercise care for the safety of the lives and property entrusted to him. The Chief Engineer goes down to the engine room to have a final look around to satisfy himself that the great mass of machinery under his care is ready to drive the liner across the ocean. The Purser meets the passengers as they embark, passes a friendly greeting to those who have previously crossed with him, gives a courteous welcome to new passengers, quiets the flustered, and receives passengers' mail, telegrams, and parcels. The Chief Steward moves about the ship supervising the many men under his orders who will be tending passengers during the voyage. The Doctor and his staff are ready to give professional attention, if needed. The chef and his many assistants prepare lunch to be served as soon as the vessel leaves the quay. Electrician and plumber pass along the decks looking to those fittings and equipment which are to be their care throughout the voyage. The printer and his "devils" are busy running off the menu cards for dinner that night and setting up other printed work that must be completed without delay. The carpenter and his mates close and secure hatches and those doors in the ship's shell that will not be used for landing the Pilot. The boatswain supervises the clearing up of all weather decks and secures movable fittings about the deck ready for sea.

Navigating officers are fully occupied with receiving passengers, mail, and parcel post from the post office officials, the care of the ship in general, and getting all navigating instruments and equipment checked and ready for the voyage. The Pilot arrives on board during the time that passengers are embarking, and reports to the Captain any changes that have taken place or are being made in the positions of the buoys marking the channel through which the ship must pass on her way to the open sea, while tugs are alongside waiting to pull her from the quay and assist in turning her into the channel.

Within a few minutes from 1 p.m. at Southampton, all the passengers and mail are on board, and the navigating and engineer officers at their stations in readiness for the voyage to begin. At 1 p.m. the passenger gangways are landed, the great hawsers holding the vessel to the quay let go, and the tugs begin pulling her off into the channel. In response to an order transmitted from the navigating bridge to the engine room, the turbines begin to rotate and turn the great four-bladed propellers, and the ship moves ahead under her own power.

The tugs are let go, and she continues on her way through the buoyed channels and restricted waters out to the open sea, acknowledging the salutes from yachts, tugs, and pleasure steamers as she passes. Away on the port hand, Netley Military Hospital is passed, a testimony to Florence Nightingale and her great work; on the starboard hand, Calshot Castle near to which are moored several flying boats—a further advancement in development from the primitive voyager's original idea. Turning into the waters of Spithead, the ship passes the entrance into Portsmouth's harbour where can be seen the long, lean hulls of naval vessels and, silhouetted against the sky, the tall wooden spars of the famous "Victory", which in her day, guided by an indomitable seaman, restored the freedom of the seas. On towards the Nab tower, the great engines are now stopped and the vessel loses headway to permit the Pilot to leave the ship in a small boat which has been sent from a pilot steamer close by. He gives a wave of the hand to the bridge indicating that he is in the boat and clear. Full speed is ordered and the great ship again forges ahead, rapidly gathering speed, out to the open sea. The chalk cliffs of the Isle of Wight disappear below the horizon astern as the distance from the port she has so recently left is increased and the distance to Cherbourg, where she is due at 6.30 p.m., is shortened.

Lunch has been rather a drawn-out meal for the waiters and kitchen staff, for some passengers hurried to lunch as soon as it was served, some sat down when they were no longer interested in the passing scenes, and others are yet to be served who have been up on deck until the land disappeared below the horizon. By 6 p.m. the high land about Cherbourg is sighted and soon after the breakwater is seen. As the ship enters the harbour the engines are stopped, and promptly at 6.30 p.m. down goes the anchor. Tenders which are waiting with more passengers and mail lose no time in getting alongside. In about an hour's time all are aboard, the tenders leave, the anchor is hove up, and the great ship turns seaward and moves to the sea acknowledging the salutes from the tenders as she goes on her way. Once she is clear of the harbour, all engines are ordered to full speed. Now passing the Channel Islands, steaming down channel at the speed of a fast train, picking up the quick flashing light on the Lizard which can be seen more than twenty miles, checking the distance, passing off by bearings taken at frequent and regular intervals, turning slightly from her course to avoid fishing craft and other vessels as they pass and in accordance with the rules for safety in approaching and passing other vessels, the "Empress of Britain" steams on past the Bishop Rock Lighthouse on the extreme western end of the reefs of the Scilly Isles, ploughing her way steadily across the North Atlantic Ocean. Land will not be seen for three days while she steams across the ocean from the Bishop Rock to Belle Isle.

Day and night she will be tended by her crew, and her passengers cared for and entertained. On the bridge, navigating officers calculate her position hourly and keep the wireless operator informed. The wireless operators keep contact with the land stations on both sides of the Atlantic Ocean, communicate with other ships, relay messages from ships fitted with less powerful equipment to the shore stations, and stand ready to switch over at a moment's notice to take wireless bearings of other ships should the weather become foggy. Lookout men on duty in the crow's nest maintain telephone communication with the officers of the watch on the navigating bridge. Engineers keep a constant watch over the machinery under their care. The Purser is responsible during the voyage for the checking and manifesting of all passengers, and for arranging entertainment and deck sports; the Chief Steward and the chef for the preparation of tasty meals and attention to the comforts of the passengers; the doctor is about and giving treatment and encouragement to those who may feel uncomfortable while the great ship moves over the waters.

Each day both emergency boats—two boats on each side of the vessel—must be inspected for readiness for immediate use if required, a lighted lamp placed in each at sunset, and boat crews mustered; water-tight doors operated and fire alarms tried; fire-fighting parties mustered and drilled; and the master-at-arms must present the night patrol's report for the previous night. This supervision is never relaxed until the voyage is ended and the "Empress" is again made fast to a quay. Meanwhile the passengers are enjoying the comfort and entertainment arranged for them—movie shows, dancing, deck sports, swimming in the spacious pool, or reading in the library, which contains about two thousand books for their selection.

About dawn on the third day, the powerful lights shining from the lighthouses erected on Belle Isle are sighted and in about two hours the great vessel is steaming through the Straits of Belle Isle, with the coast of Labrador on the starboard hand and that of Newfoundland on the port. Past Forteau Bay where the missionary settlement founded by Sir Wilfred Grenfell can be seen nestling at the foot of the high, bare hills, on past Greenly Island where the first trans-ocean east to west fliers landed, mile after mile she forges ahead, with, one hopes, a beautiful clear morning, with a westerly breeze carrying the scent of pine and balsam from the wooded lands of the interior and a steady barometer which indicates that good clear weather will prevail until the voyage is completed; rounding Cape Whittle, no nearer than ten miles because of the foul water extending some distance from its shore, over the codbanks of Natashkwan, past the extreme western end of the Island of Anticosti on to the great expanse of the famous St. Lawrence River which must be crossed before the engines will be slowed as Father Point is approached and a pilot will be embarked to con the steering, while the ship passes upstream to her destination.

That night is a gala dinner night and the dining saloon is decorated with coloured lights. Paper hats and crackers are placed at each passenger's table and an atmosphere of goodwill prevails. The orchestra plays popular selections and songs which everyone joins in singing, and many friendships begun during the voyage are strengthened into life friendship.

In the early hours of the following morning, the great engines are slowed and then stopped as the great liner approaches Father Point to embark the Pilot, passengers' mail, customs and immigration officials, and the visiting medical officer to confirm that all on board are well and are not suffering from quarantinable diseases. Here mails for the Maritime Provinces and special mail to be flown by plane to Montréal and Ottawa for further distribution are landed. As soon as the doctor passes down into the small steamer which brought him alongside, the engines are once again ordered to full speed and the ship passes upstream, turning towards the north shore and passing along the steep and wooded slopes of Cape Dogs and Cape Salmon. She rounds Cape Goose and passes Isle de Coudres and St. Joseph, where scenes of rustic beauty and villages are scattered along the shores.

During the time that has elapsed since leaving Father Point, the customs have examined passengers' baggage, immigration officers viewed each passenger's passport, and railroad representatives completed their arrangements for the seating of passengers in trains which will be ready to haul them to their many destinations after the ship has docked. As soon as the vessel has passed out of the newly-dredged channel, her speed is again increased until the western end of the Island of Orleans is passed. The great turbines are slowed as she moves upstream through the harbour of Québec slowly and majestically under the butting heights of the Citadel, passing the foreshore of the Heights of Abraham, and turning in towards the dock at Wolfe's Cove. At this spot three tugs fuss about her and assist the "Empress" into her berth. Along the wharf are many sightseers and many friends to meet the incoming passengers. Two long trains are drawn up in readiness to receive the passengers, baggage, and mails, headed by two great panting locomotives which always seem impatient at having to wait. Quietly the great ship moves into her berth, the great hawsers are passed between ship and shore and hove tight, the gangway is placed on board from shore, the engine-room telegraphs ordered to "finished with engines", and the voyage is ended.

(From *Factors in Railway and Steamship Operation.* Montréal: Canadian Pacific Foundation Library, 1937.)

APPENDIX IX
Sidelights on a World Cruise

by A.M. Irwin
Assistant Editor, *Canadian Pacific Staff Bulletin*

The operation of a cruise round the world might rightfullly be termed "big business". In the Canadian Pacific organization it is merely a part of the many activities of the Cruise Department. Each year for the past fifteen a cruise has been operated from New York to New York with the entire management, afloat and ashore, in the hands of the Company. This cruise, lasting 128 days, involves the steaming of 30,478 nautical miles in 70 days, 10 1/2 hours by the Empress of Britain, and the land travel of literally countless miles by the passengers during the 57 days, 11 hours they are ashore. It involves, too, the provision of practically every kind of transport known to man.

To provide shore transportation in 23 countries, arrangements have to be made five years in advance for: Bullock-drawn sleds, man-power sleds and a funicular railway in Madeira; automobiles and horse-drawn victorias in Gibraltar; automobiles in Algeria, Monaco, Italy, Greece and Palestine; camels, donkey-carts and automobiles in Egypt; tongas, rickshaws, palanquins and automobiles in India; automobiles and elephants in Ceylon; automobiles in the Federated Malay States, Siam, Java, Bali and the Philippines; rickshaws, donkeys and automobiles in China; rickshaws and automobiles in Japan; automobiles in Hawaii, California and Panama. In addition, in order to cover a maximum amount of sightseeing within the time limit, the Cruise Department must make provision for 37 special trains and a variety of launches, steam tenders, river steamers and sampans.

A crew of 639 staffs the Empress of Britain for her annual cruise. This number includes the Captain and 125 members of the deck department; the chief engineer and 107 of the engine-room staff; and the purser's, surgeon's and chief steward's staff of 405.

For passenger entertainment and assistance ashore there is a Cruise Director, assisted by a staff of 18—in which are included Protestant and Roman Catholic chaplains. The Cruise Director and his staff make final arrangements with hotels and shore services affecting passengers and accompany all shore excursions in charge of the native staffs. To carry out the 54 major shore excursions, a total of 8,671 persons are employed in the roles of couriers, guides, dragomen, camel drivers, elephant mahouts, rickshaw men, small boat pilots, donkey drivers, personal servants on special trains and lecturers. In the course of the cruise the Cruise Director and his assistants are thousands of miles distant from headquarters. In India, they are 11,500 miles from Montréal, 3,100 miles from the nearest Canadian Pacific office, and in the case of the Across India party, 1,500 miles from the Empress of Britain. Members of the Cruise Director's staff are recruited from passenger offices in Canada, Great Britain, France, and the United States. There are 130 cruise-trained men available for selection.

As an impresario, the Empress of Britain produces: a rhumba band; devil dancers in Kandy, Ceylon; religious dances at Darjeeling in the Himalayas and Angkor Wat under a Cambodian moon; Siamese dancers at Bangkok; Balinese folk opera and Gamelon orchestra at Den Pasar, Bali; Hula dancers in Honolulu. Balls are arranged at Funchal, Madeira; Jerusalem; Darjeeling; Colombo; Batavia; Hong Kong; Peiping; Yokohama.

On three occasions during the cruise the whole passenger list is transferred bodily to the shore starting with a special train movement from Haifa to Jerusalem. Two nights are spent in the Holy City; then, again by special trains, a transfer is made to Cairo and thence, after three nights, to the ship at Suez. In India, several special trains are required for the tour of Delhi and Agra. From Chinwangtao to Peiping and back two special trains are operated via Tientsin. Two other important inland movements are the Across India train, which is home for eleven days to 80 of the passengers with the exception of a night spent in the hotel at Darjeeling prior to the sight of sunrise over Mount Everest, and the Angkor Wat expedition which starts from Penang and finishes at Bangkok. Here, too, hotels are used at Siemreap in Cambodia and Bangkok.

The special trains used in India are similar in appearance to English locomotives and carriages with the addition of a "cowcatcher" to the engine. A gauge wider than standard is used with the exception of the Darjeeling and Himalayas railway from Siliguri to Darjeeling and the South Indian Railway from Madras to Danushkodi at the southern tip of India.

For the Across India party an all-corridor train of two-berth compartments is used from Bombay to Madras via Calcutta, and from Calcutta to Siliguri where passengers transfer to the narrow-gauge railway that winds about itself for 51 miles in order to travel 10 miles in a straight line while it climbs 7,000 feet.

Compartment cars unconnected with each other are used for the shorter Indian journeys. Stops are made at proper intervals to allow passengers to and from the dining car.

From Penang to Aranya Prades, the nearest railway station for Angkor Wat, and back to Bangkok the train is operated over the rails of the Straits Settlement Railway and the State Railways of Siam. Both were built by British engineers. In the Straits Settlement the railway is paralleled by well-made highways—and loses money; in Siam, where there are no motor roads, the railway shows a profit. The compartment cars, in which, like the Indian railways, berths are made up transversely, were the first to be ventilated by the ball-louvre air-conditioning systems which were in operation before the first air-conditioned car appeared in North America.

On all Indian trains a notable feature is the large number of personal servants.

Accommodation at hotels, arrangements for automobiles and other transport and many other details necessary to the movement of the passengers while ashore are booked five years ahead, and confirmed many months in advance of each cruise. The Empress of Britain's Baggage-Master accompanies the trains.

For the 70 1/2 days at sea equally fore-handed preparations are necessary. During the cruise 14,132 tons of fuel are consumed and 46,050 tons of fresh water. These quantities must be taken aboard at various ports selected with regard to necessity, quality and price. Before the Empress sails tides, water levels and other contingencies for each harbour or anchorage have to be studied and provision made for prevailing winds.

Catering for an average of 450 passengers for a voyage lasting 128 days calls for no mean effort, particularly when it is borne in mind that provisions—with the exception of fresh vegetables, fish, eggs and fruit, sometimes purchased locally subject to rigorous medical inspection—must be loaded before the cruise starts.

Assistant Cruise Directors frequently find themselves called upon to display ingenuity and resourcefulness—particularly when the passengers are ashore. On the occasion of the first visit to Siemreap for the Angkor Wat excursion a breakdown of the shore contractor's motor-car resulted in the non-arrival of hotel room lists until after the cruise members had arrived. It did not matter, thanks to members of the staff who took over the Room Clerk's job and allotted space according to the accommodation held on the ship. It is of interest that only one change had to be made when the proper list arrived.

Summed up, a cruise around the world in all its aspects is big business, a business that in every way upholds the Canadian Pacific traditions afloat and ashore.

(From *Canadian Pacific Facts and Figures*. Montréal: Canadian Pacific Foundation Library, 1937.)

BIBLIOGRAPHY

Books

Some books published during and since the 1930s have touched briefly on the *Empress of Britain*. A few deal with the ship more fully, including those by Braynard, Musk and Winchester. Brinnin and Maxtone-Graham, although they say little or nothing about the *Empress of Britain*, give fascinating accounts of crossing the Atlantic by ship and, in Maxtone-Graham's *Liners to the Sun*, of cruises. Bridie kept a comprehensive diary of the first world cruise. Irwin, a journalist on the 1934 world cruise, wrote mostly about the ports the *Britain* visited rather than the ship herself. Seamer gives a detailed account of the bombing and sinking of the ship.

Bonsor, N.R.P. *North Atlantic Seaway*, Vol. 3 and Vol. 5. Jersey: Brookside Publications, 1979 and 1980.

Braynard, Frank O. *Lives of the Liners*. New York: Cornell Maritime Press, 1947.

Bridie, M.F. *Around the World Without a Pinprick*. Birmingham: Jones & Co., n.d.

Brinnin, John Malcolm. *The Sway of the Grand Saloon*. New York: Delacorte Press, 1971.

Gibbs, Commander C.R. Vernon. *British Passenger Liners of the Five Oceans*. London: Putnam, 1963.

Irwin, Alan Maurice. *''—and ships—and sealing-wax.''* Toronto: Macmillan, 1934.

Maxtone-Graham, John. *Liners to the Sun*. New York: Macmillan, 1985.

Maxtone-Graham, John. *The Only Way to Cross*. New York: Macmillan, 1972.

Musk, George. *Canadian Pacific: The Story of the Famous Shipping Line*. Toronto: Holt Rinehart and Winston of Canada Ltd., 1981.

Seamer, Robert. *The Floating Inferno: The story of the loss of the Empress of Britain*. Wellingborough: Patrick Stephens Limited, 1990.

Turner, Robert D. *The Pacific Empresses*. Victoria: Sono Nis, 1981.

Winchester, Clarence (ed.). *Shipping Wonders of the World*. London: Waverley, n.d.

Newspapers

By far the most useful was the Montréal *Gazette*, which had a daily page of shipping news in the 1930s. Others included:

The *Chronicle-Gazette* (Québec)
The *Dominion* (Wellington, New Zealand)
The *Evening Telegram* (Toronto)
The *Glasgow Herald*
The *Montreal Star*
The *New York Times*
The *North-China Herald* (Shanghai)
The *Southern Daily Echo* (Southampton)
The *Times* (London)
The *Toronto Daily Star*

Magazines

The May 1931 issue of *The Shipbuilder and Marine Engine-Builder* was a souvenir number devoted exclusively to the *Empress of Britain*. It is indispensable in the scope of its coverage of the ship's construction and fitting out. There were also articles or short references in the following:

Canadian Railway and Marine World
Canadian Transportation

Canadian Pacific publications

Two books give accounts of the operation of a passenger ship company, with much information on what happens behind the scenes:

Canadian Pacific. *Canadian Pacific Facts and Figures*. Montréal: Canadian Pacific Foundation Library, 1937.

Canadian Pacific. *Factors in Railway and Steamship Operation*. Montréal: Canadian Pacific Foundation Library, 1937.

The *Canadian Pacific Staff Bulletin* provided useful information.

The Publicity Department of Canadian Pacific issued a steady stream of folders and brochures in the 1930s, some dealing exclusively with the *Empress of Britain*, others with all the passenger ships in the company's North Atlantic fleet. Among the items consulted were booklets on the launching of the ship, sailing schedules from 1931 to 1939, fare schedules, embarkation notices, deck plans, world cruise booklets and folders, West Indies cruise folders, brochures advertising the transatlantic service, the memorial booklet issued after the sinking and other material.

The *Britain* had her own printing press which produced passenger lists, menus, log abstracts, the ship's newspaper (*C.P. Gazette*), and the *Flagship* (the official organ of the C.P. *Empress of Britain* Social and Athletic Club), copies of which have been consulted.

ACKNOWLEDGEMENTS

Many individuals and institutions have made notable contributions to this book. Without their assistance, it simply would not exist. To all of them I offer my thanks.

The idea to write a book on the *Empress of Britain* began when Barbara Howard was kind enough to let me have the large collection of photographs, brochures, deck plans and other material about the ship gathered by her husband, Alan, to whom this book is dedicated.

Several crew members helped considerably, particularly Reg Lucas and Fred Sammé, who were always ready to answer queries, clarify details and offer highly useful comments on parts of the manuscript. Other crew members who assisted were Harry Lynch, John E. Jones, Harry Keane and one who wishes to remain anonymous. George Musk, author of *Canadian Pacific: The Story of the Famous Shipping Line* was instrumental in locating three of the crew named above. He also read parts of the manuscript and made a number of valuable observations.

My letters to the *Sunday Star* (Toronto) and *Legion* (the magazine of the Royal Canadian Legion) drew many replies from people who had been passengers in the ship in peace and war, all of whom added to my knowledge of the *Empress of Britain*, even if their stories are not quoted directly in the text in each case. Several of them lent me photographs, menus, deck plans and other useful material. Peacetime pasengers included Mrs. Joan Anderson (Joan Davis), Ian Baxter, J.C. Campbell, Patrick J. Campbell, Len Childs, Senator David M. Croll, Mrs. Aileen Grassby (Aileen Bettesworth), Mrs. Ruth Green, Donald Hamilton, Terry Higgins, John W.H. Hopper, Maurice Laudie, Donald McCuaig, Mrs. Peggy Milliken (Peggy McCuaig), Joseph Morris, Mrs. Gertrude Morris, Mrs. W. Neilson, Mrs. R.G. Robarts (Eleanor Thomas), J.H.H. Scandrett, Mrs. Erik Seidler, Mrs. Mary Shapiro (Mary Shiman), Hugh C. Slaght, Mrs. Florrie Sloman, Mrs. Grace Tyre, Rev. L.M. Watts, Mary Webb and Mrs. Therese Zwetschkenbaum.

Wartime passengers who got in touch with me were Jack Bruce, R.K. Code, Gordon Collinson, Frederick Ewart, John H. Ferguson, Jack Gill, Ronald Light and Percy Mansell. Raymond Davis, a signalman aboard the ship when she was bombed, gave details of the attack. Victor Mordasiewicz wrote a particularly comprehensive account of the rescue operation.

A number of institutions co-operated in the research. Foremost was Canadian Pacific, whose assistance was indispensable. Dave Jones of the Corporate Communications and Public Affairs Department was always helpful. James Shields in the Archives located documents that could not have been found elsewhere. Nancy Williatte-Battet of the Archives supplied many photographs.

The Historical Resources Branch of the National Archives of Canada provided information on the ship's wartime service, as did the Directorate of History at the Ministry of National Defence in Ottawa. The Marine Museum of the Atlantic in Halifax furnished details on the royal voyage. The Robarts Library at the University of Toronto and the Metropolitan Toronto Reference Library gave me access to newspaper and magazine collections from the 1930s and early 1940s.

I consulted several institutions in Britain, including the University of Glasgow, where Mrs. Alma Topen of the Archives was very helpful. The World Ship Society and the Imperial War Museum also co-operated in the research, as did the Southampton Maritime Museum (Mrs. Simone Clark).

In the United States, the Steamship Historical Society of America in the person of its librarians, Laura Brown and Ann C. House, was always ready to assist. The Mariners' Museum in Newport News, Virginia, and the J. Porter Shaw Library in San Francisco also helped.

Jack Churchouse of the Wellington Harbour Board Museum in New Zealand located several photographs and newspaper clippings. The Australian War Memorial and the Department of Defence in Canberra supplied information on a wartime convoy.

Dietmar Borchert made carefully detailed drawings showing the *Empress of Britain* in her peacetime and wartime livery.

Many other individuals assisted me considerably in the preparation of this book. I would like to thank Roger Chapman for making copies of many photographs that were lent to me. Les Carson, a photographer on the *Britain*'s first world cruise and some of the later ones, shared his memories with me and lent me photographs. Everett E. Viez told me his impressions of the ship and supplied me with some photographs. Jay Bascom provided a copy of the May 1931 issue of *The Shipbuilder and Marine Engine-Builder* and many photographs. Among others who assisted in various ways were Reginald V. Badcock, Kenneth Barlow, John H. Bascom, Ronald F. Beaupre, Kenneth J. Blume, Gerard D. Bourke, Frank Bunker, Fred Cherney, Carl V. Ehrke, John B. Essex, Lt.-Cdr. Arnold Hague, Ted Hindmarsh, Joan Hindmarsh, Gordon C. Kemp, Peter C. Kohler, John Lang, Diana Lang, J. Louis Loughran, Gordon C. Kemp, James F. Marr, Elsie McConachie, J.E. Roué, Bruce Smith and Alexander Sosnkowski.

Sheila Anderson, William A. Breaker, Mark Harris, John Marshall and Cecil Porter read all or part of the manuscript in its various stages. They made many valuable suggestions and I appreciate their assistance.

I owe an especial debt of thanks to Philip Dawson, author of *British Superliners of the Sixties* (London: Conway Maritime Press, 1990), who assisted me almost from the day I began writing this book. He introduced me to the esoteric world of word processing, rescued me on many occasions when a recalcitrant computer would not co-operate, read parts of the manuscript at various stages, offering constructive criticism and sound advice. He copied several photographs that have been reproduced in the book. His help was invaluable.

Acknowledgement is made to the following for permission to reprint from copyrighted material:

Southam Communications Limited (publishers of *Canadian Transportation & Distribution Management*) for the article 'The Steamship Empress of Britain's Machinery" in the May 1931 issue of *Canadian Railway and Marine World*.

Marine Publications International Ltd. for material from the May 1931 issue of *The Shipbuilder and Marine Engine-Builder*.

Royal Canadian Horse Artillery History Committee for an excerpt from the book *R.C.H.A. Right of the Line*.

Maclean's for an excerpt from "The Empress of Britain" by Leslie Roberts in the August 1, 1931, issue of *MacLean's*.

John E. Jones for an excerpt from his book *The Earnest Struggle*.

Upper Clyde Shipbuilders records, held by Glasgow University Archives, are reproduced by courtesy of the Archivist and permission of the Keeper of the Records of Scotland.

At the Boston Mills Press, John Denison and his staff offered encouragement and support at all times.

I am, of course, very grateful to all who assisted me in the preparation of the book. However, I must state clearly that whatever shortcomings the book possesses are attributable only to the author.

The first Empress of Britain, *14,000 tons, was launched in 1905 at the yard of the Fairfield Shipbuilding and Engineering Co., Ltd., Glasgow. The 570-foot-long ship was renamed* Montroyal *in 1924 and was sold for demolition in 1930.* Author's Collection

The third Empress of Britain, *also a product of Fairfield's, was a 25,500-ton, 640-foot-long ship which entered service between Britain and Canada in 1956. Sold to the Greek Line in 1964, she was renamed* Queen Anna Maria. *In 1975 she was sold to Carnival Cruise Lines, renamed* Carnivale, *and began a new career as a Caribbean cruise ship the following year.* Author's Collection

INDEX